D0812571

Targeted

Targeted

**My Inside Story of
CAMBRIDGE ANALYTICA and How
TRUMP, BREXIT and FACEBOOK
Broke Democracy**

BRITTANY KAISER

HarperCollins*Publishers*

The names of some characters have been
changed to protect their privacy.

HarperCollins*Publishers*
1 London Bridge Street
London SE1 9GF

www.harpercollins.co.uk

First published by HarperCollins*Publishers* 2019

1 3 5 7 9 10 8 6 4 2

All photographs courtesy of the author unless marked otherwise

A catalogue record of this book is
available from the British Library

HB ISBN 978-0-00-836389-5
PB ISBN 978-0-00-836390-1

Printed and bound in Great Britain by
CPI Group (UK) Ltd, Croydon

MIX
Paper from
responsible sources
FSC
www.fsc.org   FSC™ C007454

This book is produced from independently certified FSC™ paper
to ensure responsible forest management.

For more information visit: www.harpercollins.co.uk/green

To the Truth:
May it set us all free.

Contents

Prologue

There's nothing like a car ride with federal agents to make you question your life choices. That was exactly where I found myself the morning of July 18, 2018, winding through the streets of Washington, DC, heading toward an interview with Special Counsel Robert Mueller's investigators.

My trip that morning consisted of riding in two cars, actually—the first took me to a coffee shop that the Department of Justice had randomly selected. This had been the driver's instructions when I initially slid into the backseat: they had chosen a place unexpectedly, without planning it out or telling anyone beforehand. Then, once we were on our way, he was to radio in our destination. At the coffee shop, the second driver was waiting. Like the first driver, he was wearing a dark suit and dark glasses, but there was a second man with him as well. From the second car—outfitted like the first with tinted windows—I watched as the city's gleaming monuments, bright and sudden and very white, flashed by us like camera bulbs.

When I was settled in the backseat between my two attorneys, it was hard not to consider just how I'd ended up here, on my way to talk to federal prosecutors about my role with the now-infamous political communications firm, Cambridge Analytica. How a situation that I'd entered with the best of intentions for me and my family had ended up so horribly and irrevocably twisted. How in the process of wanting to learn how to use data for good, and while helping my parents through a difficult financial moment, I'd ended up compromising my political and personal values. How a mixture of naïveté and ambition had landed me squarely and disturbingly on the wrong side of history.

A little more than three and a half years earlier, I'd joined Cambridge Analytica's parent company, the SCL Group—specifically, their humanitarian division, SCL Social—working on projects under the company's CEO, a man named Alexander Nix. In the years since that leap of faith, nothing had gone as I'd envisioned it. As a lifelong Democrat and devoted activist who had worked for years in support of progressive causes, I had started my work with Cambridge Analytica under the pretense that I would be separate from the company's Republican client base and outreach. It didn't take long, though, to find myself gradually pulled away from my principles by the difficulty of securing funding for humanitarian projects and the allure of success on the other side. At Cambridge Analytica there was the promise of real money for the first time in my career, and a way to buy into the vision that I was helping to build a revolutionary political communications company from the ground up.

In the process, I had been exposed to the vast sweep of Cambridge's efforts, both to acquire data on as many U.S. citizens as possible and to leverage that data to influence Americans' voting behavior. I'd also come to see how Facebook's negligent privacy policies and the federal government's total lack of oversight about personal data had enabled all of Cambridge's efforts. But, most of all, I understood how Cambridge had taken advantage of all these forces to help elect Donald Trump.

As the car drove, my lawyers and I sat quietly, each of us preparing for what was to come. We all knew I would share any part of my story in full; the question now was what everyone else wanted to know. Mostly people seemed to want answers, both professional and personal, about how this could happen. There was a variety of reasons why I'd allowed my values to become so warped—from my family's financial situation to the fallacy that Hillary would win regardless of my efforts or those of the company I worked for. But each of those was only part of the story. Perhaps the truest reason of all was the fact that somewhere along the way I'd lost my compass, and then myself. I'd entered this job believing I was a professional who knew how cynical and messy the business of politics was, only to learn time and again how naïve I'd been.

And now, it was on me to make it right.

The car drifted smoothly through the streets of the capital and I began to sense that we were closing in on our destination. I had been warned by the special counsel's team not to be afraid or surprised if, upon arriving at the secure building where I was to be questioned, throngs of press awaited me. The location, it was said, was no longer secure. Reporters had caught on that the site was being used for the interviewing of witnesses.

A reporter, the driver said, was hiding behind a mailbox. He recognized her from CNN. He had seen her loitering around the building for eight hours at a time. In heels, he said. *"What they wouldn't do!"* He exclaimed.

As we neared the place and turned a corner into a garage in the back, the driver told me to turn my face away from the windows, even though they were tinted. In preparation for my conversation with the special counsel, I had been told to clear my day. Completely. I had been told that no one knew how long I would testify or for how long I would then be cross-examined. However long it would be, I was ready. After all, my presence there had been my own doing.

A year earlier, I'd made the decision to come forward, to shine a light in the dark places that I had come to know and to become a whistleblower. I did this because, as I'd come face-to-face with the realities of what Cambridge Analytica had done, I saw all too clearly just how misguided I'd been. I did this because it was the only way to try to make up for what I'd been a part of. But, for more than any other reason, I did this because telling my story to anyone who would listen was the only way we could learn, and hopefully prepare for, what comes next. That was my mission now—to raise the alarm about how Cambridge Analytica had operated and about the dangers that Big Data posed, so that next time voters on both sides would understand the full stakes of the data wars that our democracy is up against.

The driver took us deeper and deeper into the garage, circling, circling farther down.

Why so deep? I wondered. But of course, I already knew: Privacy is a hard thing to come by these days.

1

A Late Lunch

EARLY 2014

The first time I saw Alexander Nix, it was through a thick pane of glass, which is perhaps the best way to view a man like him.

I had shown up late for a business lunch that had been hastily arranged by my close friend Chester Freeman, who was acting, as he often did, as my guardian angel. I was there to meet with three associates of Chester's, two men I knew and one I didn't, all of whom were looking for talent at the intersection of politics and social media. I counted this area as part of my political expertise, having worked on Obama's 2008 campaign; though I was still busy researching my dissertation for my PhD, I was also on the market for a well-paying job. I had kept the fact secret from nearly everyone except Chester, but I was in urgent need of a stable source of income, to take care of myself and help out my family back in Chicago. This lunch was a way for me to obtain a potentially short-term and lucrative consultancy, and I was grateful to Chester for the well-timed assist.

By the time I arrived, however, lunch was nearly over. I'd had appointments that morning, and though I'd hustled to get there, I was late, and I found Chester and the two friends of his I already knew huddled together in the cold outside the Mayfair sushi restaurant, smoking post-meal cigarettes in view of the neighborhood's

Georgian mansions, stately hotels, and expensive shops. The two men were from a country in Central Asia, and like Chester, they, too, were passing through London on business. They had reached out to him for help in connecting with someone who could aid them with digital communications (email and social media campaigns) in an important upcoming election in their country. Though I knew neither of them well, both were powerful men I'd met before and liked, and by gathering us there for the lunch, Chester intended only to do all of us a favor.

Now, in welcome, he rolled me my own cigarette and leaned in to light it for me. Chester, his two friends, and I caught up with one another, chatting brightly and shielding ourselves from the rising wind. As Chester stood there in the afternoon light, ruddy cheeked and happy, I couldn't help but be impressed by his journey. He'd recently been appointed as a diplomat for business and trade relations by the prime minister of a small island nation, but back when I'd first met him, at the Democratic National Convention in 2008, he'd been an idealistic, shaggy-haired nineteen-year-old wearing a blue dashiki. The convention had been in Denver that year, and Chester and I had both been standing in a long line outside Broncos Stadium, waiting to see Hillary Clinton endorse Barack Obama as the party's nominee, when we bumped into each other and started talking.

We had come a long way since then, and each of us now had a hodgepodge of political experience under our proverbial belts. He and I had long shared the dream of "growing up" to do international political work and diplomacy, and recently he'd proudly sent me a picture of the certificate he received upon his diplomatic appointment. And while the Chester who now stood before me outside the restaurant looked the part of a newly minted diplomat, I still recognized him as the genius chatterbox friend I'd known from the beginning, as close to me as a brother.

As we smoked, Chester apologized to me for the last-minute, cobbled-together lunch. And by way of acknowledging what a motley crew he'd assembled there, he gestured to the plate glass window, through which I glimpsed the third person he'd invited—the man, still seated inside, who would change my life and, later, the world.

The fellow appeared to be an average, cut-from-the-cloth Mayfair business type, cell phone held tightly to his ear, but as Chester explained, he was not just any businessman. His name was Alexander Nix and he was the CEO of a British-based elections company. The company, Chester went on, was called the SCL Group, short for Strategic Communications Laboratories, which struck me as the sort of name a board of directors would give a glorified advertising firm it wanted to sound vaguely scientific. In point of fact, Chester said, SCL was a wildly successful company. Over a span of twenty-five years, it had procured defense contracts worldwide and run elections in countries across the globe. Its basic function, he said, was putting into power presidents and prime ministers and, in many cases, ensuring that they stayed there. Most recently, the SCL Group had been working on the reelection campaign of the prime minister for whom Chester now worked, which was how I presumed Chester had come to know this Nix character.

It took me a moment to digest it all. Chester's intention in putting us all together that afternoon was certainly a tangle of potentially conflicting interests. I was there to pitch my services to the two friends, but it now seemed clear that the elections CEO was there to do so as well. And it occurred to me that in addition to my lateness, my youth and lack of experience no doubt meant that, instead, the CEO would likely already have secured the business I wished to have with Chester's two friends.

I peered through the window at the man. I saw him now as

someone more than average. With his phone still to his ear, he suddenly looked terribly serious and consummately professional. Clearly, I was outclassed and outdone. I was disappointed, but I tried hard not to let it show.

"I thought you might like to meet him," Chester offered. "You know," he went on, "he's a good connection and all that," meaning, perhaps, future paying work. "Or," Chester suggested, alternatively, "at least interesting fodder for your dissertation."

I nodded. He was probably right. As disappointed as I might be about what I presumed was already a lost business opportunity, I was academically curious. What did the CEO of such a company actually do? I'd never heard of an elections company.

From my time with Obama and from my recent volunteer work in London with the Democratic Party expat organization Democrats Abroad and with the super PAC Ready for Hillary, my own experience was that campaign managers ran campaigns, working in their own country with, of course, the support of a small but elite group of highly paid experts and an army of underpaid staff, volunteers, and unpaid interns, as I had been. After the 2008 Obama campaign, I'd certainly come across a few people who later became professional campaign consultants, such as David Axelrod, who had been chief strategist for Obama and had gone on to advise the British Labour Party; and Jim Messina, once called "the most powerful person in Washington that you haven't heard of,"[1] who had helmed Obama's 2012 campaign, had become Obama's White House chief of staff, and would go on to advise foreign leaders ranging from David Cameron to Theresa May. Still, it had never occurred to me that there existed entire companies dedicated to the goal of getting people elected to political office abroad.

I regarded the figure through the restaurant's plate glass window with equal parts curiosity and puzzlement. Chester was right.

I might not get any work at the moment, but maybe I would in the future. And I certainly could use the afternoon as research.

The restaurant was pleasant enough, brightly lit from above, with pale wooden floors and cream-colored walls along which Japanese artwork had been tidily hung. Approaching the table, I surveyed the man whom I had been watching from outside. He'd finished his phone call, and Chester made the introductions.

At closer range now, I could see that Nix wasn't your typical Mayfair business type after all. He was what the British call "posh." Immaculate and traditional, he was dressed in a dark, bespoke navy suit and a woven silk tie knotted at the neck of a starched button-down—pure Savile Row, right down to his shoes, which had been shined to a blinding polish. He had beside him a well-worn-in leather briefcase with an old-fashioned brass lock; it looked like it could have been his grandfather's. Though I was a full-blooded American, I had lived in the United Kingdom ever since I graduated from high school, and I knew a member of the British upper crust when I saw one.

Alexander Nix, though, was what I'd call *upper-upper* crust. He was handsome in a British boarding school sort of way—Eton, as it turned out—and he was trim, with a sharp, arrow-like chin and the slightly bony build of someone who doesn't spend any time at the gym. His eyes were a striking, opaque bright blue, and his complexion was smooth and unwrinkled, as though he'd never known a moment of worry in his life. In other words, it was the face of utter privilege. And as he stood before me in that West End London restaurant, I could easily have imagined him helmeted astride a galloping polo pony with a custom-made wooden mallet in hand.

I tried to guess his age. If he were as successful as Chester had claimed, he was likely older than I was by at least a decade, and his posture, equal parts upright and confident, yet somehow also relaxed, suggested an early middle-aged life, one that was aristocratic with a pinch of meritocracy thrown in. He looked as though he'd come into the world with a pretty good leg up, but that he'd used those legs, if Chester was right, in order to stand on his own two feet.

Nix greeted me warmly, as if I were an old friend, shaking my hand with vigor. As we took our seats at a large table tucked away from most of the others in the restaurant, he quickly, though not impolitely, turned his attention to Chester's other two friends and effortlessly picked up the thread of what must have been the conversation they were having before I arrived.

With little revving up, Nix entered full-pitch mode. I recognized what that was because I knew how to do it myself. In order to support myself through all my studies, I'd taught myself how to pitch clients for consulting work, although I could see how skilled Nix was at it. I had neither half his charm nor his experience, and I certainly didn't have his polish. His delivery was as bright as the shine on his expensive shoes.

I listened as he laid out the long history of the company for which he worked. The SCL Group had been established in 1993. Since then, it had run more than two hundred elections and had carried out defense, political, and humanitarian projects in some fifty countries worldwide; when Nix listed them, it sounded like the roster of countries on a United Nations subcommittee: Afghanistan, Colombia, India, Indonesia, Kenya, Latvia, Libya, Nigeria, Pakistan, the Philippines, Trinidad and Tobago, and more. Nix himself had been with SCL for eleven years at that point.

The sheer accumulation of experience and the volume of his work was astonishing to me, and humbling. I couldn't help but note that I was six years old the year of SCL's founding, and in the period of time when I was in kindergarten, grade school, and high school, Nix had been part of building a small but powerful empire. While next to those of my peers, my résumé looked pretty good—I'd done a great deal of international work while living abroad and since my time interning on the Obama campaign—but I couldn't compete with Nix.

"So, we're in America now," Nix was saying, with barely contained enthusiasm.

Just recently, SCL had established a nascent presence there, and Nix's short-term aim was to run as many of the upcoming American midterms in November 2014 as he could, and then go on and corner the elections business in the United States as a whole, including a presidential campaign if he could get his hands on it.

It was an audacious thing to say. But he had already secured the midterm campaigns of some notable candidates and causes. He'd signed the likes of a congressman from Arkansas by the name of Tom Cotton, a wunderkind Harvard grad and Iraq War veteran who was running for a seat in the Senate. He'd signed the entire slate of GOP candidates across *all* the races in the state of North Carolina. And he'd snagged the business of a powerful and deep-pocketed political action committee, or super PAC, belonging to UN ambassador John Bolton, a controversial figure on the right with whom I was all too familiar.

I had lived in the United Kingdom for years, but I knew at least some of the American neoconservative standouts such as Bolton. He was the kind of figure it was hard to ignore: a hawkish lightning rod who, along with a host of other neocons, had recently been revealed to be the brains and cash behind a shadowy organization called Groundswell, the intention of which, among other things, was to undermine the Obama presidency and hype the Hillary Clinton Benghazi controversy,[2] the latter issue with which I was personally familiar. I had worked in Libya and had known Ambassador

Christopher Stevens, who died there due in part to the poor decision making of the U.S. State Department, I thought.

I sat sipping my tea and took careful note of Nix's list of clients. At a glance, they may have sounded like many other Republicans, but the politics of each was so profoundly the opposite of my own beliefs that they formed a veritable rogues' gallery of nemeses to most of my heroes, such as Obama and Hillary. The people Nix named were, to my mind, political pariahs—or even better, piranhas, fish in whose pond I could never have imagined myself taking a safe swim.

Never mind that the special interest groups Nix was working for, with causes ranging from gun rights to pro-life advocacy, were anathema to me. For all my life, I had supported causes that leaned distinctly to the left.

Nix was thrilled with himself, with his company, and with the people and groups he'd managed to lasso. You could see it in his eyes. He was terribly busy, he said, so busy and so hopeful for the future that the SCL Group had had to spin off an entirely new company just to manage the work in the United States alone.

That new company was called Cambridge Analytica.

It had been in business for just under a year, but the world had best pay attention to it, Nix said. Cambridge Analytica was about to cause a revolution.

The revolution Nix had in mind had to do with Big Data and analytics.

In the digital age, data was "the new oil." Data collection was an "arms race," he said. Cambridge Analytica had amassed an arsenal of data on the American public of unprecedented size and scope, the largest, as far as he knew, anyone had ever assembled. The company's monster databases held between two thousand and five thousand individual data points (pieces of personal information) on every individual in the United States over the age of eighteen. That amounted to some 240 million people.

Nix paused and looked at Chester's friends and at me, as if to let the number sink in.

But merely *having* Big Data wasn't the solution, he said. Knowing what to do with it was the key. That involved more scientific and precise ways of putting people into categories: "Democrat," "environmentalist," "optimist," "activist," and the like. And for years, the SCL Group, Cambridge Analytica's parent company, had been identifying and sorting people using the most sophisticated method in behavioral psychology, which gave it the capability of turning what was otherwise just a mountain of information about the American populace into a gold mine.

Nix told us about his in-house army of data scientists and psychologists who had learned precisely how to know whom they wanted to message, what messaging to send them, and exactly where to reach them. He had hired the most brilliant data scientists in the world, people who could laser in on individuals wherever they were to be found (on their cell phones, computers, tablets, on television) and through any kind of medium you could imagine (from audio to social media), using "microtargeting." Cambridge Analytica could isolate individuals and literally cause them to think, vote, and act differently from how they had before. It spent its clients' money on communications that really worked, with *measurable* results, Nix said.

That, he said, is how Cambridge Analytica was going to win elections in America.

While Nix spoke, I glanced over at Chester, hoping to make eye contact in order to figure out what opinion he might have formed of Nix, but I wasn't able to catch his attention. As for Chester's friends,

I could see from the looks on their faces that they were duly wowed as Nix went on about his American company.

Cambridge Analytica was filling an important niche in the market. It had been formed to meet pent-up, unmet demand. The Obama Democrats had dominated the digital communications space since 2007. The Republicans lagged sorely behind in technology innovation. After their crushing defeat in 2012, Cambridge Analytica had come along to level the playing field in a representative democracy by giving the Republicans the technology they lacked.

As for what Nix could do for Chester's friends, whose country didn't have Big Data, due to lack of internet penetration, SCL could get that started for them, and it could use social media to get their message out. Meanwhile, it could also do more traditional campaigning, everything from writing policy platforms and political manifestos to canvassing door-to-door to analyzing target audiences.

The men complimented Nix. I was well enough acquainted with the two by now, though, to see how his pitch had overwhelmed them. I knew their country hadn't the infrastructure to carry out what Nix was planning to do in America, and his strategy didn't sound particularly affordable, even to two men with reasonably deep pockets.

For my part, I was shocked at what Nix had shared—stunned, in fact. I'd never heard anything like it before. He'd described nothing less than using people's personal information to influence them and, hence, to change economies and political systems around the world. He'd made it sound easy to sway voters to make irreversible decisions not against their will but, at the very least, against their usual judgment, and to change their habitual behavior.

At the same time, I admitted, if only to myself, that I was gobsmacked by his company's capabilities. Since my first days in political campaigning, I had developed a special interest in the subject of Big Data analytics. I wasn't a developer or a data scientist, but like other Millennials, I had been an early adopter of all sorts of technology and had lived a digital life from my earliest years. I was predisposed to see data as an integral part of my world, a given, at its worst benign and utilitarian, and at its best possibly transformative.

I myself had used data, even rudimentarily in elections. Aside from being an unpaid intern on Obama's New Media team, I had volunteered for Howard Dean's primary race four years earlier, and then both John Kerry's presidential campaign, as well for both the DNC itself and Obama's senatorial run. Even basic use of data to write emails to undecided voters on what they cared about was "revolutionary" at the time. Howard Dean's campaign broke all existing fund-raising records by reaching people online for the first time.

My interest in data was coupled with my firsthand knowledge of revolutions. A lifelong bookworm, I'd been a student forever but had always engaged in the wider world. In fact, I had always felt that it was imperative for academics to find ways to spin the threads of the high-minded ideas they came up with in the ivory tower into cloth that was of real use to others.

Even though it involved a peaceful transfer of power, you could say that the Obama election was my first experience of a revolution. I had been a part of the spirited celebration in Chicago on the night Obama won his first presidential election, and that street party of millions felt like a political coup.

I'd also had the privilege, and had sometimes experienced the danger, of being on the ground in countries where revolutions were happening silently, had just broken out, or were about to. As an undergraduate, I studied for a year in Hong Kong, where I volunteered with activists shuttling refugees from North Korea via an underground railroad through China and out to safety. Immediately upon graduating from college, I spent time in parts of South Africa, where I worked on projects with former guerrilla strategists who'd helped overthrow apartheid. And in the aftermath of the Arab spring, I worked in post-Gaddafi Libya, and have continued to be interested and involved in independent diplomacy for that country for many years. I guess you could say I had the uncanny habit of putting myself in the middle of places during their most turbulent times.

I had also studied how data could be used for good, looking at how people empowered by it had used it to seek social justice, in some cases to expose corruption and bad actors. In 2011, I had written my master's thesis using leaked government data from Wikileaks as my primary source material. The data showed what had happened during the Iraq War, exposing numerous cases of crimes against humanity.

From 2010 onward the "hacktivist" (i.e., activist hacker) Julian Assange, founder of the organization, had declared virtual war on those that had waged literal war on humanity by widely disseminating top secret and classified files that proved damning to the American government and the U.S. military. The data dump, called "The Iraq War Files," prompted public discourse on protection of civil liberties and international human rights from abuses of power.

Now, as part of my PhD dissertation in diplomacy and human rights, and a continuation of my earlier work, I was going to combine my interest in Big Data with my experience of political turbulence, looking at how data could save lives. I was particularly interested in something called "preventive diplomacy." The United Nations and nongovernmental organizations (NGOs) across the globe were looking for ways to use real-time data to prevent atrocities such as the genocide that occurred in Rwanda in 1994, where earlier action could have been taken if the data had been available to decision makers. "Preventive" data monitoring—of everything from the price of bread to the increased use of racial slurs on Twitter—could give peacekeeping organizations the information they needed to identify, monitor, and peacefully intervene in high-risk societies before conflicts escalated. The proper gathering and analysis of data could prevent human rights violations, war crimes, and even war itself.

Needless to say, I understood the implications of the capabilities Nix was alleging the SCL Group possessed. His talk of data, combined with his words about revolutions, left me unsettled about his intentions and the risks his methods might pose. This made me reluctant to share what I knew about data or what my experience with it was, and I was grateful that day in London to see that he was already wrapping up with Chester's friends and preparing to leave.

Fortunately, Nix had paid me little attention. When he wasn't talking about his company, we had chatted in general about my work on campaigns, but I was relieved he hadn't picked my brain about anything specific to do with Obama's New Media campaign, any of my work on prevention and exposure of war crimes and criminal justice, or my passion for the use of data in preventive diplomacy. I saw Nix for what he was: someone who used data as a means to an end and who worked, it was clear, for many people in the United States whom I considered my opposition. I seemed to have dodged a bullet.

I thought Chester's friends wouldn't choose to work with Nix. His presence and presentation were too large and extravagant, too big for them and for the room. His ebullience had been charming and persuasive; he had even tempered his immodesty with exquisitely honed British manners, but his bluster and ambition were out of proportion with their needs. Nix, though, seemed oblivious to the men's reserve. As he packed up to leave the restaurant, he prattled on about how he could help them with specially segmented audiences.

When Nix got up from the table, I realized I'd still have time to pitch Chester's friends. Once Nix was out the door, I intended to approach them now privately, with a simple and modest proposal. But as Nix began to go, Chester gestured to me that I ought to join him in saying a proper good-bye.

Outside in the cold, with the afternoon light waning, Chester and I stood with Nix in a few long seconds of awkward silence. But for as long as I had known him, Chester had never been able to tolerate silence of any length.

"Hey, my Democrat consultant friend, you should hang out with my Republican consultant friend!" he blurted out.

Nix flashed Chester a sudden and strange look, a combination of alarm and annoyance. He clearly didn't like being caught off guard or told what to do. Still, he reached into his suit coat pocket and pulled out a messy stack of business cards and began shuffling through them. The cards he'd taken out clearly weren't his. They were of varied sizes and colors, likely from businessmen and potential clients like Chester's visiting friends, other men to whom he must have pitched his wares on similar Mayfair afternoons.

Finally, when he fished out one of his own cards, he handed it to me with a flourish, waiting while I paused to take it in.

"Alexander James Ashburner Nix," the card read. From the weight of the paper stock on which it was printed to its serif typeface, it screamed royalty.

"Let me get you drunk and steal your secrets," Alexander Nix said, and laughed, but I could tell he was only half joking.

2

Crossing Over

OCTOBER–DECEMBER 2014

In the months after I first met Alexander Nix, I still wasn't able to secure any work that would substantially improve my family's current financial situation. In October 2014, I reached out again to Chester for help in finding the right kind of part-time job, and he responded by arranging a meeting for me with his prime minister.

It was a rare opportunity for me to offer digital and social media strategy to a nation's leader. The prime minister was a multiterm incumbent running for reelection, but this time he was facing strong opposition in his country and was concerned about losing. Chester wanted to introduce me to him to see how I might be of help.

This was how, quite inadvertently, I ran into Alexander Nix a second time.

I was in the lounge of a private jet hangar at Gatwick Airport, waiting for a morning meeting with the prime minister, when the door of the lounge flew open and Nix burst in. I was early for my meeting; his was the first one of the day, and of course it *had* to have been scheduled before mine. My poor luck again.

"What are you doing here?" he asked, his expression both threatening and threatened. He clutched his beaten-up briefcase to his chest and leaned backward in mock horror. "Are you stalking me?"

I laughed.

When I told him what I was doing there, he let me know that he had been working with the prime minister on the past few elections. He was fascinated to hear that I was there "hoping" to do the same thing.

We exchanged some small talk. And when he was called in to his meeting, he tossed an invitation over his shoulder. "You should come to the SCL office sometime and learn more about what we do," he said, and then he was gone.

Although I was still wary of him, I would indeed choose to visit Alexander Nix at the SCL office. A few days after our chance encounter at Gatwick, Chester called to say that "Alexander" had been in touch, and could the three of us get together and perhaps chat about what we all might be thinking about the prime minister's upcoming election?

I found myself strangely and pleasantly surprised at the idea. Something about running into me at the hangar must have caught Alexander's attention. Perhaps he wasn't used to boldness in someone of my age and gender. Whatever his reason, the proposed meeting was about working *together*, which struck me as far more positive than working against each other, given that he obviously had the upper hand and especially because I truly needed work.

In mid-October, Chester and I visited the SCL office together. It was tucked away off Green Park, near Shepherd Market, down an alley and off a road called Yarmouth Place, and it occupied a worn-looking building that appeared not to have been rehabbed since the 1960s. The building was filled with offices of unknown small start-ups, such as the drinkable-vitamins company SCL shared a hallway with. Wooden crates filled with tiny bottles nearly blocked our way into the ground-floor conference room, which was shared among all tenants and needed to be rented by the hour—not exactly what I expected of such a seemingly-posh crew of political consultants.

But it was that room where Chester and I met with Alexander and Kieran Ward, whom Alexander introduced to us as his director of communications. Alexander said Kieran had been on the ground for SCL in many foreign elections; he appeared to be only in his mid-thirties, but the expression in his eyes told me they had seen a lot.

There was a great deal at stake in the election of the prime minister, Alexander told us. The PM had "an inflated ego," he said. Chester nodded in assent. This was the PM's fifth bid for office, and amid dissatisfaction, his people were calling for him to step down. In his meeting with him at Gatwick, Alexander had warned the PM that if he "didn't batten down the hatches," he was certain to lose, but there was little time left. The election was coming up in a few months, after the turn of the New Year.

What SCL was hoping to do, Alexander began, and then he stopped himself. He looked at Chester and me. "But you don't even know what we do, do you?" and before we knew it, he'd slipped out the door and slipped back in again, laptop in hand. He turned down the lights and pulled up a PowerPoint presentation that he projected onto a big screen on the wall.

"Our children," he began, clicker in hand, "won't live in a world with 'blanket advertising,'" he said, referring to the messaging intended for a broad audience and sent out in a giant, homogenous blast. "Blanket advertising is just too imprecise."

He pulled up a slide that read, "Traditional Advertising Builds Brands and Provides Social Proof but Doesn't Change Behavior." On the left-hand side of the slide was an advertisement for Harrods department store that read 50% OFF SALE in large type. On the right were the McDonald's and Burger King logos, arches and a crown.

These kinds of ads, he explained, either were simply informational or, if they even worked, merely "proved" an existing customer's loyalty to a brand. The approach was antiquated.

"The SCL Group offers messaging built for a twenty-first-century world," Alexander said. Traditional marketing like these ads would never work.

If a client wanted to reach new customers, "What you have to do," he explained, was not just reach them but "convert" them. "How can McDonald's get somebody to eat one of their burgers when they've never done so before?"

He shrugged and clicked to the next slide.

"The Holy Grail of communications," he said, "is when you can actually start to change behavior."

The next slide read, "Behavioral Communications." On the left was an image of a beach with a square, white sign that read, "Public Beach Ends Here." On the right was a bright yellow, triangular placard resembling a railroad crossing sign. It read, "Warning. Shark Sighted."

Which one was more effective? The difference was almost comical.

"Using your knowledge of people's fear of being eaten by a shark, you know that the second would stop people from swimming in your piece of sea," Alexander said. *Your piece of sea?* I thought. *I suppose he's used to pitching to those that have their own.*

He continued without pause: SCL wasn't an ad agency. It was a "behavior change agency," he explained.

In elections, campaigns lost billions of dollars using messages like the Private Beach sign, messages that didn't really work.

In the next slide was an embedded video and an image, both campaign ads. The video was composed of a series of stills of Mitt Romney's face and clips of audiences applauding over a soundtrack of a Romney speech. It concluded with the phrase "Strong New Leadership." The image was of a parched front lawn littered with signs on which candidates' names had been printed. Romney, Santorum,

Gingrich—it almost didn't matter who it was. It was so clear how static the signs were, how easy to ignore.

Alexander let out a little chuckle. You see, he said. None of these signs "converts" anyone. He held out his arms. "If you're a Democrat and you see a Romney yard sign, you don't suddenly have this 'Road to Damascus' moment and change party."

We laughed.

I sat there amazed. Here I'd been in communications for many years, and I'd never thought to examine the messaging this way. I'd never heard anyone talk about the flatness of contemporary advertising. And until this moment, I had seen the Obama New Media campaign of 2008, for which I'd been a dedicated intern, as so sophisticated and savvy.

That campaign had been the first to use social media to communicate with voters. We'd promoted Senator Obama on Myspace, YouTube, Pinterest, and Flickr. I'd even created the then-senator's first Facebook page, and I'd always treasured the memory of the day Obama came into the Chicago office, pointed at his profile photo on my computer screen, and exclaimed, "Hey, that's me!"

Now I saw that, however cutting-edge we'd been at the time, in Alexander's terms, we had been information-heavy, repetitive, and negligible. We hadn't *converted* anyone, really. Most of our audience consisted of self-identified Obama supporters. They'd sent us their contact information or we gathered it from them with their permission once they posted messages·on our sites. We hadn't reached *them*; they had reached *us*.

Our ads had been based on "social proof," Alexander explained; they had merely reinforced preexisting "brand" loyalty. We had posted endlessly on social media Obama content just like the Private Beach sign, the repetitive Romney video, and the lame lawn signs that didn't cause "behavioral change" but were "information-heavy" and provided mere "social proof" that our audience loved Barack Obama. And once we had Obama lovers' attention, we sent them even more information-heavy and detailed messaging. Our intention might have been to keep them interested or to make sure they voted, but according to Alexander's paradigm, we had merely flooded them with data they didn't need.

"Dear so-and-so," I remembered writing. "Thank you so much for writing to Senator Obama. Barack's out on the campaign trail. I'm Brittany, and I'm responding on his behalf. Here are some policy links for you on blah, blah, blah, blah blah."

As enthusiastic as we had been—and our New Media team was hundreds strong and the campaign occupied two full floors of a skyscraper in downtown Chicago that summer—I saw now that our messaging was simple, perhaps even crude.

Alexander pulled up another slide, one with charts and graphs showing how his company did much more than create effective messaging. It sent that messaging to the right people based on scientific methods. Before campaigns even started, SCL conducted research and employed data scientists who analyzed data and precisely identified the client's target audiences. The emphasis here, of course, was on the heterogeneity of the audience.

I had been particularly proud that the Obama campaign was known for how it segmented its audience, separating them according to the issues they cared about, the states in which they lived, and whether they were male or female. But seven years had elapsed since then. Alexander's company now went far beyond traditional demographics.

He pulled up a slide that read, "Audience Targeting Is Changing." On the left was a picture of the actor Jon Hamm as Don Draper, the 1960s Madison Avenue advertising executive from the AMC series *Mad Men*.

"Old-school advertising in the 1960s," Alexander said, "is just loads of smart people like us, sitting around a table like this, coming up with ideas like 'Coca-Cola Is It' and 'Beans Means Heinz' and spending all our clients' money pushing that out into the world, hoping that it works."

But whereas 1960s communication was all "top down," 2014 advertising was "bottom up." With all the advances in data science and predictive analytics, we could know so much more about people than we ever imagined, and Alexander's company looked at people to determine what they needed to hear in order to be influenced in the direction *you*, the client, wanted them to go.

He clicked over to yet another slide. It read, "Data Analytics, Social Sciences, Behavior and Psychology."

Cambridge Analytica had grown out of the SCL Group, which itself had evolved from something called the Behavioural Dynamics Institute, or BDI, a consortium of some sixty academic institutions and hundreds of psychologists. Cambridge Analytica now employed in-house psychologists who, instead of pollsters, designed political surveys and used the results to segment people. They used "psychographics" to understand people's complex personalities and devise ways to trigger their behavior.

Then, through "data modeling," the team's data gurus created algorithms that could accurately predict those people's behavior when they received certain messages that had been carefully crafted precisely for them.

"What message does Brittany need to hear?" Alexander asked me, and clicked over to another slide. We need to create "adverts just for Brittany," he said, looked at me again, and smiled. "Just for the things she cares about and not for anything else."

At the end of his presentation, he pulled up an image of Nelson Mandela.

Mandela was in my pantheon of superheroes. I had worked with one of his best friends in South Africa, someone who had been imprisoned with him on Robben Island. I had even helped run a Women's Day event in South Africa for Mandela's longtime partner, Winnie, but I'd never gotten the chance to shake the hand of the man himself. Now, here he was, right before me.

Alexander said that in 1994, the work SCL did with Mandela and the African National Congress had stopped election violence at the polls. That had affected the outcome of one of the most important elections in the history of South Africa. On the screen was a ringing endorsement from Mandela himself.

How could I not have been impressed?

Alexander had to jump out of the meeting abruptly—something had come up—but he left us in the capable hands of Kieran Ward, who walked us through more of what SCL did.

It had started out running elections in South Africa, and now it ran nine or ten elections each year in places such as Kenya, Saint Kitts, Santa Lucia, and Trinidad and Tobago. Kieran had been on the ground in some of those countries.

In 1998, SCL had expanded into the corporate and commercial world, and after September 11, 2001, it had begun to work in defense, with the U.S. Department of Homeland Security, NATO, the CIA, the FBI, and the State Department. The company had also sent experts to the Pentagon to train others in its techniques.

SCL had a social division as well. It provided public health communications, in case studies where he explained they persuaded people in African nations to use condoms and people in India to drink clean water. It had had contracts with UN agencies and with ministries of health worldwide.

The more I heard about SCL, the more I was taken with it. And when we regrouped and Alexander joined us for dinner at a nearby restaurant, I learned more about him and warmed to him as well.

He had a much broader view of the world than I'd initially thought. He had a degree in art history from Manchester University. After graduating, he had worked in finance at a century-old securities merchant bank in Mexico, a country I loved dearly. He'd gone on to work also in Argentina, then had returned to England, thinking he could make much more of the SCL Group than it currently was—which was more a loose collection of projects than a company, really. He had built it from almost scratch into a mini-empire in just over a decade.

Alexander had loved running elections in the Caribbean and Kenya. And when he mentioned that he had overseen the company's work in West Africa, I was moved. In Ghana, SCL had undertaken the largest research project on health in that country, and since my own most recent work had been on health care reform in North Africa, we found common ground.

I shared with him what I had been working on, and I told him about some of my work in South Africa, Hong Kong, The Hague, the European Parliament, and for NGOs such as Amnesty International. I still said nothing about my campaign work, and I suppose that hung in the air between us, but I wasn't ready. Cambridge Analytica was working for the opposition.

Still, I enjoyed the conversation, and next to me, all evening long, Chester boasted so much about my accomplishments that he was a veritable walking, talking recommendation letter.

"Well," Alexander said when he heard all that I'd done. "A person like you doesn't wait around for new opportunities, does she?"

I was only half surprised when Chester called the next morning and said that Alexander had gotten in touch with him and asked if he thought I'd be willing to come back in for a formal interview. I knew that Alexander likely had few occasions to meet a young woman like me, not because I was so rare a bird but because of the world in which he lived.

I was a twenty-six-year-old American woman who seemed unafraid to have entered high-stakes, high-testosterone arenas. He had emerged from a closed society of young, privileged men destined to operate in a world of others who looked just like him.

I was of a mixed mind, though, about a job at Cambridge Analytica.

It was exhilarating to understand how such a small company in Britain could be so bold and have such an impact on political systems, cultures, and economies. I was intrigued by the sophisticated technology and its potential to be used for social good. But I was concerned about the company's current clients in America. How could I not be? I was who I was: a dyed-in-the-wool Democrat.

But I needed a job. A scrappy self-starter, I wasn't afraid of doing things that might make me money, even if they weren't my first choice. I'd pushed myself out of my comfort zone at an early age, volunteering on Howard Dean's 2003 primary campaign bid for the presidency and then on John Kerry's run when I was only fifteen years old. To support the unpaid work I was passionate about, throughout university in the UK, I'd taken odd jobs, such as training in wine as an in-house sommelier, and less glamorously waited tables—and when really stuck for money, I'd taken bartending and cleaning shifts to remove vomit from the floors of gritty local pubs.

Then, when I was beginning my MPhil/PhD studies in 2012, I leapt to more entrepreneurial endeavors. I started up an events company that put government officials and businesses in conversation with Libyans to discuss how to help stabilize that country in the wake of the Arab Spring. I had gone on to work on a part-time basis as director of operations for a UK trade and investment association

that specialized in fostering relationships between the United Kingdom and nations, such as Ethiopia, where it was difficult to do business or easily engage in diplomacy.

Earlier in 2014, while I was still working on my doctorate, I had
aspired to find a plum job with the Ready for Hillary (RFH) super
PAC and with Hillary Clinton's presidential campaign itself, working all the connections I had cultivated over the years in the DNC
and, more recently, in Democrats Abroad in London. But none of my
recent efforts to work with the Democrats or with liberal or humanitarian causes had led to opportunities that would truly pay the bills.
All the (poorly paid) positions at the small RFH super PAC were
already filled, and the Hillary campaign wasn't up and running yet.

I'd then pursued a dream job working for my friend John Jones
QC, a barrister at the Doughty Street Chambers and one of the
world's most prominent human rights attorneys. (On his team was
the equally formidable Amal Clooney, née Alamuddin.)

John was an unparalleled champion of global civil liberties. He'd
defended some of the world's most controversial bad actors, from
Saif al-Islam Gaddafi, second son of Muammar Gaddafi, to Liberian
president Charles Taylor. At tribunals in the former Yugoslavia and
in Rwanda, Sierra Leone, Lebanon, and Cambodia, he'd confronted
thorny issues such as counterterrorism, war crimes, and extradi-
tions, and he did this in the service of upholding international human rights law. More recently, he had taken on the case of WikiLeaks
founder (and the source of primary material for one of my master's
theses) Julian Assange, who was evading extradition to Sweden and
had sought asylum in the Ecuadorian embassy in London.

John and I had become friends. We talked about and bonded over
our admiration for the infamous whistleblower, and we joked about
the rivalry between the prep schools we'd attended; he was British but
had attended Phillips Exeter Academy, the rival school to my own,

Phillips Academy Andover, both started in the late eighteenth century by two members of the Phillips family. I didn't yet have my credentials as a barrister, but John had kindly seen in me keenness and the potential to do good work, and he'd been trying to find funding for a position he wanted me to fill in The Hague, where he aimed to open a new branch of Doughty Street called Doughty Street International.

But the money hadn't come through yet. Even if it had, it wouldn't have been the type of money commercial lawyers make. That was the world of human rights work. John and his small family sacrificed for their belief in the law, living much more modestly than other world-famous lawyers, as John did pro bono work most of the time. As much out of principle as practicality, he was a no-frills vegetarian who rode his bicycle everywhere.

While I had imagined a close-to-the-bone and ethically authentic life like John's someday, that didn't seem in the cards right now. Back home, my parents were on the verge of poverty, the culmination of events over a decade in the making.

For many years, my father's family owned commercial real estate and a string of upscale health clubs and spas; my mother had been able to stay home to raise her children herself; and my younger sister, Natalie, and I had grown up in a privileged upper-middle-class household, enjoying a private school education, dance and music lessons, and family trips to Disney World and Caribbean beaches.

But when the subprime mortgage crisis hit in 2008, my father's family businesses suffered. A number of other problems occurred, and these, too, had been out of my parents' control. Soon, we had no savings left. Years before, my mother had been an employee at Enron, and when that Houston house of cards collapsed in 2001, she lost all her retirement money.   •

My father was now jobless; my mother, who hadn't worked in twenty-six years, had to retrain herself to reenter the workforce.

In the meantime, my parents refinanced our family home and sold off their assets until, when the bank came calling, they had literally nothing at all but the belongings in our house.

During all this, something deeply troubling was happening to my father's state of mind. He was strangely emotionless. When we tried to speak to him about what was going on, he wasn't really all there. His eyes were eerily vacant. He spent his days in bed or in front of the television, and if anyone asked him how things were, he answered flatly, saying that things were fine. We assumed it was clinical depression, but he refused to seek therapy or take medication. He refused even to be seen by a doctor. We wanted to shake him, to wake him up, but we felt helpless to reach him.

By the time Alexander Nix called Chester to invite me in for a job interview at SCL, in October 2014, my mother had found a job as a flight attendant. She'd had to move to Ohio, where the airline was based, and she was living in hotels with her coworkers. Back home, my father was surviving on food stamps. My mother, who had grown up with limited resources on American military bases, never thought she'd go back to struggling. But here it was, staring us in the face.

As much as I had my reservations about SCL, I couldn't afford to be picky. I would somehow try to balance finishing my PhD with working as a consultant. I needed a job that could help sustain me and my family. I was thinking not only of the present, but of the long term as well.

Alexander was landed gentry. In the eighteenth century, his family had its hand in the famed East India Company. He was married to a Norwegian shipping heiress.

Although I had been raised with plenty of privilege, there wasn't anything left to draw on. I was now a poor student who had a habit of overdrawing my already meager bank account, with nothing in the way of savings. My home was a ramshackle flat in East London. I had plenty of work bona fides, but I knew if I wanted to run around with Alexander, I needed to spruce myself up.

I researched new developments in digital campaigning and data analysis. I brushed up on nonprofit marketing and campaigning techniques. Then I pressed my best suit, a hand-me-down from my mother's Enron days.

When I arrived for my interview, Alexander was in the middle of an urgent phone call. He thrust into my hands an oversized, nearly sixty-page document and told me to read it while I waited. It was a mock-up for a new SCL brochure, and it was a veritable encyclopedia. I thumbed through it, knowing I'd get to the rest of it later, but I zeroed in on a section about how the company used "psyops" in defense and humanitarian campaigns.

I was familiar with the term, and it intrigued rather than troubled me. Short for "psychological operations," which itself was a euphemism for "psychological warfare," psyops can be used in war, but its applications for peacekeeping appealed to me. Influencing "hostile" audiences can sound terrifying, but psyops, for example, can be used to help shift young men in Islamic nations away from joining Al-Qaeda or to de-escalate conflict between tribal factions on Election Day.

I was still gobbling up the information in the brochure when Alexander invited me into his office. I expected the inner sanctum of a man who presented as so worldly to bear evidence of the universe in which he lived, but the room was little more than an unadorned glass box. There were no personal photos, no mementos. Its furnishings consisted of a desk, two chairs, a computer monitor, and a narrow shelf of books.

Alexander sat back in his chair and steepled his fingers. Why, he asked me, was I interested in working for the SCL Group?

I joked that he was the one who had asked me to come see *him*.

He laughed. But, really, he pressed, kindly.

I told him that I had just organized an enormous international health care conference with the British government, MENA Health, and I knew another was coming up soon, this one on security. As exciting as the work was, it had also been exhausting.

As I talked, he listened carefully, and as he spoke more about the company, I found it ever more interesting. At one point, I sneaked a glance at his bookshelf, and when he caught me doing it, he burst out laughing.

"That's just my collection of fascist literature," he said, and he waved a hand in the air dismissively. I wasn't sure what he meant, so I laughed, too. Clearly there was something on that shelf about which he was embarrassed, and it put me at ease to know that some of those conservative titles I noticed, and shunned, might not be quite his cup of tea, either.

We talked for a while longer, and when we came to my work in public health in East Africa, he jumped out of his chair and said, "I have some people here that you *must* meet." He then took me into the larger office and introduced me to three women, each more interesting and vibrant than the next.

One had worked for over a decade in preventive diplomacy for the Commonwealth Secretariat, protecting people in Kenya and Somalia caught in tribal disputes by negotiating with warlords. Her name was Sabhita Raju. She had held my dream job and was now at SCL.

Another staff member had been the former director of operations for the International Rescue Committee (IRC) and had been dedicated to saving lives for more than fifteen years. She was Ceris Bailes.

And the third had won awards from the United Nations for her work on the environment. Back home in her native Lithuania, she had worked for the liberal political party. Her name was Laura Hanning-Scarborough.

I liked all of them, and I was cheered to hear that they had strong backgrounds in humanitarian work and yet were employed at SCL. Clearly, there had been a good reason for each to choose it.

They seemed as interested in my work as I was in theirs. I shared with them my time in eastern South Africa, when I brought seventy-six volunteers out to Pienaar, a poverty-stricken township, to work for a charity called Tenteleni, tutoring children in math, science, and English. I also shared with them a lobbying project I had done at the European Parliament, when I had the privilege of briefing members on how to pressure European countries to include North Korea in their foreign policy priorities. And I expressed a deep interest in do-ing work in post-Ebola Africa, particularly Sierra Leone and Liberia.

They seemed excited about the possibility of my bringing these kinds of projects to SCL.

Shortly after the interview, Alexander called and made me an of-fer. I could work for the company as a consultant, just as I wished.

Wouldn't it be great, he said, to have the logistics and expenses for my projects covered by the SCL Group? It employed smart, effective people; used cutting-edge technologies and methodologies; and had a supportive infrastructure—and, not to mention, it would offer me an opportunity to learn how to use data-driven communications in practical applications such as preventive diplomacy. I'd see up close and personal how it worked and where it needed improvement, and all that would enable me to write my dissertation and finish up my PhD.

And the job was niche work. I could use it as a springboard for ful-filling any number of dreams: becoming a diplomat, an international human rights activist, or even a political adviser like David Axelrod or Jim Messina.

It was tempting, but I still had reservations.

I had no desire to work for the Republicans. Cambridge Analytica had just signed the Ted Cruz campaign and Alexander had made it very clear that he was out to conquer the Republican Party in the United States.

Also, as much as I desperately needed the money, I didn't want to commit to staying at Cambridge forever. I wanted to come on as a consultant at a good rate, but be able to move on when I wanted to.

Alexander must have read my mind. He told me my work at the company would only ever be under the SCL Group. No need to work on the American side, he said.

He offered me a part-time consultancy and what seemed at the time a decent wage, with the promise of more if I performed well.

"Let's date before we get married, yuh?" he said. "So, what do you want to do?"

In my early grassroots work, I had been surrounded by others who looked like me and thought the way I did—young, progressive activists on a shoestring budget. I first encountered people unlike me when I began working in human rights. In that arena, I met members of Parliament, top thought leaders, and successful business-people across the globe. Some were wealthy, but all had power. I was face-to-face with those on "the other side," and I was always ambivalent about how I felt about them and what it meant to engage with them.

I remember the moment I realized I had to find some way to marry my grassroots beliefs with an efficacy in the wider world. It was April 20, 2009. I was standing outside the United Nations building in Geneva. I was there with others to protest the appearance of Mahmoud Ahmadinejad, then the president of Iran. He had been invited to give the opening keynote address at the Durban II World Conference Against Racism and Intolerance.

Ahmadinejad, a religious hardliner, had been in power for nearly four years, and in that time, he had breached civil liberties and violated human rights. Among other things, he had punished women appearing in public in what he called "improper hijab." In his view, and under his rule, homosexuality simply didn't "exist"; the HIV virus had been created by Westerners to disrupt developing nations like his; the State of Israel ought to be wiped off the map; and the Holocaust was a Zionist invention.

In short, he was a man I, and much of the educated world, had come to despise.

As I stood that day outside the UN building with members of an organization called UN Watch—as one man after another, ambassadors and princes, kings and businessmen, passed through its doors—I thought about these men: whether they agreed with him or not, they had the power and the clout to be in the room with Ahmadinejad, to hear him speak, and to engage with one another in dialogue about it.

I looked at the crowd of protesters of which I was a part. Many looked just like me—some were graduate students, young, in torn jeans and worn sneakers and rugged boots. I respected these people, I believed in what they did, and I believed in myself.

But that day, I put down my protest sign and slipped through the glass doors without anyone noticing I had entered. At the registration desk, I obtained a badge, the kind of pass students can get in order to use the library there: white with a blue stripe at the top, but almost identical to the badges diplomats wore on their lapels.

And wearing my finest hand-me-down power suit, adorned with that badge, I made my way to the auditorium without being questioned.

When Ahmadinejad began his anti-Israel rant, I watched as Chancellor Angela Merkel of Germany and other European leaders walked out. These were powerful people, and their act of protest made headlines that day. It put pressure on the United Nations to reconsider Iran's position in the global conversation. My friends outside and their protest had gone nearly unnoticed. To make a bigger difference, it seemed, one had to be on the inside, no matter how much compromise that took, and you couldn't be afraid to be in a room with people who disagreed with your beliefs or even offended you.

For most of my life, I'd been a staunch, intense, and even angry and oppositional activist, refusing to engage with those who disagreed with me or whom I judged to be in some way corrupt. I was more pragmatic now. I had come around to the realization that I could do a lot more good in the world if I stopped being mad at the other side. I began to learn this when Barack Obama, in the early days of his first term, announced that he would sit at the table with anyone willing to meet with him. There needn't be any conditions, even for those considered "rogue leaders." And the older I got, the more I understood why he'd said that.

I knew that working for Cambridge Analytica was going to cause a sea change in my life. At the time, I believed that what I was about to do would give me a chance to see up close how the other side worked, to have greater compassion for people, and the ability to work with those with whom I disagreed.

This was what was in my head when I said yes to Alexander Nix. Those were my hopes when I crossed over to investigate the other side.

3

Power in Nigeria

DECEMBER 2014

SCL was made up of ten to fifteen full-time employees—some British, some Canadian, an Australian, three Lithuanians, and an Israeli among them—and I made my rounds to meet them and learn a little more. Each was my age or a bit older, most with master's degrees, but also many with PhDs. All had already amassed impressive experience working in the for-profit and nonprofit worlds, in everything from banking to high-tech to the oil and gas industry to running humanitarian programs across Africa.

They had come to the company because it offered them the unique opportunity to work at a place in Europe that had the feel of a Silicon Valley start-up. They were supremely hardworking and serious. Their tone was subdued and professional, with an undercurrent of urgency that, though quiet, seemed more characteristically New York than London. They worked long hours and gave 200 percent of themselves. Some had been embedded in the recent American election campaigns and had just returned to the London office to a hero's welcome. They'd been living for a year in offices in Oregon and North Carolina and Colorado, where the most contested races had been. Those who'd stayed behind in London had worked just as hard, as experts on the countries where the SCL Group also did business.

Each of my colleagues possessed highly specialized skill sets that gave him or her very specific roles in the company.

Kieran, the director of communications, whom I had met during my interview, did everything from political party branding to global messaging strategy. His list of advertising awards was impressive, and his work in corporate branding was better than most I had seen. After Alexander, he'd been with the company the longest, and he showed me a thirty-strong shelf of political party manifestos and platforms SCL had written and he'd designed.

Though with the company for only a few years, Peregrine Willoughby-Brown—Pere, for short; pronounced "Perry"—a Canadian, had already worked in multiple countries, handling elections, running focus groups, gathering data, and organizing locals. He had recently been in Ghana, working on the enormous public health project Alexander had told me about. Pere helped orient me to what it was like to be embedded in foreign campaigns in places other than the United States. In developing nations, logistics could be a nightmare. Even getting access to certain regions was difficult; roads could be washed out or nonexistent. But most problems, he said with a grin, were with people, such as when local pollsters and canvassers didn't show up or simply blew off their jobs after a first paycheck.

Jordan Kleiner was a jovial Brit with an enormous peacock tattoo on his chest. His job was to make sense of the company's research and serve as liaison between the research team and the communications and operations teams. He also acted as a kind of bridge between the data people and the creatives, and he knew how to translate research into effective copy and images.

To a new person on the inside, the team comprised big thinkers and problem solvers who were politically liberal and who, in the early winter of 2014, didn't seem terribly bothered by the fact that the company had taken on conservative clients—in part, I think, because they hadn't gotten in too deep yet. The American midterms had introduced them to hawks and eccentrics, but it might have been possible for them to think of the latter as one-offs, and the company was only just beginning to secure contracts for the Republican primaries.

At the time, the mood in the office was cheerful, the camaraderie strong, and the members of the group uncompetitive with one another, as there were so few of them and their jobs didn't overlap too often.

The SCL and Cambridge Analytica staff were energized by Alexander's vision. The opportunity open to them was the equivalent of that at Facebook in the early days, and it hadn't taken Facebook too many years to go public to the tune of an $18 billion valuation. Alexander wanted a similar outcome, and as Millennials, the staff looked to Mark Zuckerberg's baby as a model of remarkable innovation in spaces no one had even thought to occupy until the company came along.

Cambridge Analytica was based on the same idealistic notion of "connectivity" and "engagement" that had fueled Facebook. The company's raison d'être was to boost engagement in uncharted territory, and those who worked there clearly believed, as those at Facebook had, that they were building something real that the world simply didn't yet know it couldn't do without.

Alexander occupied one glass box at the front of the office, and the data scientists occupied one at the back. Theirs was filled with computer stations where the company's small team of scientists were glued to multiple screens.

Some were eccentric and kept to themselves. One, a Romanian with dark brown eyes, looked up from his work only from time to time. His specialty was research design; he could break up a country into regions and make statistically accurate samples of populations others could use to identify target audiences. Another Lithuanian, who dressed like a posh Brit, often coming to work in a smoking jacket, specialized in data collection and strategy.

The two codirectors of Data Analytics were Dr. Alexander Tayler, a taciturn, ginger-haired Australian, and Dr. Jack Gillett, a dark-haired, friendly Englishman. Tayler and Gillett had been classmates at Cambridge University and, after graduation, each had spent a few years as cogs in the wheels of larger outfits—Gillett at the Royal Bank of Scotland and Tayler at Schlumberger, an oil field services company. Both had come to SCL for the opportunity to design cutting-edge data programs and run their own shop.

Tayler and Gillett had at their disposal a robust but supple database that gave the company a great advantage whenever it had to run a new political campaign. Usually, every time a campaign begins, those in charge of data have to build a database from scratch or buy a database from a vendor. SCL's database was its own, and it could buy more and more data sets and model those data points more accurately with each client project. While I would later learn the true cost of this "advantage," and the legal wrangling it took to convince clients to share their data with SCL permanently, for now it seemed to me an incredibly benign and powerful tool.

On the first Obama campaign, we'd had no advanced predictive analytics at all. In the six intervening years, things had changed so much. Alexander said that data was an incredible "natural resource." It was the "new oil," available in vast quantities, and Cambridge Analytica was on track to become the largest and most influential data and analytics firm in the world. It was an unprecedented opportunity for those with an adventurous, entrepreneurial spirit. There were claims to be staked, data to mine. And it was a honeymoon period in a completely new industry. It was the equivalent, Alexander said, of the "Wild West."

Alexander wasn't in the office very often. The company had just achieved a massive political upset in America, winning an unheard-of thirty-three out of forty-four races in the U.S. midterms. A 75 percent success rate for a communications agency coming in from the outside for the first time was astounding, and Alexander was out and about, using the company's success to drum up new business. I understood him to be flying here and there to meet Bill Gates and others like him when in America and, when in London, entertaining British billionaires such as Sir Martin Sorrell.

The SCL office wasn't the sort of place where one brought important businessmen or heads of state. The space itself was dingy and windowless, dark even at noon. Its carpet was a worn-in industrial gray, its drop ceilings pockmarked, uneven, and curiously stained. With the exception of the two glass boxes, one for Alexander and the other for the data scientists, it consisted of a single room of roughly a thousand square feet into which the entire staff was crammed, clustered at two sets of pushed-together desks. The only other private meeting space was a tiny room of about eight by ten feet, with a table, a couple of chairs, and no ventilation; it was dubbed "the Sweat Box." While his employees packed into "the Sweat Box" like sardines, Alexander preferred to entertain potential clients at a nearby swanky bar or restaurant.

When I finally had a chance to sit down with him in his office in the second week of December, he and I talked about various projects I could pursue. He made it clear that if I wanted to chase social or humanitarian projects, I had to bring in money to fund them. He gave me his blessing to continue my work on post-Ebola Africa, a project I was interested in doing with the World Health Organization and the governments of Liberia and Sierra Leone. With Chester's help, and with his unrivaled Rolodex of contacts, I would approach each and see if I could get a literal buy-in.

Alexander also suggested that I look into upcoming elections. He asked me to follow up with Chester's prime minister and with the Central Asian men he had pitched at the sushi restaurant where he and I first met. We looked at other leads as well. Some were mine, and some were connections that I had through Chester and other worldly friends.

In contacting clients, I needed to determine three things right away, Alexander said. The first was "Is there a need?"—meaning was there a project? The second was "Do you have a budget?" And the third, which was as important as the second, was "Are you on a time line?" If someone didn't have a time line, then there was no urgency to go ahead with the project and, regardless of how much money the client had, the lead would probably go nowhere.

I needed a title, Alexander said, something that "sounded impressive but that's not too overinflated." It wasn't meaningful in-house, he explained, just a tag of sorts by which I could identify myself when addressing clients.

I suggested "Special Advisor," which Alexander liked because it reflected my part-time status and was sufficiently vague. I liked it because it was the title given to UN envoys whose jobs I coveted, such as "Special Advisor on Human Rights."

Now all I had to do was earn it.

In my early days as a street fund-raiser in Chicago, when I had all of sixty seconds to persuade someone to hand me over their credit card information and sign them up to make monthly donations to a charity they'd never heard of, I'd become inured to rejection and unafraid of approaching strangers. And in my more recent work, I'd called up ambassadors and other dignitaries and foreign businesspeople and had spent many days a week sometimes in both the House of Commons and the House of Lords. I could talk with a businessman who had been born under the Raj or a prime minister who ran any nation, big or small.

It was with such boldness that in December 2014, I reached out to Prince Idris bin al-Senussi, of Libya, a country I had come to know intimately, face-to-face. A friend had kindly made the introduction for me. The prince had some friends who needed our help. The Nigerian presidential election was just a few months away, the prince said, and the men, very wealthy Nigerian oil industry billionaires who were aligned with the incumbent, were terrified that their candidate would lose. "The men are very religious," Prince Idris said. "They fear for their lives and the lives of their families" if the incumbent doesn't prevail, he told me.

I told the prince that SCL had done election work in Nigeria in 2007. This thrilled him. He wanted to make an introduction right away. Could Alexander and I fly immediately to Madrid to meet the Nigerians?

Alexander was more than game, but skeptical of my beginner's prowess. He had a slight scheduling conflict and couldn't get there right away. I would have to read through as many case studies as I could, put together a proposal for the Nigerians, and then fly into Madrid alone first. Alexander would arrive only on the second day, at which point he'd pitch them more formally. Was I up for the challenge of doing everything else that was involved before he got there?

I was terrified and excited all at once. This would be the first time I'd represent the company, and my understanding of the depth and breadth of it was still so shallow. I had been on the job for a little more than two weeks. I also knew next to nothing about Nigeria, except that it was the most populous country in Africa, with a quarter of a billion people. I had only beginner-level knowledge of its history and the present state of its politics, not to mention the issues and players in its imminent presidential election. Still, even this early, a viable contract seemed to be in front of me, one, Alexander had told me, that could be worth millions. The Nigerian prospect met all the criteria: it was a clear project, the clients had money, and the time line was urgent. Yes, I told Alexander. I'd go to Madrid.

In advance of the meeting, I made my way around the SCL office looking for any information I could find on the 2007 Nigerian campaign—there wasn't much on it, so I pored over documents and case studies from other projects around the world. I pulled an all-nighter and threw together a proposal with a junior member of staff. It was sufficient as a start, especially under the rushed conditions, but with the election scheduled for February 14, 2015, there was so little time left that we didn't even expect to win the contract—not that this deterred me in the least.

The situation in Nigeria was complex. The potential clients were backing a man named Goodluck Jonathan, the incumbent president. Jonathan was a Christian and a progressive, my human rights attorney friend John Jones QC informed me, a leader who had brought substantial reforms to the Federation of Nigeria since taking office in 2010. He was seen by some as a champion of youth and the underprivileged; he had worked to clean up environmental disasters, including lead poisoning that had killed some four hundred children in an impoverished region of the country; and he had endeavored to stabilize the nation's energy sector by privatizing its wholly unreliable power grid. But his administration was corrupt, and he had recently become unpopular when he failed the country in a number of ways, not the least of which was his very public inability to bring home two hundred schoolgirls who had been kidnapped by the militant group Boko Haram. Not long before, he had been accused of masterminding a terrorist bombing. But as my friend John Jones informed me, in the election, Jonathan was the lesser of two evils.

The alternative was Muhammadu Buhari.

In three decades, Buhari had been involved in two military coups. In the first, he was appointed provincial governor, and in the second he claimed the presidency. Under his repressive rule, he had voiced support for Sharia law and persecuted both scholars and journalists. Various groups had filed complaints against him at the international criminal court, accusing him of human rights abuses and crimes against humanity (which Buhari denied and in the end the ICC did not pursue the complaints).[1] In fact, according to international law, if the accusations were true, it should have been illegal for him to run for president at all. John agreed with the prince and his oilmen friends that if Buhari won, the country could descend into violence.[2] With not much time left until the election, it was an imperfect situation, but as a human rights activist, I felt assured that at least SCL would be on the better side of the fence.

Alexander arranged for me to entertain the Nigerians at a luxury hotel, directing me to host them for a lavish meal. I'd never been given so much responsibility with so much hanging in the balance.

When I arrived in Madrid, I found Prince Idris waiting with only one Nigerian, and even he was not the one I had expected. The clients, it appeared, had flown in a representative to take the meeting. He was a tall, looming, thick-bodied man of early middle age, but I could see that he was terribly nervous, which made me feel better.

I made it through the first day, showing our potential client the proposal and talking through the basics of what I understood SCL could do for his boss. The company offered services such as opinion polling, caste and tribe research, opposition research, and even "competitive intelligence"—that is, state-of-the-art information gathering that could be used to research candidates' personal and financial backgrounds and explore historic party dealings or "hidden activities." I wasn't so naïve as to think that this wasn't negative campaigning, but I knew that at this late stage in the game, it might be necessary to show results quickly.

There was no time to do what SCL called a "party audit," a census to collect members' details, including their polling station and political affiliation. Nor could we clearly identify swing voters. But we could do strong get-out-the-vote work in regions where there was already great support for Goodluck Jonathan. And if we achieved a wide enough margin, that would serve to quell mistrust in the results and perhaps prevent violence in the postelection period.

I was relieved when Alexander arrived on the second day to do the formal pitch. To see him in full pitch mode was undeniably a thing of beauty. He was eloquence and elegance personified. He was self-assured and unhalting in his delivery, an appealing figure in his crisp navy suit and silk tie and more charismatic than most gentlemen one would ever meet. I regarded him with warmth and a degree of admiration that it had not occurred to me before I would ever feel for him.

The start of his pitch included much the same material he covered when Chester and I visited the SCL office back in October—the same slides with pictures of beaches and signs about sharks, the same points about Mad Men, the same top-down-versus-bottom-up creativity and blanket versus targeted advertising based on scientific and psychological research, but it felt more fluid, theatrical, and persuasive now. It seemed effortless, as perfectly managed and choreographed as the best TED Talk. With the small remote control firmly in his hand, Alexander, it seemed to me, had his finger on a button that had the potential to control the world.

The billionaires' representative was rapt, and he leaned in, as did the prince, and nodded from time to time approvingly. And when Alexander got to the part of the presentation about how the company had the ability to, as he put it, "address individual villages or apartment blocks, even zoom right down to particular people," their eyes widened.

How SCL did that was just a part of what made it different from all other election companies in the world. It was not an advertising firm, Alexander said, but a psychologically astute and scientifically precise communications company.

"The biggest mistake the political campaigns and communication campaigns face is starting where they are and not where they want to be," Alexander said. "They tend to start with a preconceived idea of what is required. And that's normally based on the subject matter."

So, he said, SCL often walked into situations where clients tried to tell it what to do. Usually, a client's idea was that they needed posters everywhere and TV adverts, Alexander said.

"Well," he asked, "how do you know that that's the right thing to do?"

The client raised his eyebrows.

"Because we're not interested in the president or the party or whoever the client is," Alexander said dismissively. "We're interested in the *audience.*" He paused for a second for effect and pulled up a slide. On it was a picture of an audience in a movie theater staring up at the screen.

"The way to illustrate this," he said, pointing to the slide, "is you want to sell more Coca-Cola in a movie theater, yeah?"

The client nodded.

"You ask an advertising agency what their plan is, and they'll say, 'You need more Coke at point of sale, you need Coke branding, you need a Coke advert before the main movie.'" Alexander shook his head. "And it's all about Coke," he said. And that's the problem with political campaigns.

"But," he went on, clicking to another slide—this one showed images zooming left, right, and center, all of Coca-Cola advertising and branding, all quickly becoming overwhelming—"If you stop and look at the target audience and ask questions like 'Under what circumstances would they drink more Coke?' and you research them, you might find that they're more likely to drink a Coke when they're thirsty."

Again, he paused.

"So," he continued, "what you want to do," he said, clicking to another slide, "is simply turn up the temperature . . . in the auditorium."

The image on the slide was of a cartoon-like thermometer, the mercury in red, risen to almost bursting.

The solution, Alexander said, isn't in the advert. "The solution is in the audience." He paused again to make sure this had sunk in.

The solution is in the audience, I thought. It had never occurred to me to think this way.

It was a stunning moment, as eye-opening to me as what he had said in his initial presentation to Chester and me about the worthlessness of blanket advertising. Here was a brilliant concept: to get people to act, you created the conditions under which they would be more likely to do what you wanted them to do. The simplicity of the concept blew my mind.

Alexander said that SCL had done this again and again across the world.

In Trinidad and Tobago in 2010, he said, pulling up slides, the company had addressed that nation's "mixed ethnicity." (Half the nation was Indian, the other half Afro-Caribbean.) "Political leaders from one group there," he said, "had difficulty making their messages resonate with those outside it." SCL had therefore designed an ambitious program of political graffiti that it disseminated as campaign messages. And the youth vote had turned out in droves.

Brilliant, I thought. Getting out the youth vote was so difficult during elections.

In Bogotá, Colombia, in 2011, SCL had found that in a country with rampant corruption, the general population mistrusted all the candidates who were running, so SCL "enlisted others" to endorse the candidates instead. Having locals vouching for the candidate was highly effective, with no trace of the candidate's face him- or herself.

How quickly could the Nigerians see results from SCL if it were to work in the upcoming election? the representative wanted to know.

I knew what Alexander was going to say, because I had read about it in the SCL brochures: SCL's services were "results oriented." The company always worked with its clients to ensure that the effects of its services were "readily identifiable and measurable."

The representative looked pleased.

After the presentation, Alexander and I had dinner together. We spoke about the Nigerian campaign and all the other campaigns he'd done through the years, and I realized that Alexander Nix could likely be the most experienced elections consultant in the world. I began to see him as an important mentor. And while it had been difficult to get to know him in the first few weeks of the job, now he invited me to come out and visit his family or come see him play in a polo match. I was surprised when I realized that both sounded quite nice, in fact.

Then, on the day we flew back to London together, he and I had a sweet moment that almost made me feel like his equal. In keeping with the frugal SCL tradition, we had tickets in economy class, but before we boarded, he invited me to join him in the business class lounge, where we toasted our future success and drank a free glass of champagne. Cheers, we said, to the future.

Back in London, Christmas was approaching. At the company holiday party, a Prohibition-themed event, I wore a flapper's dress with a pair of long, white gloves I'd borrowed from a dear friend who worked in costuming. I mingled with everyone I could—Pere; Sabhita; and Harris McCloud, a blond-haired, blue-eyed political messaging expert from Canada. I spoke with a few of the data scientists, including Dr. Eyal Kazin and Tadas Jucikas, Alex Tayler's right and left hands. I wasn't part of the team just yet; I was new, a curiosity, and it was quite hard to introduce myself in such a noisy venue. Still, I mingled and chatted with people as much as I could.

Alexander wasn't there; he was in Ghana with Ceris, to see if he could revive discussions with that country's president. I envied his having work to occupy his mind.

Suddenly, one of the data scientists I hadn't met yet came up to say hello. "So, how goes it in the elections-fixing business?" he asked.

I had no idea how to reply. I stood there for a moment looking at him, at the drink he was holding: an ice-cold, freshly shaken espresso martini. I was drinking the same; the glass would've been too cold to hold without my long, white gloves. Despite our icy beverages, I remember feeling the temperature in the room rise uncomfortably.

I don't recall how I responded; probably with something light-hearted. After all, what was one supposed to say in reply to such a comment? And what was such a comment supposed to mean?

Around the time that I began my consultancy at SCL, I had started dating a lovely Scottish man called Tim. He was different from most of the men I had dated, and he reminded me somehow of Alexander. Tim, too, had attended British boarding schools, and came from old family money. Like Alexander in my professional life, Tim was more conservative than most people in my personal life. He worked in business development, as I had just begun to do. He was a social butterfly, the loudest and happiest person in any room. He dressed formally, in three-piece tweed suits, and was as handsome as any man gracing the cover of GQ.

I didn't tell my family much about him—not just yet. I hadn't had a very good experience sharing recent news. After all, when I told my mother about my new job, she had fretted.

"Oh, no," she said, and told me she hoped I wouldn't be giving up my PhD. I assured her I had no plans to.

There was really no home to go back to that Christmas. My family had already started packing boxes to leave our home. The idea of even trying was too dreary to contemplate. So, instead, I threw myself into my work at SCL, as if in those few short days between Christmas and the New Year, I might be able to stop things happening far away from crumbling. I followed up on the Nigerians. Perhaps that project would come through. I wanted it to; I wanted something to go right. I wished I could continue working through the holidays, to keep my mind off personal things, but the office was open only until Christmas.

In the end, Tim invited me to his family home in Scotland. Going away seemed a good way to distract myself. Tim's parents lived in two adjoined turn-of-the-century country cottages surrounded by a perfectly manicured lawn. They were a warm and welcoming group, and I was diverted through Christmas Day with talking and drinking tea and sipping fine wine, with conversation and laughter. They made me feel right at home. Though, given what was going on with my family—something I didn't share with Tim's family or even Tim—this made me feel both wonderful and melancholy at the same time.

The house was so deep into the countryside that there was little cell service there. I'd asked Tim's parents for permission to give out the number for their land line, in case of an emergency. I'd shared the number only with my mother, Alexander, Prince Idris, and the Nigerians. Alexander had said that if things went well in Madrid, we'd possibly be hearing from the prince or the Nigerian representative over the holidays.

"It's now or never," he had said before he left for Ghana and then a vacation with his family. The election was just over a month and a half away.

One night the phone rang. Tim's brother ran to pick it up. I listened from the other room.

"We don't want any of what you're sellin'!" I heard him say in a gruff brogue. Tim's mother was nearby, and I could hear her scrambling to take the receiver from him. She knew I was expecting important calls. When the scuffle was over, Tim's brother returned to the room I was in, his face bright red.

"Uh, Brittany, it's for you." He paused. "It's . . . a prince?" he said and shrugged.

Prince Idris. I gathered myself together quickly and picked up the phone. "Good evening, Your Royal Highness," I said.

He had very good news. He had already called Alexander to tell him, and now he was reaching out to me. The Nigerians wanted to move forward—immediately. And they wanted to talk through the proposal in person. They were in DC.

Alexander, the prince said, was on holiday and couldn't get away. "You must prepare to go and meet them yourself right away," Prince Idris said.

After we hung up, I could hardly breathe. Surely SCL wouldn't send me. They had senior people they could put on this. I was merely a graduate student who'd been working there for only three and a half weeks part time.

Suddenly, the phone rang again. This time it was Alexander. Before I could say anything beyond "hello," he jumped in.

"Okay, Brits," he said, using a nickname for me neither he nor anyone else had ever used. "Are you ready to prove yourself? These guys say they are ready to go but want to agree to the deal in person. *Always* close in person."

I kept listening.

Everyone else was on vacation or unreachable, Alexander said. "That leaves you, my dear!"

I had no idea if I could really do it.

"If you really want it and you don't think they are bullshitting us, then it's now or never," he continued. "If we close this, I'll owe you one."

4

Davos

The trip to DC went better than I could have imagined—better than anyone could have imagined.

Just after Christmas, I left Tim's family home in Scotland and met one of the Nigerian billionaires behind it all. By the time I arrived, he had already met with government officials and businessmen from whom he was hoping to elicit a public outcry about challenger Muhammadu Buhari, but he had met with little success, and he was interested in a contract with SCL.

He was a large and physically powerful man, imposing, serious, and rich—the latter of which he made sure to impress upon me. I found him intimidating. He wasn't used to doing business with women, let alone a young American woman, and I had the sense that he wasn't entirely pleased that Alexander had sent me instead of coming himself.

I had my proposal with me, and I did the best I could to make clear what Alexander felt SCL, with six weeks left before the Nigerian presidential election, was capable of doing.

Nigeria was split down the middle between the two most powerful political parties in the country: Goodluck Jonathan's People's Democratic Party (PDP) and the party backing Buhari. There was no time to win over swing voters. Our work would be to activate Jonathan's base to promote voter turnout and, more important, ensure a wide margin of victory in order to avoid an uncontested election and therefore prevent violence from breaking out afterward.

We'd use radio, one of the most reliable means of communication in the country's rural areas, as our primary medium, filling the airwaves with ads, paid interviews, and vox-pop pieces. We'd do some TV as well as print newspaper ads and op-eds. Given that only 10 percent of households had internet, our digital campaign would be limited to urban areas, where we'd put out Facebook posts, tweets, and YouTube content and banner ads. We'd also rely on billboards in targeted areas, as there wasn't enough data to microtarget in any way or enough time to do modeling, a scientific way of analyzing data to predict individuals' behavior, even if the data had allowed.

Even with all these strategies, I told the Nigerian billionaire, SCL couldn't guarantee a win for Goodluck Jonathan. But at this point, I said, telling him what Alexander had told the man's representative in Madrid, we were the best chance he had.

The man nodded. How much would it cost? he wanted to know.

Alexander had said that it would take at least $3 million.

The man balked, and countered with $1.8 million. And: would I mind if he filled a private jet with cash and sent it our way? Or, if that wasn't suitable, they could line the interior walls of a car with the cash instead, and deliver it to a secret, prearranged set of coordinates, removing its doors and slitting its tires so that no one else could steal it, he added. It was in this way that contracts were settled in his country, he said. Shocked and out of my depth, I frantically called Alexander.

When I reached him, he casually explained that we did not accept cash, as if he were often offered that option, and he demanded a wire transfer. It wasn't an issue—by the time I arrived back in England, on January 2, the money had hit the account whose number Alexander had provided. He was over the moon. The $1.8 million deal was the largest SCL had ever achieved in so short a time. He said he knew that I was going to continue to show him amazing things. The deal with the Nigerians hadn't been just beginner's luck, he was sure of it.

I was thrilled as well. I presumed I'd make a healthy commission or a split of the profits, maybe even enough to save my parents' home from the banks and set them up comfortably for a time. I called my sister to share the good news.

But Alexander had other ideas. We hadn't talked about a commission for me, and Prince Idris was expecting one, too, because he'd made the introduction. Also, it was Alexander who had chosen the team to work in-country, and had set the budget, which was going to be expensive.

I was crestfallen. Here I had made an enormous deal for the company, and the only compensation I'd be getting was my per diem. It didn't seem fair.

I called Chester to vent.

I don't know precisely when in our friendship it had dawned on me that Chester was more privileged than I would ever have imagined being myself. I knew he'd gone to boarding school in Switzerland. I knew he'd traveled everywhere—but then I learned that, some of the time, it was in a private jet. He didn't have access to his family funds, so he had to work for his own money and live on whatever he made, but because the family he came from was a cushion he could rely on if anything went wrong, he was clearly in an entirely different class.

Still, every now and then, he would say or do something that reminded me of the stratum he was a part of, the experiences he'd had, and I would suddenly realize just how different we were. As he sat on the phone listening to me vent, he agreed that what I'd done for SCL was remarkable, that I deserved better than that. And that was when he said he had an idea for an opportunity to make even more connections and possibly drum up additional business for myself that would lead to an actual commission from SCL: together, he and I could go to Davos for the annual conference of the World Economic Forum, slated for late January, only a few weeks away.

His merely suggesting that we attend Davos was one of those things that made me realize at a much deeper level that Chester was extremely well connected. I knew he'd attended the conference before, but I had had no idea what that meant. I'd certainly read about "Davos." Since 1971, the mountain resort town in the Swiss Alps had hosted a world-famous international conference of the World Economic Forum (WEF), a nonprofit organization whose members were the world's billionaires and executives of the most valuable companies on the planet. Attending the conference each year along with the uber rich were public intellectuals, journalists, and the heads of state from the top seventy nations ranked by GDP. They came to "shape global, regional and industry agendas,"[1] in sessions that focused on everything from artificial intelligence to solving economic crises. Davos attendees that year were to include Angela Merkel of Germany; the premier of China, Li Keqiang; U.S. secretary of state John Kerry; and business leaders from a number of Fortune 200 companies.[2]

For all its good intentions, Davos had in recent years become known for its decadence—the partying, the hijinks, the poseurs and movie stars who had begun to crash it. In 2011 in Davos, Anthony Scaramucci, who would go on to become Donald Trump's spokesman for the briefest time in history, held a wine tasting that devolved, as one reporter wrote, into "a drunken mess." There were rumors of orgies, but Chester said that that was ridiculous, as no one would risk that kind of reputational damage on the world stage.[3]

No, he assured me. Davos was mostly a place where people did a year's worth of business in one week, and it was important to keep as low a profile there as possible.

How could you *not* go? Chester said. It wasn't really a question.

But "be prepared," he said. "The people are vultures. Don't let them take advantage of you. Don't drink too much, and don't talk to people that you don't need to."

His last piece of advice? There was no use bringing heels, he warned. Davos was high in the mountains, and the streets of the village were precipitous. The Swiss, Chester said, were so persnickety about their wooden floors that they refused to salt the sidewalks, and in January, the ground was so slippery that it had become a pastime for residents and forum attendees alike to watch passersby, from presidents to prime ministers, fall on their rear ends.

One didn't want to do that, Chester said. Best to be prepared.

Alexander had chosen his team for Nigeria in the early days of January. It included Pere, Harris, and James Greeley, SCL's jack-of-all-trades. Alexander had thought of sending me, but because I had done so well wrapping up the contract itself, he felt it better that I stay behind and pursue other leads. You have a knack for sales, he would say, buttering me up and making me overlook my interest in working on the campaign in-country.

Anyway, *a knack for sales*? It didn't sound like me just yet, although I could tell I was getting the hang of it.

"Stick with me," he said. "You have a future here. You might even become CEO someday."

I thought he was joking at first, but he said it often enough for me to believe that he actually saw that level of potential in me.

Codirecting the Nigerian team were Ceris and a man I had never met before. His name, Alexander said, was Sam Patten. A senior adviser to the SCL Group, he was one of the most experienced consultants on our global roster for running campaigns on the ground in foreign countries. Sam had worked on the 2014 parliamentary election in Iraq, and in 2012, he had played a critical role in the election of the opposition government in the former Soviet Republic of Georgia. He had also served as a senior adviser to President George W. Bush.[4] Unfortunately, though we couldn't know it in 2015, Sam Patten would become an infamous figure in the Robert Mueller investigation into Russia's involvement in the 2016 U.S. presidential election. His business partner, a Ukrainian named Konstantin Kilimnik, would come to be of interest to Mueller with regard to Donald Trump's connection to the Russians, and would be accused of being a spy for the Russian intelligence services.

At the time I met him, though, Sam struck me as a consummate professional, trustworthy and serious, the kind of person who looked you dead in the eye and told it like it was. He arrived at the Mayfair office on January 3, 2015, dressed in a proper suit, but wearing a polo shirt and carrying a worn laptop bag that made it clear he was distinctly American and that he had likely carried the bag around the world for years.

I brought Sam up to date on my limited experience with the Nigerians and then handed off control. The plan was basically "crisis comms," or crisis communications: getting out as much material as possible and as fast as possible to make as significant an impact as we could. I had given the campaign the name "Nigeria Forward," and I assumed that in the few short weeks we had left, it would be an upbeat, all-out fight to support Goodluck Jonathan. I imagined the radio spots, the videos, and of course the rallies—held on the back of a truck that folded out into a stage, which I had been told were used for SCL-organized campaign events in Kenya.

Only two weeks later, the picture in Nigeria had changed significantly. News came that the Electoral Commission was planning to postpone the February 14 election until late March. The insurgents of Boko Haram in the north were disruptive and threatened to make polling impossible. There were technological and logistical problems as well. It was difficult to distribute voter ID cards, and the biometric card readers weren't working, the Election Commission reported. The new elections were scheduled for March 29. While that should have been good news, as it meant the team would have more time to accomplish its goals, the delay, along with other factors, would lead to a situation with the Nigerians that would become ever more complicated.

There was an international outcry about the postponement, including from Secretary of State John Kerry, who insisted that the elections be held on time, and he warned the Nigerian government against using "security concerns as a pretext for impeding the democratic process."[5] The All Progressives Congress (APC), challenger Buhari's party, called the move "highly provocative" and "a major setback for democracy."[6] And UN Secretary-General, Ban Ki-moon "urged officials to take all necessary measures to enable Nigerians to vote 'in a timely manner.'"[7]

The project and the contract were valid only through February 14, the day originally set for the elections. Our team had expected to lift off from Abuja the day before, to avoid any problems. We therefore reached out to the clients to let them know that if they wanted to extend the contract, and have the SCL team stay longer, they would have to provide more funding, probably as much as or more than they already had. The team seemed happy to stay longer, according to feedback I heard around the office—by day they worked in their "war room" at the Abuja Hilton, by night they drank with David Axelrod's team that consulted for the opposition—and they never complained to us at HQ.

Personally, I was thrilled with the idea. If I closed another deal with the Nigerians, I'd have the chance to earn that commission I had hoped to win in the first place. But the Nigerians were dubious about a re-up. They hadn't seen enough progress yet to warrant it. Our team might be working tirelessly on the ground, but where were the results?

I didn't know how to answer. I had enough elections experience to know that it takes time to see results, and in the case of the Nigerian campaign, the proof was going to be in the election results themselves. But the Nigerians said they needed to see what the team had actually done. Where were the billboards? Where were the radio spots? Where had their money gone? I knew that it took at least two weeks to get most of those things up and running, but I also knew that they had to be in progress.

To reassure the Nigerians, Alexander had Ceris write a report that detailed everything being done to date in the project. As for me, I called Chester to ask for suggestions as to what I could do.

His idea: let's invite the Nigerians to Davos—and Alexander as well, so he can meet with them and reassure them. I asked if I could invite my friend John Jones, the human rights lawyer. He'd be perfect, I said, because his expertise could help the Nigerians use Davos as a platform to speak out against Buhari and gain the international outcry they wanted.

It sounded brilliant to me.

There's always a hitch.

One of the things that Chester had on his Davos to-do list was to throw a party on one of the evenings—and not just any party, but a really odd one. The party would be for a consortium of billionaires who had formed a company that was endeavoring to mine precious metals in space, on asteroids, Chester explained.

Asteroids?

Yes, he said. The idea was that the billionaires would launch rockets to land on asteroids and set up mines there. They hadn't done it yet, but they wanted to meet at Davos. They had asked Chester to help them set up a party as a venue for them to do so. If I came to Davos, I could help, Chester said. The asteroid mining company would pay us handsomely.

It was more money earned in one day than I could have made at SCL that whole month. I knew nothing about how to throw a party in Davos, but I was game.

I arrived in Davos a week early to prepare for a week of the highest-level meetings, and of course, the party, and it was a good thing I did. There was so much to do, and party logistics were so complicated in that village and at that crazy time of year. Chester had rented an apartment in the middle of the high-security zone, directly across from the Davos Congress Centre, the site of most of the key sessions for the World Economic Forum, and it wasn't easy getting things in and out of that area. There would be caterers, bartenders, trucks filled with liquor, food, furniture, and other supplies; and the area just around the venue was almost as hard to penetrate as Fort Knox.

The temperature the night of the party was frigid, as it often is in January in Davos, but everything was ready. We set up heaters outside on the apartment building's vast rooftop terrace, where the bar was located and where we'd placed glow-in-the-dark chairs and stools, which gave the place an otherworldly vibe, in keeping with the outer space theme.

And we spread salt to prevent the guests from slipping.

Indoors, I hung the banners and helped lay out the food. Here and there, I laid down business cards of my own and SCL brochures.

Alexander and John Jones were early arriving. They were thrilled to be there. Neither had been in Davos before.

I stood at the door and welcomed guests. Each was more famous than the last: the entrepreneur Richard Branson, Ross Perot Sr. and Jr., members of the Dutch royal family, and at least a hundred others. They spilled out onto the terrace, where they watched the bartenders performing magic tricks, mixing cocktails and juggling with fire. Inside, in the middle of the living room, they stood around watching a giant demonstration that the aspiring asteroid miners had set up: a model of an asteroid atop of which was perched a contraption that looked like a tripod and was meant to resemble something like an oil rig.

Milling among the guests, John Jones looked happy. While Alexander clearly felt that SCL was in a far smaller class than the other businesses represented in the room, he was glad to have the chance to network, and he was particularly happy to see Eric Schmidt, the CEO of Google. Before he ventured over to Schmidt, he shared with me that it was Sophie Schmidt, Eric's daughter, who had been partly responsible for inspiring the inception of Cambridge Analytica.

The party was going swimmingly until my phone buzzed: the Nigerians had arrived and were downstairs, just outside the apartment building.

We had planned a literally flashy welcome for them. When they landed at Zurich airport, a limo was waiting for them, and on the drive into town, they were accompanied, in front of the limo and behind, by police cars, sirens blaring and lights flashing, announcing the arrival of visitors of significance.

But when the Nigerians reached me by phone, they weren't pleased.

They were hungry. Where was their dinner?

I had invited them to the party; there was plenty of food there, I told them. Chester and I had spent hundreds of dollars of our budget on it.

No, they said; they were tired. They wanted to eat, be shown their lodgings, and go to bed. They weren't interested in coming to a party.

They had not eaten on the plane—a twelve-hour flight—and they wanted, they said, fried chicken. I would need to find it somewhere and bring it to them.

I had no choice but to throw on my boots and coat and head down to meet them on the icy streets below. They were standing outside the apartment building, where people were still lining up to get into my party. All five men again claimed they couldn't possibly go up-stairs and were demanding to be fed, chicken preferably.

I explained that we wouldn't be able to drive anywhere to get it— the limo wasn't allowed in the central area. Walking was the only choice, so I led them through the streets in the bitter cold.

They weren't prepared for the weather. They had neither boots nor coats. They wore thin collared shirts and flat loafers. We slipped and slid, walking from closed restaurant to closed restaurant, finding, of course, no fried chicken in a Swiss mountain town, and little else as well. Finally, I happened upon a restaurant that served pasta atop of which the chef agreed to put some grilled chicken. Takeout contain-ers in hand, I led the Nigerians back onto the slippery streets again, the men, freezing, following along behind me, barely able to stay up-right. I carried the stack of chicken-and-pasta meals all the way to their lodgings, where I made sure they were settled in, and I said my good-nights. They looked cold, hungry, and far more unhappy with me than I would have liked.

I was away from the party for almost two hours. When I got back, it was 2:00 a.m., and the party was still raging.

Chester was nowhere to be found. No one had been at the door to welcome guests. No one had been in charge. The bartenders had run out of alcohol. The food had been devoured. Just before I returned, the guests had become rowdy, and a drunken princess had fallen outside and, though unhurt, was making an inebriated ruckus that had set off alarms.

For the second time that night, the air filled with the sound of sirens and the flash of spinning lights. The Swiss Police were on their way to stop the party. With the help of the son of the head of police, we managed to talk them out of arresting anyone, but not in stopping the party.

When the interaction was over, I stood in the middle of the empty room. I was starving. Like the Nigerians, I hadn't eaten for hours.

Alexander was as pleased with the results of Davos as he was of the deal I had made with the Nigerians. He had found the party festive. He had met people he wouldn't otherwise have, and of course SCL had walked away with a giant fishbowl full of business cards from some of the wealthiest and most influential people in the world.

What he didn't know yet was how disastrous the evening had been for our relationship with our Nigerian clients, and how angry they were the next morning when they woke to discover that Alexander had flown back to London without even bothering to meet them.

When they learned that he was gone, they demanded that I come to see them immediately. They didn't want to go out themselves. It was too cold.

So, I made my way through the slippery streets in my inadequate boots, cringing.

I'd never been yelled at by an African billionaire before. He and the other Nigerians didn't understand why they weren't being treated better. They were VIPs, they said, just as important as the other VIPs at the conference. Why had no reception been arranged especially for them? Why hadn't the CEO of my company, to which they had just paid nearly $2 million, stayed to meet them? They were unhappy, too, with the work we were doing in Nigeria. Where were the radio spots? Where were all the billboards? What's our money going toward? they demanded to know.

I didn't know how to reason with them. They had never invested in an election before. They didn't know what to expect. Perhaps they had thought they would see a giant rally on the back of a truck with LED screens flashing and megaphones blasting. That hadn't been part of the team's plan. Measuring the impact of elections work is a complicated task, and, having been a part of the company for just over a month, I couldn't explain to them right then and there why everything SCL had done wasn't more obvious to the naked eye. The fruits of SCL's labors might be borne out only on Election Day in March, and they needed to be patient.

But they wouldn't listen to me. It wasn't just that I was young; it was also that I was a woman. This attitude was eminently clear, and made me incredibly uncomfortable. It even began to feel threatening. These were powerful, wealthy men, the kind who thought nothing of filling a jet with naira, the Nigerian currency. What might they be capable of if they were unhappy with how that money had been spent?

When I put them on a conference call with Alexander, they were calmer, and much more respectful. They didn't yell, but they weren't assuaged. Yet Alexander seemed oblivious to how serious the situation was.

I arranged for John Jones to come over and visit with them. Perhaps they could find a way of working together. We discussed strategies for showing up Buhari in the press and making his alleged war crimes known, but when I left the Nigerians with him to head back to our apartment, I had the sinking feeling that there would be no second contract after February 14. The Nigerians hadn't said as much, but the way they'd treated me was demeaning. How could I possibly return to them and close another contract? Things were trending in a bad direction, and even worse, while taking care of them, I'd had no time even to pursue any SCL leads, so the trip would not even result in new business.

As if all that weren't bad enough, that morning the website Business Insider published a story about the evening before: "Davos Party Shut Down After Bartenders Blow Through Enough Booze for Two Nights," the headline read.[8]

When the phone rang, it was Alexander. Maybe he had seen the article. Even if my name wasn't in it, it could look bad for SCL. Maybe the Nigerians had called to give him a piece of their minds.

But he was buoyant. Neither had happened, it seemed.

"Brittany," he said. "Davos was wonderful. Thanks to you and Chester for the excellent hosting! I'm calling to let you know that I'm offering you a permanent position with SCL that you've been waiting for!" he said, likely winking on the other end of the phone. "No more consulting. You'll be a full member of the team."

There'd be a bonus, he added: ten thousand dollars more per year; a regular salary, benefits; a company credit card. I could pursue the types of projects I liked, as long as they brought in the same kind of money as the Nigerian campaign. It was a high bar, but it had been an auspicious start.

Welcome aboard, he said.

5

Terms and Conditions

FEBRUARY–JULY 2015

It didn't take long for full-time employment at SCL to afford me entry into the higher echelons of the company. In an email copying only a handful of people—Pere, Kieran, Sabhita, Alex Tayler, and me—employees whom Nix considered important and "good fun," he said, he invited us out for lunch one weekend at his home in Central London.

Located in Holland Park, it was a city house—he had a country one as well—a four-story stone mansion, the interior of which resembled a private members-only club or rooms you would find in Buckingham Palace, except that the art that hung from ceiling to floor weren't Old Masters but, instead, provocatively modern.

We started at midday with vintage champagne in the drawing room and continued at the dining table for hours, all through which the champagne flowed. Alexander and the others told war stories about their time together in Africa. In 2012, for example, Alexander had moved a team from SCL and his entire family to Kenya, so that he could run the country's 2013 election himself. He hadn't too many staff members at the time, and it had been difficult. Research was limited to door-to-door surveys, and messaging was done through roadshows on those convertible stage-trucks I've mentioned before.

"That's why what we're doing in America is so incredibly exciting," Alexander said. "Knocking on doors isn't the only way to get data now. Data is everywhere. And every decision is now data-driven."

We stayed at his house until dinnertime, and then all of us, woozy and lightheaded, made our way to a bar somewhere for cocktails, and then for a meal somewhere else, and then to another bar, where we capped off the evening.

It was the kind of memorable event that is difficult to recollect entirely the next day, although in the office, I began to see that Alexander's excitement about America was more than just idle chat over drinks.

Indeed, while I continued to pursue global projects, my colleagues at SCL were increasingly focused on the United States, and their work was no longer confined to the Sweat Box. They were absorbed in daily conversations I could overhear, about their client Ted Cruz. He had signed on with us back in late 2014, for a small contract, but was now upgrading to nearly $5 million in services. Kieran and the other creatives were now producing tons of content for the Texas senator. They huddled at a desktop computer putting together ads and videos, which they would sometimes show off and at which they would sometimes stare, grimacing.

Meanwhile, Alexander was focused entirely on the United States, too. The Cruz campaign had agreed to sign a contract without a noncompete clause, so Alexander was free to pursue other GOP candidates as well. Soon, he had signed Dr. Ben Carson. Next up, he began systematically pitching the rest of the seventeen Republican contenders. For a while, Jeb Bush considered hiring the firm; Alexander said Jeb even flew to London to meet with him. In the end, though, he wanted nothing to do with a company that would even consider working at the same time for his competition. The Bushes were the kind of family who demanded single-minded loyalty from those with whom they worked.

The Cambridge Analytica data team busied themselves preparing for the 2016 U.S. presidential election by interpreting the results of the 2014 midterms. In their glass box, they wrote up case studies from John Bolton's successful super PAC operation, from Thom Tillis's senatorial campaign, and from all the North Carolina races. To show how Cambridge had succeeded, they put together a packet explaining how they'd broken the target audience into "Core Republicans," "Reliable Republicans," "Turnout Targets," "Priority Persuasions," and "Wildcards," and how they'd messaged them differently on issues ranging from national security to the economy and immigration.

Also, in the data analytics lab, Dr. Jack Gillett produced midterm data visualizations—multicolor charts, maps, and graphics to be added to new slide shows and pitches. And Dr. Alexander Tayler was always on the phone in search of new data from brokers all over the United States.

I was still pursuing SCL projects abroad, but as Cambridge Analytica ramped up for 2016, I was becoming privy, if accidentally, to confidential information, such as the case studies, the videos, the ads, and the chatter around me. I was never copied on CA emails at that time, but there were stories in the air and images on nearby computer screens.

This presented an ethical dilemma. The previous summer, when Allida Black, founder of the Ready for Hillary super PAC was in town, I'd been fully briefed on Democratic Party plans for the election. Now I was receiving a regular paycheck from a company working for the GOP. It didn't sit well with me, and I knew that it wouldn't sit well with others.

No one asked me to, but I began to cut my ties with the Democrats, although I was too embarrassed to tell anyone on the Democratic side why. I didn't want to put the SCL Group on my LinkedIn or Facebook page. I didn't want any Democratic operatives I knew to have to worry that I'd ever use information I had from them against them. Eventually, I stopped replying to incoming emails from the Ready for Hillary super PAC and from Democrats Abroad, and I made sure that in writing personally to friends who were Democrats, I never included the SCL name on any of my communications. To the Clinton teams, it must have seemed as though I had simply dropped off the map. It wasn't easy for me to do. I was tempted to read everything that came in, news about exciting meetings and plans. So, after a while, I just let these messages sit in my in-box, unopened, relics of my past.

I also didn't want my Cambridge Analytica colleagues or the company's GOP clients to worry about the same. After all, I was a Democrat working in a company that exclusively served Republicans in the United States. I removed the Obama campaign and the DNC from my LinkedIn profile (my public résumé) and erased all other public references I had made to the Democratic Party or my involvement in it. This was painful, to say the least. I also begrudgingly stopped using my Twitter account, @EqualWrights, a catalog of years of my left-leaning activist proclamations. As much as it hurt to close those doors and hide some of the most important parts of myself, it was necessary, I knew, in order for me to grow into the professional political technology consultant I was to become. And one day, perhaps, I could reopen both those accounts and that part of myself.

My change of identity wasn't just online. In London, I opened up a big box my mother had sent me via FedEx; because she worked for the airlines, she had virtually free international shipping privileges. She had sent me business suit after business suit from her old closet: beautiful Chanel pieces, items by St. John, and specialty outfits from Bergdorf Goodman—what she'd worn years before, when she worked for Enron. I pictured what she looked like back then, when she left for work in the mornings back in Houston. She was always impeccably put together, dashing out the door in the highest of heels and those expensive suits, her makeup perfect. Now the suits were my hand-me-downs. I hung them in the closet of the new flat I'd rented for myself in Mayfair.

The flat was tiny, just one room with a kitchen counter and an electric burner and a bathroom far down a hall, but I'd chosen the place strategically. It was close to work and, more important, in the right neighborhood and on Upper Berkeley Street. If a client asked, in that presumptuous way Brits had, "Where are you staying these days?"—meaning where did I *live*, meaning of what social class and means I was—I could say without hesitation that I lived in Mayfair. If they filled in the blanks in their imagination with an expansive flat with a view, all the better. In point of fact, my flat was so small that I was nearly already halfway through it when I walked in the door; and when I stood in the middle of it, I could reach my arms out and touch either wall.

I kept those details secret, though, and every morning I strolled out of my Mayfair address wearing a fancy old suit of my mother's knowing that no one would notice much of a difference between me and any trust-fund baby that owned half of the neighborhood.

"I want you to learn how to pitch," Alexander said to me one day. I'd been talking to clients about the company for months, but in the end, Alexander or Alex Tayler always had to come in to close the deal, so he meant he wanted me to learn to pitch *properly*, as expertly and as confidently as he did.

Although he was the CEO, Alexander was still the only real sales-person in the company, and his time was ever more in demand. He needed me in the field, he said. I had never stood up in front of a client to make a PowerPoint presentation myself. It was an art, Alexander said, and he would mentor me.

What was most important, he said, was that I learn to sell myself, and that I wow him. I could choose whichever pitch I'd seen him give: the SCL pitch or the Cambridge Analytica one.

At the time, given that I was having little luck closing SCL contracts after the Nigerian deal, it occurred to me I might need to rethink things. I was also becoming increasingly uncomfortable with aspects of SCL's work in Africa. Many of the African men I met with didn't respect me or listen to me because I was young and a woman. Also, I was having ethical qualms, as potential deals sometimes lacked transparency or even verged on illegality, I thought. For example, no one ever wanted a paper trail, which meant that most often there were no written contracts. In the rare cases that there were, the contracts weren't to include real names or the names of recognizable companies. There were always obfuscations, masks, and nebulous third parties. Those arrangements bothered me for ethical reasons as well as selfish ones: every time a deal was less than clean and straightforward, it narrowed my chances of making an argument for what I was owed in commission.

I was learning every day at SCL about other so-called common practices in international politics. Nothing was straightforward. While in discussions regarding freelance election work with contractors for an Israeli defense and intelligence firm, I heard the contractors boast about their firm doing everything from giving advance warning of attacks on their clients' campaigns to digging up material that would be useful for counter-operations and opposition messaging. At first it seemed pretty benign to me, even clever and useful. The contractors' firm was pitching clients similar to the SCL Group's, even with some overlap, and the firm had worked in nearly as many elections as Alexander had. While SCL did not have internal counter-ops capacity, its work still had the feel of guerrilla warfare. The more I learned about each firm's strategy, both appeared to be willing to do whatever was needed to win, and that gray area started to bother me. I had suggested SCL work with this firm, as I assumed that two companies working together could produce greater impact for clients, but I was quickly taken out of copy, per usual in Alexander's practice, and not kept abreast of what was actually happening to achieve said results.

While trying to show value and close my first deal, I had introduced this Israeli firm to the Nigerians. I'm not sure what I expected to come of that, besides my looking more experienced than I was, but the results were not what I had imagined they would be. The Nigerian clients ended up hiring the Israeli operatives to work separately from SCL, and as I was later told, they sought to infiltrate the Muhammadu Buhari campaign and obtain insider information. They were successful in this and then passed information to SCL for use. The messaging that resulted discredited Buhari and incited fear, something I wasn't privy to at the time, while Sam Patten was running the show on the ground. Ultimately, the contractors and SCL itself were not effective enough to turn the tide of the election in Goodluck Jonathan's favor. To be fair, the campaign hadn't even lasted a month, but, regardless, he lost spectacularly to Buhari—by 2.5 million votes. The election would become notorious because it was the first time a Nigerian incumbent president had been unseated and also because it was the most expensive campaign in the history of the African continent.

But what was of most concern to me at the time, when it came to ethics, was where the Nigerian money ended up. As I was to learn from Ceris, of the $1.8 million the Nigerian oil billionaire had paid SCL, the team had, in the short time it worked for the man, spent only $800,000, which meant the profit margin for SCL had been outrageous.

The rest of the money I had brought into the company, a cool $1 million, ended up being sheer profit for Alexander Nix. Given that normal markup for projects was 15–20 percent, this was a spectacularly high figure, in my opinion well outside of normal industry standards. It made me wary about pricing for clients in parts of the world where candidates were desperate to win at any cost. While taking high profits is of course legal, it was deeply unethical when Alexander had told the clients we ran out of money and would need more to keep the team on the ground until the delayed election date. I was sure we had more resources, but still, I was afraid to reveal to Alexander that I knew the markup, and the fact that I didn't confront him on this haunted me.

Frankly, even some of SCL's European contracts seemed less than aboveboard when I finally paid attention to the details. On a contract SCL had for the mayoral elections in Vilnius, Lithuania, someone in our company forged Alexander's signature in order to expedite the closing of the deal. I later found out that the deal itself may even have been granted to us in contravention of a national law requiring that election work be publicly tendered and that we had already received notification that we'd "won" the tender before the end of the window of time during which public firms ought to have been able apply for the contract.

When Alexander discovered that his signature had been forged and that the contract wasn't entirely kosher, he asked me to fire the person responsible, even though she was the wife of one of his friends from Eton. I did what he asked. Later, it would become clear that though he seemed to be punishing the employee for her behavior, what he was angriest about wasn't the backroom dealing but the fact that she hadn't collected SCL's final payment from the political party in question. He made me chase the money and told me to forget about Sam in Nigeria: concentrate on our next paycheck.

All this had started to overwhelm me, and I was nervous that I was in over my head at SCL's global helm. I began to look elsewhere in the firm for social projects for which I could use my expertise. I had so much to give and so much to learn about data, and I wasn't going to let some rogue clients get the better of my strong will and put me off from finishing my PhD research.

On the positive side, I was learning that the most exciting innovations were happening in the United States, and that there were dozens of opportunities in America, most of which, thankfully, had nothing to do with the GOP. In Europe, Africa, and many nations around the globe, SCL was limited in its ability to use data because most countries' data infrastructures were underdeveloped. At SCL, I'd been unable to work on contracts that both made use of our most innovative and exciting tools and that, I believed, involved our best practices.

Alexander had recently boasted of nearly closing a deal with the biggest charity in the United States, so I hopped onto that to help him close it. The work involved helping the nonprofit identify new donors, something that appealed to me greatly, as I had spent so many years in charity fund-raising that I couldn't wait to learn a data-driven approach to helping new causes. On the political side, SCL was pitching ballot initiatives in favor of building water reservoirs and high-speed trains, public works projects that could really make a difference in peoples' lives. The company was even moving into commercial advertising, selling everything from newspapers to cutting-edge health care products, an area I could dip into if my heart desired, Alexander told me.

I wanted to learn how analytics worked, and I wanted to do it where we could see, and measure, our achievements, and where people worked with transparency and honesty. I remembered my work with men like Barack Obama. He had been honorable and impeccably moral, and so had the people around him. The way they campaigned was ethical, involving no big-dollar donors and Barack had insisted on absolutely no negative campaigning, too. He would neither attack his Democratic rivals in the primaries nor go low on Republicans. I was nostalgic for a time when I'd experienced elections that ran according to not only rules and laws, but ethics and moral principles.

It seemed to me that my future at the company, if I were to have one, would be in the United States.

I told Alexander I wanted to learn the Cambridge Analytica pitch. And in choosing to do so, I was choosing to join that company, with all the bells and whistles attached.

I couldn't wow Alexander with my own pitch without first meeting with Dr. Alex Tayler to learn about the data analytics behind Cambridge Analytica's success. Tayler's pitch was much more technical and much more involved in the nitty-gritty of the analytics process, but he showed me how Cambridge Analytica's so-called secret sauce wasn't *one* particular secret thing but really many things that set CA apart from our peers. As Alexander Nix often said, the secret sauce was more like a recipe of several ingredients. The ingredients were really baked into a kind of "cake," he said.

Perhaps the most important first thing that made CA different from any other communications firm was the size of our database. The database, Tayler explained, was prodigious and unprecedented in depth and breadth, and was growing ever bigger by the day. We had come about it by buying and licensing all the personal information held on every American citizen. We bought that data from every vendor we could afford to pay—from Experian to Axiom to Infogroup. We bought data about Americans' finances, where they bought things, how much they paid for them, where they went on vacation, what they read.

We matched this data to their political information (their voting habits, which were accessible publicly) and then matched all that again to their Facebook data (what topics they had "liked"). From Facebook alone, we had some 570 individual data points on users, and so, combining all this gave us some 5,000 data points on every single American over the age of eighteen—some 240 million people.

The special edge of the database, though, Tayler said, was our access to Facebook for messaging. We used the Facebook platform to reach the same people on whom we had compiled so much data.

What Alex told me helped bring into focus two events I'd experienced while at the SCL Group, the first when I'd just arrived. One day in December 2014, one of our senior data scientists, Suraj Gosai, had called me over to his computer, where he was sitting with one of our research PhDs and one of our in-house psychologists.

The three of them had developed, they explained, a personality quiz called "the Sex Compass"—a funny name, I thought. It was ostensibly aimed at determining a person's "sexual personality" by asking probing questions about sexual preferences such as favorite position in bed. The survey wasn't just a joyride for the user. It was, I came to understand, a means to harvest data points from the answers people gave about themselves, which led to the determination of their "sexual personality," and a new masked way for SCL to gather the users' data and that of all their "friends," while topping it up with useful data points on personality and behavior.

The same was true for another survey that had crossed my desk. It was called "the Musical Walrus." A tiny cartoon walrus asked a user a series of seemingly benign questions in order to determine that person's "true musical identity." It, too, was gathering data points and personality information.

And then there were other online activities that, as Tayler explained, were a means to get at both the 570 data points Facebook already possessed about users and the 570 data points possessed about each of the user's Facebook friends. When people signed on to play games such as Candy Crush on Facebook, and clicked "yes" to the terms of service for that third-party app, they were opting in to give their data and the data of all their friends, for free, to the app developers and then, inadvertently, to everyone with whom that app developer had decided to share the information. Facebook allowed this access through what has become known as the "Friends API," a now-notorious data portal that contravened data laws everywhere, as under no legislative framework in the United States or elsewhere is it legal for anyone to consent on behalf of other able-minded adults. As one can imagine, the use of the Friends API became prolific, amounting to a great payday for Facebook. And it allowed more than forty thousand developers, including Cambridge Analytica, to take advantage of this loophole and harvest data on unsuspecting Facebook users.

Cambridge was always collecting and refreshing its data, staying completely up to date on what people cared about at any given time. It supplemented data sets by purchasing more and more every day on the American public, data that Americans gave away every time they clicked on "yes" and accepted electronic "cookies" or clicked "agree" to "terms of service" on any site, not just Facebook or third-party apps.

Cambridge Analytica bought this fresh data from companies such as Experian, which has followed people throughout their digital lives, through every move and every purchase, collecting as much as possible in order, ostensibly, to provide credit scores but also to make a profit in selling that information. Other data brokers, such as Axiom, Magellan, and Labels and Lists (aka L2), did the same. Users do not need to opt in, a process by which they agree to the data collection, usually through extensive terms and conditions meant to put them off reading them—so with an attractively easy, small tick box, collecting data is an even simpler process for these companies. Users are forced to click it anyhow, or they cannot go forth with using whichever game, platform, or service they are trying to activate.

The most shocking thing about data that I learned from Alexander Tayler was where it all came from. I hate to break it to you, but by buying this book (perhaps even by reading it, if you have downloaded the e-book or Audible version), you have produced significant data sets about yourself that have already been bought and sold around the world in order for advertisers to control your digital life.

If you bought this book online, your search data, transaction history, and the time spent browsing each Web page during your purchase were recorded by the platforms you used and the tracking cookies you allowed to drop on your computer, installing a tracking device to collect your online data.

Speaking of cookies, have you ever wondered what Web pages are asking when they request that you "accept cookies"? It's supposed to be a socially acceptable version of spyware, and you consent to it on a daily basis. It comes to you wrapped in a friendly-sounding word, but it is an elaborate ruse used on unsuspecting citizens and consumers.

Cookies literally track everything you do on your computer or phone. Go ahead and check any browsing add-on such as Mozilla's Lightbeam (formerly Collusion), Cliqz International's Ghostery, or the Electronic Frontier Foundation's Privacy Badger to see how many companies are tracking your online activity. You could find more than fifty. When I first used Lightbeam to see just how many companies were tracking me, I found that by having visited merely two news Web pages within *one* minute, I had allowed my data to be connected to 174 third-party sites. These sites sell data to even larger "Big Data aggregators" such as Rocket Fuel and Lotame, where your data is the gas that keeps their ad machines running. Everyone who touches your data along the way makes a profit.

If you are reading this book on your Amazon Kindle, on your iPad, in Google Books, or on your Barnes and Noble Nook, you are producing precise data sets that range from how long you took to read each page, at which points you stopped reading and took a break, and which passages you bookmarked or highlighted. Combined with the actual search terms you used to find this book in the first place, this information gives the companies that own the device the data they need to sell you new products. These retailers want you to engage, and even the slightest hint of what you might be interested in is enough to give them an edge. And all this goes on without your being properly informed or consenting to the process in any traditional sense of the term *consent*.

Now, if you bought this book in a brick-and-mortar store, and assuming you have a smartphone with GPS tracking switched on—when you use Google Maps, it creates valuable location data that is sold to companies such as NinthDecimal—your phone recorded your entire journey to the bookshop and, upon your arrival, tracked how long you spent there, how long you looked at each item, and even perhaps what the items were, before you chose this book over others. Upon buying the book, if you used a credit or debit card, your purchase was recorded in your transaction history. From there, your bank or credit card company sold that information to Big Data aggregators and vendors, who went on to sell it as soon as they could.

Now, if you're back home reading this, your robot vacuum cleaner, if you have one, is recording the location of the chair or couch on which you're sitting. If you have an Alexa, Siri, Cortana, or other voice-activated "assistant" nearby, it records when you laugh out loud or cry while reading the revelations on these pages. You may even have a smart fridge or coffeemaker that records how much coffee and milk you go through while reading.

All these data sets are known as "behavioral data," and with this data, it is possible for data aggregators to build a picture of you that is incredibly precise and endlessly useful. Companies can then tailor their products to align with your daily activities. Politicians use your behavioral data to show you information so that their message will ring true to you, and at the right time: Think of those ads about education that just happen to play on the radio at the precise moment you're dropping your kids off at school. You're not paranoid. It's all orchestrated.

And what's also important to understand is that when companies buy your data, the cost to them pales in comparison to how much the data is worth when they sell advertisers access to you. Your data allows anyone, anywhere, to purchase digital advertising that targets you for whatever purpose—commercial, political, honest, nefarious, or benign—on the right platform, with the right message, at the right time.

But how could you resist? You do everything electronically because it's convenient. Meanwhile, the cost of your convenience is vast: you are giving one of your most precious assets away for free while others profit from it. Others make trillions of dollars out of what you're not even aware you are giving away each moment. Your data is incredibly valuable, and CA knew that better than you or most of our clients.

When Alexander Tayler taught me what Cambridge Analytica could do, I learned that in addition to purchasing data from Big Data vendors, we had access to our clients' proprietary data, aka data they produced themselves that was not purchasable on the open market. Depending on our arrangements with them, that data could remain theirs or it could become part of our intellectual property, meaning that we could retain their proprietary data to use, sell, or model as our own.

It was a uniquely American opportunity. Data laws in countries such as the United Kingdom, Germany, and France don't allow such freedoms. That's why America was such fertile ground for Cambridge Analytica, and why Alexander had called the U.S. data market a veritable "Wild West."

When Cambridge Analytica refreshed data, meaning updating the locally held database with new data points, we struck a range of agreements with clients and vendors. Depending on those agreements, the data sets could cost either in the millions of dollars or nothing, as Cambridge sometimes struck data-sharing agreements by which we shared our proprietary data with other companies for theirs. No money had to change hands. An example of this comes from the company Infogroup, which has a data-sharing "co-op" that nonprofits use to identify donors. When one nonprofit shares with Infogroup its list of donors, and how much each gave, it receives in return the same data on other donors, their habits, fiscal donation brackets, and core philanthropic preferences.

From the massive database that Cambridge had compiled from all these different sources, it then went on to do something else that differentiated it from its competitors. It began to mix the batter of the figurative "cake" Alexander had talked about. While the data sets we possessed were the critical foundation, it was what we did with them, our use of what we called "psychographics," that made Cambridge's work precise and effective.

The term *psychographics* was created to describe the process by which we took in-house personality scoring and applied it to our massive database. Using analytic tools to understand individuals' complex personalities, the psychologists then determined what motivated those individuals to act. Then the creative team tailored specific messages to those personality types in a process called "behavioral microtargeting."

With *behavioral microtargeting*, a term Cambridge trademarked, they could zoom in on individuals who shared common personality traits and concerns and message them again and again, fine-tuning and tweaking those messages until we got precisely the results we wanted. In the case of elections, we wanted people to donate money; learn about our candidate and the issues involved in the race; actually get out to the polling booths; and vote for our candidate. Likewise, and most disturbing, some campaigns also aimed to "deter" some people from going to the polls at all.

As Tayler detailed the process, Cambridge took the Facebook user data he had gathered from entertaining personality surveys such as the Sex Compass and the Musical Walrus, which he had created through third-party app developers, and matched it with data from outside vendors such as Experian. We then gave millions of individuals "OCEAN" scores, determined from the thousands of data points about them.

OCEAN scoring grew out of academic behavioral and social psychology. Cambridge used OCEAN scoring to determine the construction of people's personalities. By testing personalities and matching data points, CA found it was possible to determine the degree to which an individual was "open" (O), "conscientious" (C), "extroverted" (E), "agreeable" (A), or "neurotic" (N). Once CA had models of these various personality types, they could go ahead and match an individual in question to individuals whose data was already in the proprietary database, and thus group people accordingly. So that was how CA could determine who among the millions upon millions of people whose data points CA had were O, C, E, A, N, or even a combination of several of those traits.

It was OCEAN that allowed for Cambridge's five-step approach.

First, CA could segment all the people whose info they had into even more sophisticated and nuanced groups than any other communications firm. (Yes, other companies were also able to segment groups of people beyond their basic demographics such as gender and race, but those companies, when determining advanced characteristics such as party affinity or issue preference, often used crude polling to determine where people generally stood on issues.) OCEAN scoring was nuanced and complex, allowing Cambridge to understand people on a continuum in each category. Some people were predominantly "open" and "agreeable." Others were "neurotic" and "extroverts." Still others were "conscientious" and "open." There were thirty-two main groupings in all. A person's "openness" score indicated whether he or she enjoyed new experiences or was more inclined to rely on and appreciate tradition. The "conscientiousness" score indicated whether a person preferred planning over spontaneity. The "extroversion" score revealed the degree to which one liked to engage with others and be part of a community. "Agreeableness" indicated whether the person put others' needs before their own. And "neuroticism" indicated how likely the person was to be driven by fear when making decisions.

Depending on the varied subcategories in which people were sorted, CA then added in the issues about which they had already shown an interest (say, from their Facebook "likes") and segmented each group with even more refinement. For example, it was too simplistic to see two women who were thirty-four years old and white and who shopped at Macy's as the same person. Rather, by doing the psychographic profiling and then adding to it everything ranging from the women's lifestyle data to their voting records to their

Facebook "likes" and credit scores, CA's data scientists could begin to see each woman as profoundly different from the other. People who looked alike weren't necessarily alike at all. They therefore shouldn't be messaged together. While this seems obvious—it was a concept supposedly already permeating the advertising industry at the time Cambridge Analytica came along—most political consultants had no idea how to do this or that it was even possible. It would be for them a revelation and a means to victory.

Second, CA provided clients, political and commercial, with a benefit that set the company apart: the accuracy of its predictive algorithms. Dr. Alex Tayler, Dr. Jack Gillett, and CA's other data scientists constantly ran new algorithms, producing much more than mere psychographic scores. They produced scores for every person in America, predicting on a scale of 0 to 100 percent how *likely*, for example, each was to vote; how *likely* each was to belong to a particular political party; or what toothpaste each was *likely* to prefer. CA knew whether you were more likely to want to donate to a cause when clicking a red button or a blue, and how likely you were to wish to hear about environmental policy versus gun rights. After breaking people up into groups using their predictive scores, CA's digital strategists and data scientists spent much of their time testing and retesting these "models," or user groupings called "audiences," and refining them to a high degree of accuracy, with up to 95 percent confidence in those scores.

Third, CA then took what they had learned from these algorithms and turned around and used platforms such as Twitter, Facebook, Pandora (music streaming), and YouTube to find out where the people they wished to target spent the most interactive time. Where was the best place to reach each person? It might be through something as physical and basic as direct paper "snail" mail sent to an actual mailbox. It might be in the form of a television ad or in whatever popped up at the top of that person's Google search engine. By purchasing lists of key words from Google, CA was able to reach users when they typed those words into their browsers or search engines. Each time they did, they would be met with materials (ads, articles, etc.) that CA had designed especially for them.

At the fourth step in the process, another ingredient in the "cake recipe," and the one that put CA head and shoulders above the competition, above every political consulting firm in the world, they found ways to reach targeted audiences, and to test the effectiveness of that reach, through client-facing tools such as the one CA designed especially for its own use. Called Ripon, this canvassing software program for door-to-door campaigners and phone bankers allowed its users direct access to your data as they approached your house or called you on the phone. Data-visualization tools also helped them determine their strategy before you'd even opened your door or picked up your phone.

Then campaigns would be designed based on content our in-house team had composed—and the final, fifth step, the micro-targeting strategy, allowed everything from video to audio to print ads to reach the identified targets. Using an automated system that refined that content again and again, we were able to understand what made individual users finally *engage* with that content in a meaningful way. We might learn that it took as many as twenty or thirty variations of the same ad sent to the same person thirty different times and placed on different parts of their social media feed before they clicked on it to act. And knowing that, our creatives, who were producing new content all the time, knew how to reach those same people the next time CA sent something out.

The even more sophisticated data dashboards that CA set up in campaign "war rooms" provided project and campaign managers with metrics in real time, giving them up-to-the-minute reads on how a particular piece of content was working and how many impressions and clicks that content was getting per dollar spent. Right in front of their eyes, they could see what was working and what was not, whether they were getting the return on investment they wanted, and how to adjust their strategy to do better. With these tools, those watching the data dashboards were able to monitor up to ten thousand different "campaigns within campaigns" we were running for them at any given time.

What CA did was evidence-based. CA could provide clients with a clear picture of what they had done, whom they'd reached, and, by scientifically surveying a representative sample, what percentage of the people they had targeted were taking action as a result of the targeted messaging.

It was revolutionary.

When I learned these things from Alex Tayler, I was dumbfounded but also fascinated. I had had no idea of the reach of data collection in America, and although it made me think back to Edward Snowden's warnings about mass surveillance, Tayler explained everything to me in such a matter-of-fact way that I saw it as just the "way things were done."

It was all so no-nonsense; nothing was dark or troubling. This was just how the data economy flowed, I imagined. Soon, I came to understand that I had been naïve to think I could achieve my goals with anything less than a big database. Didn't I want to be heard? Didn't I want to be effective? Yes, I did. At the time, I couldn't think of anything I wanted more.

As successful as this five-step approach had been, I learned in 2015 that it was about to change, when Facebook announced that as of April 30, it would, after so many years of openness, be closing its user data to "third-party app" developers, companies like CA. At that point, according to Dr. Tayler, a critical piece of CA's data gathering would be jeopardized. No longer could Tayler freely gather data from Facebook through the Friends API.

No longer could he use the Sex Compass or the Musical Walrus.

He had just a short time to grab whatever data he could before that window closed, Dr. Tayler told me.

And CA wasn't alone. Around the world, everyone else was rushing. Facebook was becoming a walled garden. After April 30, Tayler told me, it would allow data-gathering companies to use the data they had *already* harvested from it, and to advertise on its platform and use its analytics, but the companies wouldn't be able to harvest any new data.

Tayler showed me lists of thousands of categories of user data still up for grabs, if not from Facebook itself then from one of its developers. Somehow, other app developers were selling data they had gathered from Facebook, so even if CA couldn't collect it directly, Tayler could buy it easily from any number of sources. So easily, he said, that I didn't question it.

And there was so much to choose from. There were groupings of people according to their attitudes about everything from the food brands they preferred to their fashion choices to what they believed or didn't believe about climate change. All this information was there for the taking. I looked at the list and marked the groups I thought would be most interesting, based on clients I imagined we might have in the future. Tayler gave the same lists to other CA employees and asked them to choose groups, too.

The more the better, he said.

I now know this was against Facebook's policies, but one of Tayler's final purchases of Facebook data would occur on May 6, 2015, a whole week after Facebook said this was no longer possible. Strange, I thought. How did we get the data if the API was already closed?

After an extensive time with Dr. Tayler, I sat down and put together my Cambridge Analytica pitch, borrowing from Tayler and Alexander freely, using some of their slides but also adapting them and adding my own so that I would feel more comfortable with the way I personally explained the company to clients.

In the Sweat Box one afternoon, I finally pitched Alexander. When I had finished, he told me I had done a very good job, but that I needed to work on some of the details in order to demonstrate more clarity and more confidence.

"The most important thing is to sell yourself," he reminded me. The data sell will come naturally once the clients love you, he said, and he sent me out to pitch to every single person in the office. It was in that way that I gained greater knowledge about the company but also got to know my colleagues better.

Krystyna Zawal, a Polish associate project manager new to the company who accepted chocolates as currency, helped me fine-tune the part of my presentation using the case studies that had come from the John Bolton super PAC and the North Carolina midterms.

Bianca Independente, a fun-loving Italian in-house psychologist, helped me understand the larger context of OCEAN modeling, explaining that CA's expertise in it had come from the nonprofit out of which SCL had grown: the academic research center at Cambridge University called Behavioural Dynamics Institute, or BDI. As Bianca explained, BDI had been affiliated with more than sixty academic institutions, and that's what had given the SCL Group its academic bona fides. She was working diligently to add to the body of knowledge through experiments.

From Harris McCloud and Sebastian Richards, who were a messaging expert and a creative, respectively, I learned better ways to frame complex technical concepts for laypeople. And Jordan, who worked in research, provided me with visuals that could help me better explain those concepts in a slide show. Kieran literally helped me mock up new slides.

My colleagues provided me with their expertise, which was an embarrassment of riches. They clarified so much for me, and when I approached Alexander again to pitch him in the Sweat Box, I felt ready.

I made sure that I was perfectly dressed, as though for a real client. I wore bright red lipstick. I lowered the lights. Then I began.

"Good afternoon."

On the wall was the Cambridge Analytica logo, an angular abstract depiction of the human brain and the cerebral cortex, composed not of gray matter but of simple, short mathematical segments printed in white on a crimson background.

"Cambridge Analytica is the newest and most cutting-edge company in the political space in America," I said. "We specialize in what we call the science of behavioral change communication. What that means is that we've"—I pulled up another slide, one showing two equal-size puzzle pieces that fitted together perfectly—"taken behavioral and clinical and experimental psychology and combined that with world-class data analytics."

I pulled up another slide.

"We have some of the best data scientists and PhDs in this space, working with psychologists to put together data-driven strategies— that means that all your communications strategies are no longer guesswork. All your communications are based on science," I said.

Next, I discussed how blanket and informational advertising was useless and how the SCL Group had moved on from the old *Mad Men* way of advertising.

I pulled up a slide of a 1960s ad man drinking a martini.

We worked from the "bottom up" instead of the "top down." I said, and pulled up a slide that explained survey work and OCEAN scoring.

I explained that we weren't trying to fit people into categories based on what they looked like or any other preconceived assumptions we might have about them, but according to their underlying motivations and their "levers of persuasion."

Our modeling goals, I said, were to become accurate in our turnout probability (whether the person was likely to vote) and also our partisanship score (whether the Democratic- or Republican-leaning people in our database were persuadable). These would help us target our swing voters, I explained. And it was on swing voters that we largely concentrated our work.

I pulled up slide after slide after slide that segmented people categorized by OCEAN scores and hundreds of other algorithms into "persuadables." And from those persuadables, I showed how we segmented them even further and continued to test our algorithms until our models achieved 95 percent accuracy or more.

The example Alexander gave me to elucidate our process was a ballot initiative for gun rights.

If we had a database of 3.25 million possible voters, I began, we could see that, say, 1.5 million people would definitely vote against the ballot initiative; 1 million people would certainly vote for it; and 750,000 people would be considered swing voters. Then I showed how, after we had psychographically scored those voters, we could choose the messaging with which to reach them.

The most powerful of my slides compared swing voters. One group of swing voters was "Closed and Agreeable." Those people received an ad about guns that used language and images that reinforced the values of tradition and family.

I pulled up an image of a man and a boy, in silhouette, duck hunting at sunset. The text read, "From father to son . . . since the birth of our nation." It emphasized how guns could be shown as something people shared with those they loved. For example, my grandfather had taught me to shoot when I was a kid.

Another image was for a very different audience: the "Extroverted and Disagreeable" swing voter. This slide depicted a woman.

"The 'Extroverted and Disagreeable' voter needs a message that is all about her ability to assert her rights," I said. "This type of voter likes to be heard. On any topic," I said. "She knows what's best for her. She has a strong internal locus of control and hates to be told what to do, especially by the government."

The woman on the slide was wielding a handgun, a fierce expression on her face. The text below read, "Don't Question My Right to Own a Gun, and I Won't Question Your Stupidity Not To." Although I had never owned a gun, I could see part of myself in the woman on my slide.

That was my pièce de résistance.

Then I landed the plane. Looking Alexander in the eye, I said, "What Cambridge Analytica offers is the right message for the right target audience from the right source on the right channel at the right time. And *that's* how you win."

I stood there waiting for his response.

Alexander sat back for a moment, quiet.

As I looked at him, I couldn't help but consider the trajectory I'd been on during my brief time there and how heavily his response now weighed on my future. I so longed to please him.

Over the past few weeks, I'd been staying late at the office and connecting more deeply with my colleagues. After we were done for the day, usually after dark, we'd go out to dinner and to bars, staying up late.

My life had been changing. I had become a part of a whole new world, a professional world but one that celebrated with such an intensity as to drown out the maniacal working hours of the day, and reset our minds each night. I'm not sure if it was just the "work hard, play hard" mentality, but Alexander encouraged us in this; he wanted us to be friends.

Alexander came from a background in which his behavior had no consequences. He kept liquor in the office fridge, and there were times when, if there was good news to share, such as a new deal sealed, he would pop out of his desk chair like a champagne cork and open up a bottle so we could all celebrate together. In the mornings, we came in hungover, and Alexander joked about who looked the worse for wear. He himself always seemed the best recovered, although sometimes, after a late night, there were mornings when he had "off-site" meetings and wasn't in until the afternoon. The rest of us didn't have the luxury of doing that, so we worked all day, partied at night, and came back and did it all again the following morning.

Champagne, of great vintage and cost, flowed freely also at the polo matches to which Alexander invited the small, elite group of us. As the weather grew warmer and polo season arrived, it became our custom to spend the weekends at the Queen's polo grounds, called the Guards Polo Club, where Alexander was a member and where we could watch him play a match.

I knew nothing much of the game, but I knew he had played all his life and that his team was formidable in terms of both skill and pedigree. Among his teammates were members of the British aristocracy and top global players who flew in from Argentina and other countries. I understood little of the details of the game itself, except that the innings, or quarters, were known as "chukkas," but instead of learning the nuances of the game, I took to enjoying the experience of sitting in the stands or of being served meals in the clubhouse while watching Alexander ride a muscled horse about the vast green fields, smack a little ball around with a club, and then, during breaks, gallop over for a glass of champagne—which I'd pour for him and which he'd drink while still astride his pony, like a prince.

In the evenings, we'd repair to his nearby cottage, which, like his home in London, was adorned with modern art and stocked with liquor. Through the haze of it all—through the late nights of drinking and dancing and telling silly stories and experiencing no sleep and all gaiety, I found myself believing that this was a world I wanted to be a part of. This was a world of comfort and success, and I wanted it like nothing I had ever wanted before—and I was determined to have it.

Now, in the Sweat Box, I wondered if Alexander would toast me and my presentation. Would we open a bottle of champagne and celebrate?

Finally, he leaned forward and uttered the fateful words: "Fantastic, Brittany. You've done it," he said. "Bravo. You're ready at last for me to take you to America."

6

Meetings and Reunions

Cambridge Analytica's creation story didn't involve Facebook. No, it was another internet behemoth that gave birth to Alexander's baby.

In 2013, a young woman named Sophie Schmidt landed an internship with Alexander at SCL.[1] Sophie was a graduate of Princeton whose father, as I've mentioned, just happened to be Eric Schmidt, the executive chairman of Google. During her internship, Sophie regaled Alexander with the new developments at her father's company. He would ask her as often as possible to show him these new features, and she would log into dashboards and explain the importance of all the metrics. Alexander would take notes privately, absorbing the innovations that seemed to fit perfectly with his current business model.

In particular, he was enthused about the new developments in Google Analytics. Everything was becoming data-driven, and Google Analytics was now being used to collect and analyze the data from visitors to almost half the world's top-performing websites. By placing tracking cookies on the devices of people worldwide, Google Analytics was amassing a behavioral data set on a huge number of people across the globe—allowing Google to provide clients with everything in the form of data visualization and tracking measurements of a given website's effectiveness. Clients could see click-through rates, what people were downloading, what they were reading and watching, and how much time they spent doing those things. They could literally see the mechanisms that got people's attention and engaged them the longest.

Google's advancements in analytics didn't stop at Web page performance; the company had innovated track ads and had enabled Google Search to rank content and put high-performing materials at the top of its feed. The better the content performed, the higher up it went in the feed.

Immediately after Sophie Schmidt finished her internship, Alexander began avidly pursuing setting up a company that made use of the kind of cutting-edge predictive analytics Google had. It made perfect sense to integrate advanced, predicted data analytics into what SCL had been doing all over the world for two decades. It would allow SCL to reimagine and remarket its already data-driven services.

SCL had been reinventing itself from the beginning. In 1989, brothers Nigel and Alex Oakes, friends of Alexander's father, founded the nonprofit think tank that Nigel himself had taught me about: the Behavioural Dynamics Institute. BDI began to look at the ways in which human behavior could be understood, and then influenced, through communication. Out of this research, BDI produced significant findings useful for stopping violence, and it began to consult in the defense industry. When the Oakes brothers ran a defense campaign to stop election violence in South Africa in 1994, they helped to bring about the peaceful election of Nelson Mandela. As Alexander had shown me when I first visited the SCL offices, Mandela himself had endorsed SCL.

The company's first golden age began after September 11, 2001, when SCL became an essential partner with governments, including the United Kingdom, in the fight against terrorism. It was an integral part of helping to fight Al-Qaeda messaging. It ran training programs for armies all over the world, and won accolades from NATO. Nigel could never have envisioned that when defense spending dried up again in the second decade of the twenty-first century, there'd be another way to make SCL remain profitable and relevant in the digital age.

In this post-9/11 work, SCL used the social and behavioral psychology developed at BDI to interpret data. Back then, there hadn't been much data to purchase, the sample sizes were crude and small, and the data collection process was broad, mostly in the form of focus groups, door-to-door surveys, and phone calls. SCL could match some information it had about people to census or UN data, but the most it was able to do with it was identify common issues and do basic segmentation among large groups.

What Alexander was after when he created Cambridge Analytica was to bring the power of behavior predictability to the elections business. He needed to amass as much data as possible from a variety of sources and be able to "hygiene" it more thoroughly than anyone else could. "Hygiene-ing" is the process by which data engineers match new data to old and fix errors. At Cambridge Analytica, what it usually involved in the first stage was something as rudimentary as making sure the first and last names of an individual in both data sets were correct, with basics such as zip code and birthday lined up. Then there were more and more specific "cleanings." The cleaner the data, the more accurate the algorithms, and hence, the better the predictability. Data analytics could take what SCL already did and make it ever more accurate, scientific, and granular.

The place to launch such a business was in the United States. Because the United States lacked fundamental regulations about data privacy, and individuals were automatically opted in to their data being collected without additional consent required besides just being in the country—and the buying and selling went on unabated almost entirely without government oversight. Data was everywhere in the United States; the same is true today.

As Alexander looked to the United States for clients to whom he could sell new data-based products, he quickly began to focus on Republicans. This draw to the right had little to do with his own personal leanings. Alexander's politics were middle-of-the-road conservative. A Tory who liked to think of himself as above some of the antediluvian thinking on the far right, he was fundamentally a fiscal conservative who could run liberal on social issues such as equal marriage rights. If the U.S. market had been loaded with clients who were Democrats, he would have pursued them with equal vigor. The problem was, that market was already saturated.

In the wake of the 2008 and 2012 Obama campaigns, plenty of companies had arisen that served the data needs of liberal candidates. The big five were Blue State Digital, BlueLabs, NGP VAN, Civis Analytics, and HaystaqDNA. BlueLabs was the brainchild of a classmate of mine from Andover, Chris Wegrzyn, with whom I had worked on the Obama campaign. The Obama team's New Media strategy had gone on to produce a new era of digital gurus competing for communications work for political clients.

After serving as Obama's chief digital strategist for both the 2008 and 2012 campaigns, Joe Rospars founded Blue State Digital. Rospars and his team at Blue State described themselves as pioneers who understood that "people don't just vote on Election Day—they vote every day with their wallets, with their time, with their clicks and posts and tweets."[2] Other senior-level members of the Obama for America analytics team founded BlueLabs in 2013.[3] Daniel Porter had been director of statistical modeling on the 2012 campaign, "the first in the history of presidential politics to use persuasion modeling" to identify swing voters.

Sophie Schmidt's father, Eric, founded Civis in 2013, the same year that Sophie interned at CA. Civis's mission was to "democratize data science so organizations can stop guessing and make decisions based on numbers and scientific fact." Interestingly enough, one of the pillars of its mission statement was also "No a**holes."[4]

With the new media landscape already cluttered on the left, Alexander's target clients would have to be on the right—it was the only opportunity to bring data science into politics. It was a business decision, pure and simple.

For investment money and ideas, Alexander turned to America's most prominent conservatives, many of whom were inextricably linked. In his first trip to America, he visited with conservative media figure Steve Bannon. When I came on board the SCL Group, and even after I met Bannon, I had no idea who he was. Little did I realize at the time, but he was an avid producer of conservative media: audiovisual, print-, and Web-based. Breitbart News, the company Bannon began to helm after the death of its founder, Andrew Breitbart, would soon become the fourth-most-popular media agency in the country. And Steve's company Glittering Steel churned out everything from full-length anti-Clinton films to digital ads for super PACs.

Most important, the others whom Alexander approached included father and daughter Robert and Rebekah Mercer.

Steve Bannon apparently once said that Bob and Bekah, who was in charge of the disbursement of funds from Bob's vast empire, were "really incredible folks. . . . Never ask[ed] for anything." According to Steve, the Mercers were people of "very middle-class values" who came to their "great wealth late in life." By the time Alexander approached the Mercers, they were billionaires, and donors to conservative causes.

Bob Mercer had indeed started out modestly. He had been a brilliant IBM data scientist whose early work was largely in artificial intelligence. He built the first algorithms that enabled computers to read human speech, and he authored or coauthored many of IBM's early papers on "Watson," its famous computing system.

Bob left IBM and went on to become the first person to use predictive modeling in the stock market, which gave rise to his status as a hedge fund baron. His fund, Renaissance Technologies, based on Long Island, was and still is the most successful hedge fund in the world, with included assets of over $25 billion.[5] Bekah, one of Bob's three daughters with his wife, Susan, was the most politically active, and took control of the family's conservative giving strategies.

Now, what more could a conservative donor family want than a media baron to produce messaging and a data science company to target those messages to their audience? Steve Bannon would become, by many accounts, the Mercers' Obi-Wan Kenobi.

Steve, Bob, Bekah, and Alexander were an obvious match—all connected via Wisconsin GOP politico Mark Block. In 2013, Block was on an airplane when he met, by chance, a U.S. Air Force cyberwar expert who sang the praises of SCL. Block then sought out Alexander. Block had been aware of the Obama campaign's data analytics, but after meeting Alexander, he realized that Nix's vision was "light-years ahead" of what the Democrats had.[6]

Block went on to get everyone on board—literally. As he once described the Nix-Bannon-Mercers meeting to a journalist, he and Alexander arrived at a "grungy sports bar" on the Hudson River, where they had been told they were to meet up with the Mercers. Block and Alexander were baffled as to why the billionaire and his daughter would have chosen such a spot. "What the f**k?" Block remembered saying. After Bekah Mercer texted to say that her father would soon arrive, the "Mercer family's 75 million dollar 203-foot super yacht," the *Sea Owl*, "pulled up to the dock behind the sports bar." Steve

Bannon was already on board with Bob and Bekah.[7] Block and Alexander hopped on, and the rest is history.

It was no coincidence that Bob Mercer invested in a new data science company. One of his favorite sayings was "There's no data like more data."[8] And his choice of right-wing politics was a no-brainer: his political beliefs were uber-conservative and libertarian. Mercer's extreme views, if true, have garnered much press. It's been said that he believes, among other things, that passage of the 1964 Civil Rights Act was a terrible mistake—unbeknownst to me at the time.

Alexander never spoke directly to me about the amount Bob Mercer put into Cambridge Analytica, but he said that the minute he finished pitching Bob for the first time—pitching everything from how to use data to target people to how to tell if someone was a true supporter, and if not, then how to turn them into one—Bob Mercer was on board. The Mercers' generosity to conservative causes is well known, but Bob saw in Alexander a marriage between his love for data science and his political motivations. Alexander recalled Bob's reaction as something like "How much do you want, and where should I send it?"

From there, Steve and Bekah and Bob formed the triumvirate that was the board of directors of the new company known as Cambridge Analytica, with Alexander Nix at the helm. Alexander had already hired some data scientists by then, but he went on to hire more, and he began to instruct SCL Group employees to split their time between international work and building the U.S. business. The data scientists began to purchase as much data as they could get their hands on, and within months, Cambridge Analytica had taken off.

I first met Bekah Mercer in June 2015, when Alexander took me to the States for the first time. I had "wowed" him in London, and this felt very special to me. Though I'd traveled to the States many times while in college and graduate school, the fact was, I had lived solidly abroad for ten years, mostly as a student, and I hadn't been able to afford going back home often. Sometimes I'd go for two years at a time without setting foot on American soil.

Now, being in America felt good to me. I had to admit that as much as I had seen myself living in England forever, the United Kingdom had grown tiresome to me in terms of doing business, and not just SCL business. The British were polite to a fault, which meant that you never knew whether they truly liked you or whether they had any intention of doing business with you.

What I loved about America, and what I loved about New York City in particular, which is where Alexander and I went to meet Bekah, was that, as in London, everyone there was so involved in their important lives that they were too busy to stop and talk. That kind of self-preoccupation might have bothered some people, but, to me, New York and London shared an urgency I found appealing.

I'd spent hardly any time in New York City before—just weekends here and there when I was in high school, and friends and I would take the train down for a holiday—but now I was reminded of how the city worked: people rushed by, completely absorbed in their own concerns, not making eye contact with strangers on a bus or a train.

At the same time, when it came to doing business, Americans in general were so refreshingly direct. If someone didn't like you or didn't have the money to work with you, there was no delay in finding out. And you always knew if you were being bullshitted. At least, that's what I thought back then.

At least that's how it seemed with Bekah Mercer. With Bekah, what you saw was what you got. She didn't have much time to spend with us on June 15, when we walked in the door of her office, but she was straightforward and kind, pleasant, and cheerful. She made direct eye contact. Dressed in a pretty business suit and heels, she was tall and fit looking, with red hair, pale skin, and a regal forehead. She wore dark glasses embellished with glittery stones. Her hands were delicate, but her handshake was definitive and strong, befitting the kind of powerbroker she was.

I didn't know that much about her at the time, except that she was powerful. I had heard her voice on conference calls; it was firm, and her statements direct. I would soon learn that she had a dual bachelor's degree in biology and mathematics and a master's in operations research and engineering economic systems. She'd worked as a trader for a New York financial firm.[9] She was said to be the Mercer family's fiercest "political animal."[10]

Bekah knew what she wanted, and I was now a part of the team that would be giving it to her. As for Alexander, he called Bekah his "work wife," a title about which he offered little explanation, except to say that he had more in common with Bekah than his own wife, Olympia. Between art collecting and riding polo ponies, Alexander seemed to spend more than just Cambridge Analytica time with Bekah and her family. In fact, the more I learned, the more it seemed to me that he was closer to the Mercers than to his own family.

When I first met Bekah, I had recently learned that it was she who had connected Alexander and Cambridge Analytica to the Cruz campaign back in 2014. The story went that after Senator Cruz met with Alexander and Steve Bannon in DC in the fall of 2014, just before I came on board at SCL, the Mercers invested $11 million to support Senator Cruz.

At the time, Cambridge had scores of smaller races. Alexander had thought that for his first time in America, he'd be able to land, at best, a senatorial race, or a gubernatorial if he got really lucky. But that wasn't enough for the Mercers.

As reported in the press, Bekah and Bob's vision was to find a presidential candidate to challenge the Democrats in 2016, one who would fit the profile of a disrupter and who would come to Washington to change the way DC worked. Bob and Bekah would become known as the "Blow-It-All-Up Billionaires."[11] They were drawn, it's been said, to a set of ideas and a narrative about Washington's future laid out by a political operative named Pat Caddell. Caddell's vision was that what American politics needed was a figure like the James Stewart character in the 1947 film *Mr. Smith Goes to Washington*. Caddell wanted to "identify a new class of leadership for American politics, business and civic life," and he set out to find that figure, initially calling his quest "Desperately Seeking Smith."

Bob and Bekah were attracted by the notion, and they, too, sought an Everyman, someone "who went to Washington, took on corruption and stood on principle."[12]

That Senator Ted Cruz was the Mercers' choice was interesting. Cruz's poll numbers were terrible, he had very low name recognition, and those who knew him seemed universally to dislike him. Senator Lindsey Graham once famously opined that if someone shot Ted Cruz on the Senate floor, no one would bother calling an ambulance. Bekah and Bob certainly saw Cruz's disadvantages, but they liked a great deal about what he stood for, and they were counting on Cambridge Analytica to propel him to the White House.

Little by little, Cambridge's efforts succeeded. In early testing, Alexander boasted of a higher-than-30-percent uplift in performance for Cruz's campaign messaging. More people started to know and recognize the candidate, and eventually many of those people began to change their tune. They were clicking through, joining the campaign, and donating en masse. Cruz's viability as the Republican nominee began to become a reality, and people in politics started to notice Cambridge Analytica.

While Bekah and Bob were behind CA, both liked to keep a low profile. Some labeled them anti-Semitic, anti-immigrant promoters of hate speech and tribalism. Others described Bekah as being as "smart at politics as you could be without ever having been at the grunt level." Some saw her as an evil genius, an image she abhorred.[13] In an op-ed in the *Wall Street Journal* in 2018, Bekah wrote that her "natural reluctance to speak with reporters has left me vulnerable to the media's sensational fantasies." She described herself as someone committed to research and the scientific method; to small and localized government; and, among other things, to "fighting entrenched corruption on both sides of the aisle."[14]

In New York City in June 2015, Alexander introduced me to Bekah at her office on the twenty-seventh floor of the Newscorp Building near dusk. He kindly told Bekah that I was the "new genius in the crew," that I had already quite a bit of success at SCL, and that I'd be heading up all Cambridge's business development from then on.

Bekah greeted me warmly and welcomed me to the team. She said she had to leave soon, because it was the end of the day. (I knew she had four children.) But she hoped we'd meet again.

I did, too.

Alexander had an ulterior motive for arranging the meeting for so late in the workday. He liked Bekah, but he had not come to see her. His purpose was to visit with Brandon Muir, the executive director of a nonprofit Bekah funded. Alexander was not fond at all of Bekah's project. Called Reclaim New York, it had been created ostensibly to increase government transparency in New York State. Steve Bannon had founded it with about $3 million in Mercer Foundation money, but Alexander thought it a waste of Bekah's energy. All the nonprofit did was file Freedom of Information Act requests to find out which companies might have corruptly bid to fix potholes or who had bought public schoolbooks throughout the city but had never paid for them.

Alexander wanted Bekah's attention and her time. He wanted her connections and her help in reeling in big-fish clients. Even if those clients couldn't afford to pay Cambridge, Bekah would support the cause, make a strategic donation to the client, and Cambridge would have plenty of work to do.

So, Alexander's scheme that afternoon wasn't to spend time with Bekah. It was to woo the executive director of Reclaim New York away from Bekah's pet project and cause it to collapse.

Brandon Muir had been with Reclaim New York for a year at that point. He had broad experience in elections in South America, was a staunch Republican, and spoke fluent Spanish. He could be a perfect addition to CA if it expanded into América del Sur, where the data frontier had yet to be tamed.

Because I'd never had a chance to pitch for real, Alexander's plan was to have me practice my pitch on Brandon, a potential CA employee, and he introduced me to him not as the company's newest genius but as its sole "Dirty Democrat."

Alexander had picked a historic moment for our trip to the States. On June 16, 2015, the day after our visit to the offices of Reclaim New York, Donald Trump grandly descended a gilded escalator in Trump Tower and announced his bid for the presidency of the United States. Introduced to the gathered crowd by his daughter Ivanka, he took to the stage as speakers on either side of him bellowed out Neil Young's 1989 song "Rockin' in the Free World."

"When Mexico sends its people, they're not sending their best. They're not sending you. They're not sending you. They're sending people that have lots of problems, and they're bringing those problems with us [*sic*]. They're bringing drugs. They're bringing crime. They're rapists. And some, I assume, are good people," he said.

He wanted to build "a great wall," he said. "Nobody builds walls better than me, believe me, and I'll build them very inexpensively, I will build a great, great wall on our southern border. And I will have Mexico pay for that wall."

The potential Trump bid had been a source of gossip and a subject of concern in our London offices for some time. In March 2015, Trump had formed a presidential exploratory committee. In May, he'd announced the creation of a leadership team while in New Hampshire, the state that is always home to one of the nation's first presidential primaries.

Would Trump be significant competition to Senator Cruz, our main client? I doubted it.

I couldn't take Trump seriously. So many others in America couldn't, either. At that time, a poll had shown that about seven in ten voters nationwide, including 52 percent of all voters said they would definitely not vote for him.[15]

I was fairly certain that he was a threat to neither CA's other clients nor me. He would never win.

Alexander agreed. That's why we were in DC on June 16. We had come to see Steve Bannon, who, Alexander said, could help us get to Trump, a useful cash cow for commercial purposes, and an experiment for politics.

The only thing I knew about Steve Bannon when I met him was that he was the guy who had founded CA with Alexander and the Mercers, and that he was "big" in media and film production. Alexander always spoke about "Steve" with such reverence: He was a power broker, the go-between for CA and Mercer money, the person who made campaigns happen. He was the "godfather of CA." And although it was supposed to be an honor for me to be presented to him, I was a bit frightened even to think that I was about to meet him.

Steve's house was on A Street, in the heart of Capitol Hill, a two-story brick Georgian that Alexander called "the Embassy." I'd heard it was owned by the Mercers, but only Steve lived there. Alexander had the keys, so we let ourselves in. The house was dark. We stood on a threshold carpeted in American flags. Steve was probably in the office, Alexander ventured, and led me down to the basement, a poorly lit space in which a handful of young people worked quietly at computer stations.

We passed through a set of French doors into a large boardroom. No one was there. Alexander took out his phone and made a call. In a few moments, Steve Bannon burst through the doors of the basement boardroom and headed directly over to Alexander to greet him. Bannon was dressed casually, much more so than I had expected, given how prim and proper Alexander and I looked. He quickly shook both our hands before using the hand I had just shaken to toss his hair messily back out of his face, revealing bright red cheeks and bloodshot eyes. He seemed to have had quite a late night—I didn't know at the time that Steve was sober, but with the bloodshot eyes and red face, I assumed he was hungover, and it made me feel less nervous.

Alexander introduced us, making sure to out me as a Democrat, as he had with Brandon.

"So, we've got a spy, do we?" Bannon said, and laughed.

"She's an Obama girl, not a Hillary girl, though," Alexander said, and explained my campaign work in '08.

"You ran against Hillary, then," Steve said. He pulled out his phone and pulled up a video. "Check this out."

It was a thirty-to-forty-second advertisement in which an actress dressed as Hillary sat at a desk and, looking over her shoulder, suspiciously exchanged an envelope with someone.

"That's one of our babies," Steve said of the video. He was beaming. "Have you read *Clinton Cash*?" he asked, referring to a book that would later become a feature-length documentary. He showed me how to find it online. "You should read it," he said. "We are making a film of it, too."

The three of us sat for about ten minutes in the boardroom, chatting about which clients Alexander was targeting for Cambridge to work with these days—nonprofits such as the Heritage Foundation and political groups such as For America. But when the topic of Republican presidential candidates came up, Alexander asked me to excuse myself so the two could talk privately. I assumed they were going to talk about Trump. Alexander thought that Steve could get a meeting for us with Trump's campaign manager, Corey Lewandowski.

I closed the French doors and made my way around to the computer stations, introducing myself. The people in the room reminded me of my colleagues at Cambridge Analytica—young, bright, although everyone there was American—and clearly seemed just as devoted as SCL employees to whatever they were working on.

They identified themselves as reporters, digital designers. Some oversaw the social media. "For Breitbart," they said.

I drew a blank but pretended I knew what they were talking about. I'd never heard of Breitbart back then, and by the time Alexander and Steve emerged from the boardroom, I still didn't have a full idea of what it was, except that it was some kind of conservative website.

"Well," Steve said to the group, "we're all done here."

He wasn't speaking only about Alexander and me.

It was time, Bannon announced, to get ready for the event. He was hosting a book signing that evening for Ann Coulter.

I loathed Ann Coulter. I might not have known much about Steve Bannon or have heard of Breitbart, but Ann Coulter was hard to miss: a bitchy conservative pundit with a syndicated column and a dark mean streak. At the sound of her name, I felt nauseated. In her new book, ¡Adios, America!: The Left's Plan to Turn Our Country into a Third World Hellhole, its pleasant little title anticipating Donald Trump's later "shithole countries" comment, Coulter claimed that "Today's immigrants aren't coming here to breathe free, they are coming to live for free."[16] She also claimed that Carlos Slim Helú, the Mexican-born billionaire and owner of the New York Times, had bought the paper because he wanted to be able to place "pro-illegal immigration coverage" in America's newspaper of record.[17]

Steve wanted us to stay to meet Ann.

"Ah," Alexander said vaguely. "But we have another important meeting," he explained.

Steve promised to send us a pair of signed copies of ¡Adios, America!, and I tried not to roll my eyes.

The second we got outside, Alexander turned to me. "Who is Ann Coulter, please?"

I was shocked. "Alexander!" I whispered. "She's the worst person ever."

"Oh, good," he said when I was done giving details. "Then we dodged a bullet." He then joked that he'd make sure, though, to get the signed copies from Steve. He'd put his, he said, with his collection of fascist literature, the shelf of books I'd spotted near his desk on my first visit to his office.

I liked traveling with Alexander. During our time in the United States, I quickly learned more about him. His hunger for modern art was insatiable, and whenever we could, we stopped at galleries along the way to look at new work. He was also a loving father, or as much as he could be with his busy schedule. While in the States, I helped him pick out gifts for his children at Lego and American Girl.

Alexander had specific rituals that were part of his travel as well. He insisted on having drinks whenever he arrived somewhere, and said that every afternoon business meeting required a business dinner to follow. He liked, as he often said, "to socialize the deal." He was the kind of businessman who subscribed to the notion that the relatively low cost of a few meals and some drinks could make a world of difference to a business relationship, and that it was worth the investment for the bottom line.

As we began to spend more time together in America, and he saw me in my new role as head of business development, Alexander began to say that I had a future at the company, a big future. Perhaps, he said, often at the time, I could even be CEO one day.

"When I'm old and ugly," he said. "You'll be running the show."

He'd recently turned forty, a veritable babe in the woods, but to me, he seemed so senior, so experienced. And as I was the only person at Cambridge Analytica training directly under him, perhaps his prophecy for my future would turn out to be true.

The evening of our meeting with Bannon, we finished dinner, and I went back to my hotel room. I'd managed to get a copy of the book on the Clinton Foundation that Steve had recommended. The title read *Clinton Cash: The Untold Story of How and Why Foreign Governments and Businesses Helped Make Bill and Hillary Rich*, by Peter Schweizer, senior editor-at-large at Breitbart. Like the film that followed, the book had been underwritten by the Mercers.

Later, Schweizer served as the film's narrator. When it came on the scene in May 2016, Pete led the viewer through a biased exposé of the Clinton Foundation, suggesting that during the period when

Hillary was secretary of state, the Clintons directly benefited from improper donations. In his unsavory tale, the Clintons—who, Hillary had claimed, left the White House "broke"—had rebuilt their financial empire during her years as secretary of state by accepting bribes in exchange for disaster relief; speeches, especially in countries such as Nigeria and Haiti; and changes in U.S. policy. Those bribes, Schweizer's film claimed, filtered through the Clinton Foundation as payments for speeches Clinton had given—always at overinflated prices. It was "crony capitalism gone awry," Schweitzer writes.

I read the book at the time and would later watch the film with both disdain and alarm. It was odd to feel that way. I was not like the Hillary-obsessed Democrats of those days, and when the film was over, I couldn't help but think that if even half of what it claimed was true, then I understood exactly why the Republicans were so dead set against Hillary ever becoming president.

During the visit to New York, I had made a side trip up to Boston, to celebrate my tenth high school reunion at Andover.

It was a powerfully emotional return for me to the place where I'd first been politically energized. I had been a freshman there in 2001. My first day of school was literally September 11. From my dorm room, I had watched as that event shook the world and those around me.

Some of my classmates lost relatives in one of the twin towers or on one of the planes that flew into the Pentagon and a field in rural Pennsylvania. My dormmate found out that her uncle had been the pilot on Flight 11, which had hit the North Tower. On that bright Tuesday in September in Massachusetts, I watched as classmates frantically tried to reach their parents or received word of the missing. I saw that, and I grieved with them.

Those events might have pushed another person toward political conservatism, but they had the opposite effect on me.

I had been born a liberal. It was my natural way of being in the world. And after September 11, I leaned ever more to the left. I saw that in the wake of these acts of terrorism, civil liberties in America eroded. The nation became a surveillance state. On October 26, 2001, the Patriot Act passed without much protest, giving the government the right to collect data on citizens entirely without their consent. (Ironically, of course, it would be the extension of the government's powers in 2001 that would lead to the Big Data free-for-all at the tail end of the same decade.)

The invasion of people's privacy troubled me; so did the militarization of the country. That's when I first became involved in national politics. That next spring, when one of the smartest girls in my grade put out an open invitation for students to attend a Howard Dean rally in New Hampshire, I signed up immediately and got on the bus. I was only fifteen but I knew Dean was a fiercely progressive candidate, and after I returned to Andover from the rally, I began to work for Dean remotely, as a volunteer, writing emails to undecided voters from the computer in my dorm room.

In my sophomore year, I received a formal invitation to participate in the youth leadership program Lead America. That's how I first met a very young Barack Obama. He was in Boston for the 2004 Democratic National Convention giving a speech at an environmental rally at the harbor, and after listening to his stirring talk in a crowd of only thirty people, I waited for him to come offstage.

He was tall, handsome, and though he was in his thirties, he looked a decade younger. He emanated so much warmth and hope that just being around him made me feel that everything was going to be okay. I introduced myself as a fellow Chicagoan and told him about my volunteer work for Dean.

"Well, I'm actually running for U.S. Senate," Obama said. "Maybe you want to volunteer on my campaign?"

Of course, I said yes. I volunteered for him when he ran for Senate, and then I left college to intern for him when he ran for the highest office in the land. I had once been so devoted to Obama and his causes that I took a leave of absence from college and dedicated days and nights to the cause of seeing him become president. I was such an Obama enthusiast that I even had my mother bake cookies with Obama's face on them for my fellow campaign staffers.

That was the girl I'd been at Andover. That's who I was before I worked for Cambridge Analytica.

Before the high school reunion, I thought about what my former classmates knew about me. I hadn't put the SCL Group on my LinkedIn page or on Facebook. The latest updates they might have seen about me on social media were my meetings with dignitaries in London or pictures of me leading a trade mission to Libya.

At the reunion, at first I didn't tell my classmates what I was currently doing. I let them assume that I was still at work in the humanitarian sphere or in diplomacy.

"What *you've* been up to since graduation must be one of the most interesting stories," some of them gushed.

Perhaps it was, but now, recently, my life had become interesting in unexpected ways. I was living a life diametrically opposed to the one I had been living just a short time before. Only a year prior, I had been a progressive activist doing human rights research in India. Now, all of a sudden, I was a business development director for a company that had once worked hand in hand with the CIA and now was dedicated to helping the GOP. With the skill of a Method actor, I had stepped into a new role.

To only a few at the reunion did I whisper what I was truly doing for work. Most of these were the wealthier trust fund kids or classmates with whom I'd once argued about politics.

"That's amazing. Never thought we'd hear that from you," they said as I described my work on Nigeria and psyops or how SCL was designing election strategies all over the world.

Meanwhile, as I explained to these few that I was now working for SCL's American spin-off, Cambridge Analytica, I tried to explain it to myself as well.

Our second trip to see Steve Bannon came in mid-September 2015. He had wanted to know what new leads Cambridge had, and Alexander and I traveled to DC to brief him.

The second time around, I knew more about him. I had read some extreme articles Steve published on Breitbart and realized that most of the beliefs were opposite to my own. I was nervous now, much more so than the last time. Did he actually believe everything he printed? He couldn't possibly. In person, he seemed to me both smart and strategic. What could he really get out of the fear-mongering articles I was seeing on Breitbart.com?

This time when Alexander and I arrived at "the Embassy," it was Steve who opened the door. He was wearing a pair of old boxers and a plain white T-shirt, which, once he saw us standing there, he must have decided wasn't the right choice. He disappeared and then met up with us in the basement wearing a sweatshirt and jeans.

We went over our leads. Among other prospects, Alexander shared that we were about to travel to France to pitch former French president Nicolas Sarkozy. We were also intending to work in Germany, Alexander proudly told Steve—for the party of Angela Merkel, the Christian Democratic Union (CDU).

Steve had opinions about both—he started to tell us that he preferred that we pitch far-right candidates, such as France's National
Front politician Marine Le Pen, but the phone buzzed.

He looked at the screen, appeared to be very pleased with himself,
and then flipped the phone to face us. The caller ID read, "Donald
Trump."

He put the phone to his ear. "Donald!" Steve said, his voice booming. "What can I do for you?" He put Trump on speakerphone, and
out came the voice of a man for whom I had about as much respect
as I had for the likes of Ann Coulter and Marine Le Pen—that na-
sal, arrogant tone I had heard on the surreal reality show in which
the billionaire held court on a golden throne in a golden castle and
berated his underlings like a king cutting off the heads of jesters and
ne'er-do-wells.

"I'm going crazy over here preparing for this anti-Iran deal rally,"
Trump said. He was in New York City—calling from the castle, I
presumed.

Alexander had said that Trump was going to co-headline with
Ted Cruz, and it was clear from what Trump was saying that he was
annoyed at having to do so. Steve had arranged the event through
backroom negotiations; it had been intended to broaden Trump's
base, while elevating Cruz, but apparently neither man had much
taste for the other.

"We're packing up over here to fly to see you and Ted tomorrow,"
Trump told Bannon. "We're so busy. Everything is getting so big.
Very big. When are you going to send me your English guys?!" he
shouted.

Steve eyed Alexander and me. "I'm actually here with them right
now," he said. "The English guy and Brittany! Shall I send them to
you now?" he asked.

I hadn't realized that there was anything truly imminent with

Trump with regard to CA, but there was. Alexander had set up a meeting with Corey Lewandowski in June 2015, before the fateful day Trump descended that escalator in Trump Tower to announce his presidential bid. The two had been introduced by Steve Bannon, and the parties involved had known long before that some kind of campaign was coming. Regardless of whether Donald planned to run for president or build a bigger commercial empire, we followed the lead with steadfast efforts to get in there somehow. Over three months since June, we had gone back and forth with Corey, without confirming a meeting. But now Donald himself was asking aloud on Steve Bannon's phone for us to come to Trump Tower and help him out. How could Corey say no to the boss? Corey Lewandowski could meet us at Trump Tower early the next morning, Trump told us. "Then we fly at ten a.m. to the Hill," he said.

Alexander had promised me that I would never have to get directly involved in Republican politics. Now he promised me that the Trump pitch wasn't necessarily political anyway—just a great business connection that could turn into any number of different contracts. A massive opportunity, he said. We must capture it.

That evening, we headed to Union Station and hopped on a train for New York. The darkened landscapes of Maryland and then Delaware slid past the train car windows, the night slipping beneath us with each mile of track.

I was wondering just what Alexander wanted me to do the next morning. "So, am I pitching commercial or political, or both?" I asked him.

"Hmm," he said absentmindedly. "Either one is fine." He looked back at whatever he had been doing. "It doesn't matter, but I need you to *wow* me." He said that to me often now.

But I needn't worry, he said. Trump was only *technically* running for president. Commercial, political—it was all the same. The real reason Donald Trump was "running" for office, Alexander explained, was to create the conditions for the launch of something called Trump TV. His candidacy was, in other words, nothing more than a shell game. The political and the commercial were inextricably connected.

This information stopped me cold: Trump's whole "campaign" had nothing to do with running for office?

No, Alexander said. It had everything to do with stirring up and solidifying the audience for his most audacious business venture to date, an endeavor that would out-rival Trump's real estate empire— in other words, the greatest multimedia empire in the world.

Could it really be true? There was no possibility of a Trump presidency?

Alexander explained that of course the idea of Trump becoming the president of the United States was ludicrous. The American people would never stand for it; the whole notion was as ridiculous as many people thought. Cruz or Rubio or someone else would likely win the nomination, and then lose to Hillary. Trump's candidacy had always been a front for the enormous business venture, and CA was going to be there at the immaculate *inception* of that empire. We were going to be on the ground floor. After all, Trump TV was all about data. And so much of what CA was already doing was to solidify its monopoly on the U.S. conservative database in order to create a product Trump TV wouldn't be able to thrive without.

By introducing us to the Trump team, Steve was essentially handing us the keys to Trump's new kingdom.

Our appointment was at eight o'clock the next morning. I'd never been to Trump Tower, so Alexander instructed me to meet him at the front entrance.

I'd hardly slept the night before. Alexander's revelation had unnerved me. I had also learned that the money behind Trump TV was the Mercers', and that Steve Bannon was the project's impresario, its thought leader and champion. During the so-called campaign, the Trump organization would be gathering data that would feed directly into an enterprise that would serve as a megaphone for Steve and Bob and Bekah's political agenda. Getting the contract would be Alexander's greatest coup. At the same time, CA would do no harm to the Cruz campaign. Our work on Trump TV could even help Cruz, by giving him a platform once elected. In other words, there was nothing to worry about, Alexander said.

Every rally, every debate, every announcement, and every outrageous utterance that came out of Donald Trump's mouth was entirely for the purpose of activating, identifying, and solidifying his hold on a rapt audience. The primary campaign was a trial balloon for the whole shebang. And Donald Trump's growing "base" would comprise the consumers of his new product. "Running," which he'd spent very little money on, was Donald J. Trump's unique, brilliant, broad, and very cost-effective way of testing his messaging, and CA would make a fortune helping him, thus becoming afterward the key communications and data analytics team for the new enterprise.

Around me on Fifth Avenue, people rushed by on their way to work, men in business suits, women with their high heels in their hands and sneakers on their feet. Children made their way to school. And none of them, I thought, had any idea what was really going on.

Once inside Trump Tower, past the bronze-plated doors, Alexander and I boarded an elevator and rose, passing floor after floor, and when the elevator doors opened, I was taken aback. The scene before me was amazingly familiar, but I couldn't place why. I was trying to sort that out for myself when Corey Lewandowski strolled out of a corner office, looking smug and confident, dressed in a blue collared shirt with rolled-up sleeves, as if he'd just been working on something important and challenging. He seemed distracted, but by what, I couldn't quite imagine. He seemed the kind of person without much of substance on the brain. His fifteen minutes of fame had already preceded him: as the story goes, once, back when Corey worked as an administrative assistant to Ohio congressman Bob Ney (the same Bob Ney who was later convicted of corruption in a lobbying scandal), he was arrested for carrying a handgun in a bag of laundry into an office building at the U.S. House of Representatives. Corey claimed it was an accident, which would have suggested that he was daft, but I'd always thought the incident revealed a certain thuggishness in him.

Now he walked up to greet us and shook our hands without much intention or strength, quickly letting go as he did. It occurred to me that perhaps he had agreed to see us only as a favor to Steve Bannon.

I glanced around. The floor we were on was largely uninhabited. The ceilings were enormously high and held up, it seemed, by columns of gold. The grand office space was vacant of people and decorated only by signs on the gilded walls reading, "Make America Great Again."

I still couldn't shake the feeling that I'd been there before.

Corey must have caught my expression. "Looks familiar, does it?" he said. He seemed amused. "Aww," he said. "You watch *The Apprentice*, don't ya?" Then, without waiting for me to answer—I had, in fact, seen it—he jumped in. "Of coooooourse you do!" he said. He was from Lowell, Massachusetts, and even after years in Washington, he still had a slight New England accent. "Well, welcome to the set!" he said with a flourish, his arms outstretched.

Corey was as close to a used-car salesman as I had ever seen in someone in a political position, and he held forth about how "slammed" he was with work, how *popul-lah* his client was. Donald was the *best*, the *absolute best*, and we were lucky to be having a conversation about supporting such a popular guy.

We had taken seats in Corey's office, but I was hardly listening to what he was saying because all I could think was, *Is Donald Trump's presidential campaign headquarters a reality TV set?*

Trump was running around in the next room, getting ready to fly to DC. I caught a glimpse of him a few times, but didn't get introduced or speak to him directly, as we spent the next hour negotiating with Corey, wanting to leave with a "win." But first, we had to hear all about Corey, and then how incredibly important and special his candidate was.

After Corey's long-winded monologue, which was essentially a pitch to us about both himself and Donald, I was finally given room to pitch him in return. Corey wasn't a stranger to Republican politics; he had worked on campaigns for much of his career, but some of my descriptions of the analytics work took him aback slightly, and he cut me off—so that he could tell us more about Donald's being so popular that he hardly needed any help.

Both Alexander and I pushed back, explaining why our work was not only important but necessary. How else would Donald compete against sixteen other players in the primaries, let alone go up against a behemoth like Hillary Clinton?

By the end of our competitive conversation, Corey seemed more open-minded. He called Steve on his desk phone and punched the loudspeaker button.

"We got your English guys here, Steve! Now, you know people are *begging* to be involved in this campaign, you know that? People are working for us for free, they want to be involved so badly! So, what kind of deal can you make me?"

7

The Face of Brexit

SEPTEMBER 2015

Paris in late September: the weather is fine, the crowds of tourists have thinned out, and children return to school. The city can be yours for the taking, and Alexander and I had come to conquer France.

I was supposed to be working exclusively for Cambridge Analytica at this time. In fact, I was in the midst of moving to DC, where CA was opening its first American office. But Alexander had asked me to accompany him to France to pitch a team for working on the presidential election of Nicolas Sarkozy. It was a one-off, Alexander promised. A favor. He knew I was busy. He wouldn't ask me to do this kind of thing again.

Even though I was busy—shuttling back and forth between London and Washington, looking at both office spaces and apartments, moving over some essential belongings, arranging to change my paycheck from pounds to dollars—I thought it was a magnificent suggestion.

The company was growing fast, but we were short-staffed: I was the only employee in international business development, a department of one, straddling both our global work and helping out in America now, too. I loved Paris. And if we were to sign Sarkozy,

I fantasized about a commute I wouldn't mind: back and forth between the U.S. capital and the City of Light.

Alexander had pitched Nicolas Sarkozy in 2012, but Sarkozy had turned him down and lost to François Hollande by a 3.2 percent margin. Alexander didn't want the Sarkozy team to make the same mistake again. This time, Sarkozy would be running under a rebranded party, his UMP (Union for a Popular Movement), now being called Les Républicains ("the Republicans"), representing the center right, and the team had to be prepared. The elections were still two years out, which seemed a long time, but Alexander always said that elections could be won in six to nine months' time only if need be, and then only if the conditions were right. Two years was the optimal amount of time for planning.

It was a single day's journey, a round trip on the Eurostar and back. We left in early morning, and by noon Alexander was in midpitch in a quintessentially nineteenth-century building in central Paris, a black-turreted, four-story affair with high ceilings and elaborately wooden moldings, speaking before a political and commercial communications consultancy with whom we hoped to partner. The French consultants were in their early forties, neatly dressed, and particularly attentive, I thought.

Some clients got dazed during the data analytics portion of a pitch, but the two executives seemed more keenly interested. They had questions about how CA obtained data, what we did with it in-house, and how microtargeting was done. But when Alexander finished up and asked if there were any questions, there was a decidedly dead pause.

One of the men cleared his throat. "*Non*," he said. "This simply will not work."

The other executive shook his head in agreement. "It is impossible," he said. "The French will never accept it."

Alexander was as genuinely puzzled as I. "Because . . . ?" he asked.

"The data, of course," one of the men said. "If people knew a candidate was doing this, it would mean defeat for certain."

Alexander and I both knew French law: as long as users opted in to share their data, they made a conscious, informed, and legal decision. The same was true in Britain.

"This is not America," one of the men said.

No, it was not, I thought. In America, users are automatically opted in through legislation that allows their unfettered data collection; there are few protections in the United States like those in France and the United Kingdom.

The subtext was obvious, though: America hadn't the baggage Europeans did. The French, like the Germans and many other western Europeans, were far more sensitive, and understandably so, about the use of people's private information. While laws allowed entities to gather data with people's permission, the precedents for data's misuse were horrifying.

The Nazis' collection of data on citizens from Jews to the Romany, on the disabled and homosexuals, was what had made the Holocaust both possible and cruelly efficient. In the aftermath of World War II and coming into the digital age, legislators in Europe made sure that data laws were strict in order to prevent something like that from ever happening again. Data privacy was, in fact, an underlying principle of the European Union—clear rules limited a rogue actor's ability to abuse data and violate human rights.

Alexander and I were well aware of these issues, but we didn't think of them as insurmountable in France or elsewhere in Europe. At least we hadn't thought so until this moment.

Alexander tried to persuade those assembled before us that our process was transparent, well within the letter and the spirit of the law, and that anyone who wished to build a campaign these days and didn't use data would get left behind. But the two men were immovable. We parted amicably, although both Alexander and I were shocked. We had never thought of the use of data in politics as offensive but rather as inevitable.

Silent, we boarded the Eurostar for London. Europe wasn't America. The wounds of World War II had not yet healed.

The train sped from Paris to Calais, but there it came to halt. I had read that delays at the entrance to the Channel tunnel, or "Chunnel," on the French side were common these days. Refugees who were part of the great migrant crisis had set up camp at the entrance, and they were known to attempt treacherous and illegal crossings, sometimes on the top of freight trains; others on the bumpers or roofs of trucks. Many had met their deaths, some having fallen, others having drowned in the canals at the border. Over the past nine months, it was reported that border guards had prevented an unbelievable thirty-seven thousand attempts to cross in this way. The guards had described "'nightly incursions' of hundreds of migrants trying to storm the route in the hope that a lucky few will make it to the other side."[1]

The refugee crisis across Europe was unprecedented. The UN High Commissioner for Refugees reported that worldwide conflicts had displaced some sixty million people, a number equal to the population of Italy.[2] In 2015 alone, more than one million had made their way to EU countries, and many of those wished specifically to enter Britain, where health care and government housing were free, and which was often the choice of last resort for a refugee who had tried every other country along the way.[3]

Most refugees were from Muslim-majority countries. The reasons for their flight were varied, ranging from armed conflict to the effects of climate change. People streamed out of Syria, Libya, South Sudan, Eritrea, Nigeria, and the Balkans.

The crossings from Africa were particularly dangerous because smugglers asked exorbitant fees and because large groups of people, sometimes in the hundreds, boarded unsteady boats or rafts to sail the treacherous Mediterranean.[4] Authorities had estimated that more than eighteen hundred migrants had drowned trying to do so that year.[5]

Our train waited at the entrance of the Chunnel forever, it seemed. When it finally sped into the dark mouth of the below-seabed route between France and England, Alexander turned to me. He had been thinking something through, he said. We had an exciting opportunity coming up in Great Britain. It had to do with a historic referendum on Britain's membership in the European Union.

The United States held referendums all the time; in nearly all our local and statewide elections, we vote on whether we want to fund new schools, pass ordinances on public drunkenness, and allow electric scooters to park on sidewalks. But the upcoming referendum in Britain was national. Britain had held only two other national referendums in its modern history, the 1975 European Communities membership referendum and the 2011 United Kingdom Alternative Vote Referendum, but this upcoming election was contentious and immensely consequential. It had the potential to change the face of Europe itself.

As the result of something called the Maastricht Treaty, England had been part of the European Union since the late 1990s, but there had long been widespread disagreement over the benefits of an open-bordered and unified Europe and Britain's participation in it.

To what advantage was it for Britain to share a currency and a market with other European nations? The EU was predicated on noble ideas: economic equity across Europe, nondiscrimination, and the shared values of democracy and human rights. It offered freedom of movement without internal borders and the enhancement of solidarity among nations. Indeed, for its commitment to peace and prosperity among its member states, the Swedish Academy had awarded the European Union the Nobel Peace Prize in 2012.[6]

But more and more Britons had become nativists and separatists. Nationalism and tribalism were on the rise in England, just as in the United States. Like America, Great Britain had a long history of fierce independence and self-rule. Lately, the populist voices in support of "leaving" the EU had become as powerful as those that supported "remaining."

The upcoming "Brexit" referendum would have two sides: The "Remainers," with their slogan "Stronger Together," supported staying in the European Union. They supported a supranational framework with joint laws and regulations that upheld both freedoms and human rights but, in doing so, cost the nation some degree of self-determination.

The "Leavers," or "Brexiters," or "Brexiteers," would campaign to leave the EU altogether. Its argument for doing so would be that Britain needed to choose its own rules, close its borders to massive numbers of immigrants, and save its funds for British institutions such as the National Health Service (NHS), which the British dearly prized.

It might be tricky for SCL to be involved in the referendum, Alexander acknowledged. After all, it was a British election, and as a British firm, SCL had always stayed out of British politics; it didn't want to be seen as taking sides in its own country, though it had done so just about everywhere else.

Alexander explained that he had been interested in working with either side, but the Remainers believed they were going to win, and didn't think they needed expensive political consultants like SCL.

An opportunity with the other side had presented itself, and it was too tempting to turn down.

Two key groups were vying to become the official campaign of the Leave movement. To get that designation, each first had to present its case to the Electoral Commission. SCL was lucky, because both of these Leave groups wanted to work with us.

The two meetings were coming up shortly, Alexander said. So, he had another favor to ask. The Leavers were, in general, a complicated group with whom to work. They included some of the most controversial and divisive political figures in modern British history. Given what had happened in Paris that day, Alexander said, he would rather not associate himself with them and be seen as a pariah. The situation was, he pointed out, not unlike my own: I was reluctant to be associated with Cruz or Trump in the United States. Alexander didn't want to be seen with people whose opinions and policies could be considered distasteful.

"I know you have a lot on your plate," he said—meaning my move to Washington—but he hoped I'd be willing to pitch the Leavers and work with them for only as long as it took to get them to sign on with us. For a short time only, Alexander said, I'd be the face of SCL for Brexit, and in exchange, he would continue to be the face of Cambridge Analytica for the Republicans in the States.

As busy as I was, it didn't seem like too difficult a thing to do. First, I had read the same newspapers as everybody else in England. I was as sure as anyone that the Leavers had not a chance of winning.

Second, meeting with them might provide me with some experience with referendums. Perhaps I could get some skin in the game during a historic election.

Third, I was dating Tim. He and his friends and family were conservative Scotsmen and Englishmen, and perfectly content to leave the European Union for more self-determination, especially the Scots, who had tried and failed three times to exit the United Kingdom. My boyfriend intended to vote "out," so if I worked for the Leavers, there'd be no lovers' quarrel.

Fourth, part of me had always secretly hoped that one day I might be able to become a British citizen. I had also dreamed of having children and raising them in a country where public services were well funded and liberal values reigned.

And fifth, there were some fine political reasons that leaving could be good for British citizens. As a human rights activist and liberal, I had watched Britain, under the EU, become ever more conservative. The EU had compelled it to enforce some supranational legislation that was, frankly, more restrictive on certain issues, such as the sale of cannabis and psychedelics, which I believed were wrongly criminalized. As a human rights activist, I believed that an independent Britain meant a Britain that had the potential to serve its people better: become more liberal, not less.

All this was why I wasn't troubled about doing Alexander the favor he was asking of me. Given the dispiriting day we'd just had with the French—never mind the fact that Alexander had suggested that working with the Leavers could lead to a plump commission—it seemed rather an innocuous task, a bargain between Alexander and me that was no more complicated than splitting the check after lunch. "I'll take the Americans, and you take the Brits," Alexander had offered cheerfully. And he promised that, after this, I'd never again have the problem of associating my public image with conservatives.

The first Leave group I had to pitch, Alexander, said, was Leave.EU. Its primary point person was a prominent businessman named Arron Banks, an insurance broker and prodigious donor to conservative causes. Banks had been a Tory but had jumped ship, Alexander said, joining the UK Independence Party, or UKIP. Alexander said that Arron was good for millions.

The Leave.EU team, a motley crew of five, arrived at the SCL offices on a Friday in late October and made an immediate impression: Arron Banks, middle-aged with a baby face and dressed in a suit and tie, waddled into the conference room like a Mob boss, his round belly arriving before he did. He introduced himself with a booming voice and a bone-crushing handshake.

Accompanying him were Chris Bruni-Lowe, communications director, and Liz Bilney, CEO of Leave.EU and a right hand to Arron. Apart from Liz's slick, long black hair that fell around her face like an oil spill, both of them were unremarkable figures.

The fourth man was the bespectacled Matthew Richardson, a jovial barrister who introduced himself as legal counsel—but counsel to whom, I wasn't sure. Did he mean legal counsel to Leave.EU? To Banks?

And the fifth was Andrew (aka "Andy," aka "Wiggsy") Wigmore, an odd duck who was some sort of business associate of Arron's but whose role in the campaign would never become clear to me. Andy looked more like an aging athlete than a politico, and it would turn out that he was a former footballer and sometime trap shooter. An eccentric, before he took his seat, he unzipped his backpack and produced from it a slew of tiny bottles of liquor, the kind you find on airplanes, and handed them out to those in the room to whom he was introduced. They were filled, he said, with Belizean rum.

My task that day was to pitch the Leave.EU team and gather enough information about their needs and data capabilities to be able to write up a formal proposal for them. Arron, whom Andy called "Banksy," was so thrilled with the presentation that he said he was interested in using SCL not only for the campaign but also for the party, UKIP, and for his insurance company.

The most pressing issue, Arron said, was to out-dazzle the competition. Leave.EU's rival, a group called "Vote Leave," was likely to have the advantage over Arron's group. It comprised mainstream Westminsterites with powerful and established connections. In just four weeks, Leave.EU planned to hold a public panel preceding its formal application to the UK Electoral Commission. It wanted to put on a dog-and-pony show that would demonstrate that it was better suited than Vote Leave to serve as the designated campaign.

Winning the designation was important because it meant financial support from the Electoral Commission (a seven-million-pound spending limit) and designated TV ad spots. The latter was a huge perk in England, as British law forbade anyone but officially designated political groups from conventional advertising.

In order to help Arron's team prepare for the presentation, I had to know what data they had. Then we would prepare a two-phase proposal, so that the first bit of work would be done before the event.

It was still early days, Arron said, but we'd better not wait. He'd have his team send what they could as quickly possible.

Vote Leave had planned to meet with SCL, but they pulled out when they learned we were meeting with their rivals. The British equivalent of Jeb Bush, they wanted loyalty. Leave.EU, for its part, was the more desperate, British version of Ted Cruz—they were so far afield from winning that they didn't risk any pride when they waived the signing of a noncompete contract.

After the meeting, two emails regarding Leave.EU crossed my desk. One, addressed to Banksy and Wiggsy, was from Julian Wheatland, SCL's chief financial officer. It described the work SCL planned to do to prepare for the press conference, which Julian called a "short programme of data analytics and creative support" that was "designed to showcase intellectual capability and a data driven approach to campaigning." The email also contained a very British request for payment for our services in advance.

The other email, from Arron, was a follow-up to the meeting we'd had. In it, he wondered if SCL might be able to do fund-raising in the United States for Leave.EU, by targeting people in America "with family ties to the UK." I wasn't entirely sure what he meant or why he thought that was a good idea. I noticed that, among others, the email had copied Steve Bannon.

This explained how Arron Banks might have found Alexander and SCL. Steve must have introduced them. After all, Bannon was an American version of Nigel Farage, and the two men were friends. The founding head of UKIP, Farage was a larger-than-life member of the European Parliament whose sole reason for being an MEP was his desire to dismantle the European Union from the inside out.[7] Having spent my entire adult life based in the UK, to me, Steve wasn't as public a figure as Nigel, but he was as fierce a disrupter. Both men were pugilistic populists, a brand on the rise all over the world.

Bannon and Farage were proponents of the kind of populism that was an "us versus them" proposition, men who argued that the "establishment" and the "elites" were corrupt and that the common man was of purer motivation. They each believed, or at least publicly professed, that political correctness was merely a smokescreen for elitism, which, they felt, squelched frank but valuable "plainspokenness."[8] They both violated social taboos and were epically rude. It made sense to me that they were friends.

As I prepared for the task ahead, I reminded myself that if Arron Banks had arrived by way of Nigel Farage by way of Steve Bannon, then I had better do a very good job for Leave.EU.

Getting data from the Leave.EU crew turned out to be a longer process than I expected. First, Arron sent us Liz Bilney, the woman from his office who turned out to know nothing about data at all, nor where any might be, despite being the CEO of Leave.EU. She put me in touch with someone else at Leave.EU headquarters, in Bristol, who told me that he didn't have much data at all, but could give us access to what little they had. After I appealed to the crew from our original meeting for guidance, Matthew Richardson got in touch and told me he could certainly help me out. Richardson made it sound as though UKIP had a massive database of information on its entire membership in addition to some useful survey data. *He* then put us in touch with the IT guys at UKIP and said he would arrange to have someone there get the data over to us as quickly and as securely as possible.

How can he have access to that? I asked Julian, who promptly replied that Matthew was in fact the secretary of UKIP.

I was stunned. How was Richardson both legal counsel to Leave .EU and in the party leadership? Fundamentally, the legal question was if the campaign could possibly use the data from the party, and someone incentivized to make this happen was not exactly an unbiased third party you would usually expect to make this kind of determination. It didn't make much sense, but I figured that as party leadership, at least he had permission to use the data. He would deliver what he had, and we'd proceed from there.

In the meantime, I had to leave for America, for a trip I'd planned with my family to New York City. I told the data scientists in the office that I'd be gone, but I asked if, once the data had arrived from UKIP, they could start working on it right away. Time was very short.

The trip to the States was a splurge on my part. I'd flown in my mother, father, and sister to treat them to a nice hotel and a few days in the city. We had good meals together, saw a Broadway show, and went to a museum. I spent every dollar in my bank account hosting them, but it was worth it to have some family time and help push out of our minds the bad memories of having given away everything we owned just months before.

Despite the festivities I'd arranged, my father was still strangely flat of affect, frequently returning to his hotel room early and alone. His living situation back home was still dreary: he was staying temporarily with his sister in a spare room at her house, and he hadn't found, or wasn't motivated to find, work. Still, I was happy I had the resources to do something nice for him and for my mother and sister, and I was looking forward to doing even more, given that I was six months into receiving a steady paycheck and starting to feel that I could stand on my own two feet. Because I'd soon be living in DC, back in America for the first time in my adult life, I would also be able to see them more often.

During the visit, I spoke very little about my job, except to share the broad outlines of what I did. My sister, Natalie, had studied psychology in college and seemed genuinely interested in the fact that Cambridge used OCEAN modeling to identify voters' personalities. We spoke about how CA's capabilities could be applied in areas that might have a positive social impact. Natalie's politics were not unlike my own, progressive, and she'd always been a down-the-line Democrat like me. So, when I let it slip that I was working with Steve Bannon, I wasn't surprised at her reaction, though it wasn't particularly comfortable experiencing it.

She put her finger in her mouth, pretending to make herself vomit. "How could you?" she said.

"He's a brilliant man," I answered, for lack of a better explanation.

It was in the middle of a conversation with her like this one that I got a curious call from one of our head data scientists in London, Dr. David Wilkinson, who was to oversee the data analytics for Leave.EU. When he phoned me, he was laughing.

"Brittany," he said grandly. "Your data has arrived!"

The joke was that Matthew Richardson had sent someone from UKIP headquarters all the way to London on a train with a giant computer tower, which he delivered to the SCL offices with some ceremony and the suggestion that there should be plenty of information on it. My colleagues at London HQ were shocked and amused, considering that there were quite a few ways to transmit data that did not include the physical delivery of a heavy 1990s computer stack.

As it turned out, there were only two small Microsoft Excel files on the hard drive, one with UKIP membership data on it and the other the results of a survey that UKIP had apparently carried out about people's attitudes toward Brexit. It was a paltry amount of data, two files that could easily have been sent over to us as email attachments or even brought on a USB stick, but it was enough to start with, David said.

When I returned to London, the results of the data modeling from the two sets were ready, and they were indeed, at least preliminarily, very useful.

David had discovered that the Leave community comprised four segments to whom our messaging team gave the following monikers: "Eager Activists," "Young Reformers," "Disaffected Tories," and "Left Behinds."

The Eager Activists were extremely politically engaged, looking for opportunities to get further involved with and donate to the cause. They were also somewhat pessimistic about the economy and the National Health Service.

The Young Reformers were single, in the education field, politically active, and comfortable with people from different ethnic groups; they tended to dislike talking too much about immigration. In general, they were also fairly optimistic about the economy and the future of the NHS.

The Disaffected Tories were fairly satisfied with the current and previous governments, but they were unhappy with those governments' stances on the European Union and immigration. Generally, they were upbeat about the economy and the NHS, and they believed that crime was decreasing. Most were fairly affluent professionals and managerial-level employees. Most weren't particularly politically active.

The Left Behinds were perhaps the most interesting. They felt increasingly alienated by globalization and society in general. They were deeply unhappy about the economy and the NHS and felt that immigration was the central issue of their time. They were suspicious of the establishment, including politicians, banks, and corporations; and they worried about their economic security, deteriorating public order, and the future in general. In other words, if David had enough time to do OCEAN scoring, the Left Behinds might have been found to be highly neurotic and, hence, most reachable when messaging appealed to their fears.

We mocked up the results in the form of slides and some documents, but both Julian and Alexander weighed in and told me not to share the actual documents with Arron, Andy, or the rest of the Leave.EU crew. They hadn't yet paid for the work we'd done, so I was instructed that I couldn't "give it away for free." I could instead present the findings and even show slides, but I was to hand nothing concrete over to anyone until they signed the contract they'd promised to us and paid for the work they'd asked us to do. This made sense, but I also pushed back, saying that we should proceed, as Arron had given us the "green light" in writing. Julian had told me so. I figured it was only a matter of some legal back-and-forth before the contract was signed and paid. Matthew Richardson had assured us that he was arranging contracts between UKIP, CA, and Leave.EU to make the data sharing legally compliant. So, I fully intended to use the data's findings to the benefit of the campaign, and worked with the SCL team to gain as much knowledge as possible out of the work we'd done in phase one.

By the run-through, which was scheduled for November 17, the day before the press conference was to take place, there was still no payment and no signed contract. We had also run into some legal difficulties, but as far as I knew, they seemed resolved. The concern had been whether it was legal to share the UKIP membership data and the surveys UKIP had done with Leave.EU. At the time their data was collected, UKIP members had not opted in to its being shared with Leave.EU or any political organization, so we needed the legal nod before handing it over.

It was that morning when Julian finally showed me a legal opinion that a barrister named Philip Coppel QC had written up that at least cleared the data work we had done for UKIP. A Queen's Counsel is the most qualified public legal expert in the country, so I trusted this implicitly. Phew! The work had already been done, so now we could proceed with presenting it. In the meantime, a contract for data sharing between UKIP and Leave.EU would be written up separately, which I was told would clear our UKIP data work for wider use in the campaign.

At the time, I didn't pay attention to anything except the legal content of the QC's document Julian had given me, and I was happy with the green light I believed it gave us to do more data work. I would only later notice that it was not only a QC's handiwork, but had been coauthored by Matthew Richardson, whom I knew as being a lawyer CA had hired specifically for this project. I had assumed that being a barrister was his main job, with UKIP leadership taking a backseat. He might have helped Philip Coppel out with the details—it made sense, given that he was an expert in what was required for the project—but looking back, I see that it was quite curious that he would have given himself permission for work he himself wanted carried out. At the time, though, I was slammed with prep work in advance of the run-through for the Leave.EU press conference, and I thought little of these details. I put the finishing touches on my talking points and worked on my slide show.

The news leading up to the run-through had been deeply disturbing. On November 13, purportedly in retaliation for a French military operation in Iraq and Syria, ISIS terrorists struck Paris in coordinated attacks. They detonated bombs outside the Stade de France, in the suburb of Saint-Denis, during a soccer game; killed people in cafés and restaurants; and carried out a mass shooting at the Bataclan theater during a concert by an American rock group— murdering a total of 131 people (which included one later suicide) and injuring 413. Two days later, in retaliation for the attacks, the French increased air strikes on an ISIS stronghold in Syria, and on November 15, President François Hollande, in an address to Parliament, declared France to be at war with ISIS.

On November 17, I made my way to the London offices of Leave.EU, in Millbank Tower, with the distinct awareness of a world in a state of chaos. The run-through, though, was truly successful. The entire team had gathered, and we introduced ourselves and gave updates on the work we'd done thus far.

Present were Arron Banks, Andy Wigmore, Chris Bruni-Lowe, and Liz Bilney. Matthew Richardson was also in attendance, having come in from UKIP headquarters. Richard Tice, a prominent Tory businessman, had joined the group, as had the very well respected demographer and expert on the Labour Party Ian Warren, whose purpose was to provide insight into how to target liberals. Most impressively, a man named Gerry Gunster, CEO of the American firm

Goddard Gunster, had flown in specially from DC. Gerry's expertise was referendums, and his work in the States was similar to CA's. He did research, data analysis, and strategic decision making for electoral campaigns (discovering which voters were key and how to get them out to vote) and enjoyed an unrivaled track record in winning for his clients, with an over 95 percent success rate in referendums, their core business.[9]

Arron reported that the campaign had raised more than two million pounds to date. Richard Tice reported that the campaign had secured more than three hundred thousand registered supporters since the previous summer and had organized some two hundred groups around the country. He shared with us that the campaign had begun to "shift the polls," and was now neck and neck for the lead in winning the desired designation from the Electoral Commission over the competing Vote Leave.

Matthew Richardson provided an update on UKIP's plans for canvassing and on upcoming events. The idea was to launch the largest voter registration drive in the history of the country. Gerry gave a presentation on strategic targeting and said that if the referendum were called for spring 2016, then six to eight months was plenty of time to prepare. Ian laid out some of the key issues concerning liberal voters. Richard Tice explained how London, the financial capital of the world, would be able to drive unprecedented growth once Britain was independent from the European Union's regulatory red tape. And for his part, Andy Wigmore (whose role in all this I still hadn't sorted out) had shown up once again with his little bottles of Belizean rum, which he handed out to those to whom he hadn't met before. He seemed more intent on promoting the exports of Belize than on keeping his head in the Brexit game.

I then presented all the intelligence I'd gathered, the results of the data modeling, and a slide show with visualizations of each group, its set of concerns, and how to message them. I also delivered a summary of the data I'd found on the British electorate that was purchasable or obtainable, which would help us create not only even more accurate models, but also an entire database on UK voting-age citizens, as we had done in America, complete with every model needed to win elections or sway consumers. This was a tool, I told the group, that we suspected no one else had yet used in the United Kingdom, one that would wield unprecedented campaigning power.

The group was duly impressed. They were amazed at how easy it was to segment people according to their personalities and issues in order to be able to microtarget them. I showed them what that could look like, whether it involved one-to-one messaging through digital campaigns, social media, and door-to-door canvassing or using the data more generally to inform the content of speeches and rallies. All seemed to understand precisely what CA's value was to the campaign.

Before we adjourned, we discussed how to develop an even more intricate proposal to prepare Leave.EU for the Electoral Commission and for the time leading up to the referendum on Voting Day.

"I'm hoping the designation is not a competition," Arron said. He hoped to rule out Vote Leave as an opponent long before the commission had to decide. Therefore, he needed as much of a PR stunt as possible: I would represent Cambridge Analytica up onstage with the other hired experts, and this spectacle would prove that Leave.EU was the campaign most prepared to stir the nation into action for the referendum.

On the morning of Leave.EU's public panel, held in a church in downtown London, the headlines were that French police had raided a terrorist cell in the Paris suburb of Saint-Denis, killing two men, including the leader of the Paris terrorist attacks of November 13. The recent events in France were on the minds of all in the room, and an obvious subtext for much of what the participants had to say. Leave.EU would make sure that the issue of immigration was central to the campaign, and it would argue that immigration was tantamount to an invasion or "a ticking time bomb."[10]

As I rose to the stage to take the first chair, I was joined by Arron Banks himself, Liz Bilney, Gerry Gunster, and Richard Tice. After Richard's opening speech highlighting the business benefits of leaving the EU, one reporter asked if the Paris attacks had sounded the death knell for the European Union as a whole. Arron dodged the question, but said that "the United Kingdom can do so much better outside the EU." The referendum was a once-in-a-lifetime opportunity for a United Kingdom that was "big enough," "good enough," and "free to set its own laws and control its own borders— free of the handcuffs of the European Union. We are a people's campaign," he said.

One reporter asked cheekily, "If this is a campaign of ordinary people, I don't see any of those people on the panel."

Then, to much laughter, a reporter from the *Daily Mail* asked, "Why is your most prominent supporter behind me and not on the panel? Are you ashamed of him?"

He was referring to Nigel Farage, seated in the audience and keeping entirely and uncharacteristically quiet—"The soothsayer with the arsonist's grin," as *Time* would later describe him.[11] Farage's contribution to the panel had been arranging for every seat in the place to have on it a Leave.EU T-shirt reading, "Love Britain, Leave EU." Wrapped inside each was a mug that read, "I Won't Be Taken for a Mug," another way of implying that staying in the European Union was only for those being taken advantage of.

Another reporter took aim at the fact that there were two Americans on the team, Gerry Gunster and me. The reporter wondered what place all that "American flag-waving" of U.S. campaigns had in Britain.

Gerry was impatient with the question. Look, he said, "In the United States, we vote on everything. We have hundreds of referendums on everything. We vote on whether we should tax ourselves. We vote on whether we should have a Walmart down the street. Just last year, the state of Maine voted on whether or not jelly doughnuts and pizza should be bait for bears." Gunster knew what he was doing, and that's why he'd been asked to be part of the team.

I said much the same. What Cambridge Analytica brought to the table was that we'd be able to run a bottom-up campaign. We'd be able to understand why people wanted to leave the European Union, and we'd turn out more voters than ever before. That's what we were all about.

8

Facebook

As 2015 came to a close, Alexander saw a bright future for Cambridge Analytica. We were a part of Brexit—or so we thought at the time. While we didn't have the signed contract in hand, we knew it was coming any day, as Julian had confirmation of it in writing from Arron Banks. That meant we were a part of possibly the most consequential event in the history of Great Britain, a movement that had the potential to reshape Europe itself and, of course, the future of the United Kingdom. Even if Brexit didn't happen, and most people were agreed that it never would, being involved in such a historic election was a big deal.

Also, on the same day that I was representing the company on the Leave.EU panel, Alexander was in the midst of pitching Germany's Christian Democratic Party (CDU) to run Angela Merkel's upcoming bid for reelection as chancellor. After the debacle in France, and our relationship with Leave.EU, Alexander was sure he'd found a way to frame Cambridge Analytica's work as something far from the data collection of World War II that still haunted her country's psyche.

Still, it was the opening of the Washington office that was perhaps our greatest achievement to date. I had moved to DC after we found the rental space, to staff it and get it up and running for what we were sure would be a busy 2016. We had found the perfect place, in a beautiful historic building along the boardwalk in Alexandria, Virginia, with a gorgeous view of the nation's capital across the Potomac. Our neighbors were all the major Republican consulting companies. We announced our arrival, and soon, we'd booked client meetings back to back, and could see greatness in our near future.

The DC offices resembled a Silicon Valley company that was beginning to come of age. We had been created in the image of Google and Facebook, and were growing as they had: in better digs and with more staff, more clients, and far more data than ever. We were moving faster and breaking more things every day.

Alexander wanted our early December holiday fête to be a coming-out party for Cambridge in America. This meant showcasing our shiny new reality and the fact that we had friends and clients in the highest of places. The invitations went out in style to the glittering guest list that included more than a hundred CA clients and connections, among them RNC communications director Sean Spicer, conservative political activist Ralph Reed, conservative pollster Kellyanne Conway, controversial Arizona sheriff Joe Arpaio, and members of the Breitbart "Embassy" crew. And because Alexander subscribed to the old saw that one should keep one's enemies close, he also invited every other political candidate who was not a client, even if they were running against one of ours.

Another awkward move was that we were cohosting the event with another microtargeting firm, Targeted Victory. The Mercers had at one point thought of acquiring the firm for Cambridge, but the founders wouldn't sell. (Instead of combining forces, we would instead later steal away one of their rock stars, a talented digital and ad tech specialist named Molly Schweickert.) Although, by the time Christmas rolled around, we were competitors with our cohosts, the joint holiday event had already been arranged. As they say, the show must go on—and it did.

Another cohost that evening was the opposition research firm America Rising. The head of it was Matt Rhoades, who would go on to found Definers Public Affairs, a PR firm later famously hired by Facebook to run a movement against George Soros—that has widely been condemned as anti-Semitic—not a far cry from some of the shocking smear campaigns America Rising had enabled against Democratic candidates up and down the ticket since its inception.

With all the controversial ducks in a row, the party took place in a restaurant we'd rented out to give our clients privacy, and which we'd bedecked with many company banners showing that CA was now part of the old guard, the real political consulting elite. In the style of its parties every year, we hired a deejay and organized an ample open bar and a good spread of food—and hoped that the evening's festive mood would not be ruined by something that had happened the day before.

On December 11, 2015, the *Guardian* of London published a shocking story about Cambridge Analytica and the Cruz campaign. The allegations were explosive: CA had allegedly obtained data from Facebook in violation of the social media site's terms of use. The data was the private information of some thirty million Facebook users and their friends, and most of those individuals had not wittingly agreed to share it. What was more, according to the article, Cambridge was using that data as a weapon to affect the outcome of the Republican primaries and make Ted Cruz the GOP nominee.[1]

The story read like the plot of a spy novel. In it, reporter Harry Davies alleged that Cambridge had covertly acquired the Facebook data set and was now "embedded" in the Cruz campaign and deploying a powerful secret psyops weapon for targeting vulnerable voters. Behind the plot was the owner of Cambridge Analytica,

Robert Mercer, who was, according to the Davies piece, a Dr. Evil–like American billionaire whose motivation was to disrupt the U.S. political system and advance a fringe right-wing agenda.

The method Cambridge had used to acquire the data put it in direct violation of Facebook's terms of service. CA had contracted with a man who himself violated Facebook's service agreement when he used a third-party app, the infamous Friends API, to "hoover up" vast amounts of private information. The man's name was Dr. Aleksandr Kogan, a lecturer at Cambridge University with a relationship to Russia. Kogan had lied to Facebook, the article said, collecting the data under the guise of doing academic research and then turning around and selling it for commercial purposes to Cambridge Analytica. If the terms and conditions hadn't stated explicitly that the data was being collected for commercial use, then Kogan was not supposed to have sold it. Data protection laws had been violated, the article implied.

The *Guardian* had reached Dr. Kogan for comment, and he proclaimed his innocence. He could produce evidence that he had secured the rights from Facebook to use the data as he wished. The *Guardian* had "failed" to reach Cambridge for comment—most of us were en route to DC for the holiday party, and no one had answered the phone, with the exception of one hurried person in our temporary New York office who had inexplicably hung up on the reporter.

The article made Cambridge Analytica look venomous, and horribly guilty. The implication was that CA had not only infiltrated the biggest and safest social media platform in the world, but, more importantly, was in violation of nothing less than the public trust.

It was hard for any of us to believe that the allegations were true. I had never heard of a Dr. Aleksandr Kogan. From my pitch training sessions with Alex Tayler, I certainly knew that SCL worked with academics at Cambridge University; that both Dr. Tayler and Dr. Jack Gillett had earned their PhDs there; and that our very name, which Steve Bannon had apparently come up with, derived from the connection. I was also well aware that we had an enormous Facebook data set. We advertised as much on our pitch materials; our brochures and PowerPoint presentations openly declared that we had data on some 240 million Americans, which included Facebook data that averaged 570 data points per person for more than 30 million people.

Why would we advertise such a thing if we had obtained the data illicitly? Didn't we have enough other data that we could have left that data out of the database and still achieve grand results?

Beginning in 2010, the infamous Friends API had allowed companies such as SCL to install their own apps on Facebook to harvest data from the site's users and all their friends. We knew this all too well, so what was the problem? When Facebook users decided to use an app on Facebook, they clicked a box displaying the app's "terms of service." Hardly any of them bothered to read that they were agreeing to provide access to 570 data points on themselves and 570 data points of each of their friends. There was nothing illegal about the transaction for the individual who consented: the terms of agreement were spelled out in black and white for the few who cared to attempt to read the "legalese." Still, in a rush to get to the quiz or game the app was providing, users skipped over reading the document and gave their data. The problem lay in the fact that they were also giving away their friends' data, friends who had not legally consented.

I knew that some of our Facebook data came from quizzes such as the Sex Compass and the Musical Walrus (which had circulated around the London office, too), but I was also keenly aware that CA had produced and used these apps on the Facebook platform well before April 30, 2015, when Facebook closed off access to third-party developers. After all, I was among the employees Alex Tayler had alerted that spring to the looming deadline. In response, I had combed through a list of the Facebook data sets available to purchase prior to that date and had helped identify what information I thought Cambridge ought to buy. The *Guardian* article alleged that the data gathering Dr. Kogan had done was back in 2013, which was well before the cut-off date.

The story gained traction overnight. It was reprinted everywhere, and led to additional reporting in influential publications such as *Fortune* and *Mother Jones* and on sites such as Business Insider and Gizmodo.

Kogan's 2013 data gathering had first taken place on an Amazon Marketplace platform called "Mechanical Turk." He had paid users a dollar apiece to take the personality quiz This Is Your Digital Life. When users completed the quiz on Facebook, the app connected to the Friends API to take their data and that of their entire list of friends. From the answers Kogan had obtained through This Is Your Digital Life, he created a training set to model all the participants' personalities and then reportedly sold the modeling and the data set to CA, where Alex Tayler and the team tested Kogan's models and then created new, more accurate ones based on similar concepts of personality measurement.

The night of the party, the Cambridge and SCL staffs discussed the *Guardian* piece and debated who was at fault. Wasn't the onus on this Dr. Kogan, if he had somehow violated Facebook's terms of service in 2013 and misrepresented himself to Facebook and to us?

Alex Tayler had worked with Kogan, and while Dr. Tayler seemed downtrodden that night, he insisted that he had licensed the data from Kogan legitimately. What desperately worried him, though, was the perception of Cambridge in the press. The blowback, he said, was going to set the company behind in reputation and sales. It would take a long, long time "to crawl back from." Also, our relation-ship with Facebook itself was in jeopardy. Dr. Tayler had spent an entire day exchanging frantic emails and phone calls with executives in Palo Alto.

We gathered around Dr. Tayler and Alexander, the latter of whom was more dismissive of the hullaballoo. He didn't see the bad press affecting the company's bottom line, and he gestured to the room: no one at the party that night would care a bit about the story, he said, and encouraged us to drink up and celebrate. It did seem curi-ous to me, though, when later that evening he declared the party a dud. Somehow it wasn't as festive as parties he'd thrown in England. The parties there were so much better, he declared, taking a swig of his cocktail.

"Republicans are boring," he pronounced. He then gathered up a group of his "favorites," including me, and we left before the party was over, for the company's new corporate apartments, where Alex-ander poured the champagne more freely and we stayed up until all hours, having, as Alexander declared when it was over, a much jollier time without the stragglers.

When I first arrived at SCL Group, it was clear to me that Alexander's excitement about his enterprise had been built with an eye toward the Facebook model as much as on the power of what he had found possible through Google Analytics. In 2011 and 2012, Facebook had gone public and become a data collection behemoth, monetizing its data assets for an extra boost in company valuation. For Alexander, it was an object lesson in having faith in a vision that might seem outlandish to others.

The young Cambridge Analytica staff were energized by Alexan-der's vision; I was, too. We worked for a company that was building something important, something real that could boost engagement across the connected world.

My own experience with Facebook was not dissimilar to that of every other Millennial. It seemed always to have been there as part of my life. I didn't know Mark Zuckerberg directly, but when he started the company in 2004, he did so with a high school colleague of mine named Chris Hughes. Chris and I had worked together on Andover's school newspaper, the *Phillipian*, and later I found it exciting to see one of our own involved in such an innovative project as "The Facebook" while still in college.

As a high-schooler, I remember links for "The Facebook" on Mark and Chris's AOL Instant Messenger profiles, and on the profiles of the rest of my friends who had graduated from Andover and headed to Harvard. Then the only users of the site, Harvard students were inviting people to "Facebook Me." You could click on the link and see what dorm they were in and when their birthday was. By September 2005, now-"The"-free Facebook was open for use by students at top U.S. high schools and universities abroad. I couldn't wait to get a Facebook profile of my own, and I signed up for one the moment my college acceptance letter arrived in July 2005. I used that email as a Facebook log-in before opening my actual college email box. In 2006, by the end of my first year in college, anyone with a registered email address could be a Facebook user. The protected landscape of only college students had been opened to the world.

Just a year later, Chris Hughes came to work for the Obama campaign, when I did. He was the first person who had direct Facebook experience to be embedded in a political campaign, and he brought his expertise to the Chicago headquarters, helping to transform the way the Democrats connected with their base. I worked beside Chris on the New Media team. Looking back, I saw it as an exciting and innocent time.

Back then, Facebook had so few of the mechanisms that would soon be built to serve the campaigning process. One day, our New Media team realized that our volunteers were spending too much time accepting or rejecting Senator Obama's Facebook friend requests. After all, the presidential candidate, according to the campaign's policies, could not be "friends" with anyone whose profile featured guns, drugs, or nudity. The influx of hundreds of thousands of requests forced our hand. To control our workload, we decided to make a change, and turn "friending" the senator impossible. The Barack Obama profile page I had created was therefore transformed into the first "entity" page, a place where politicians, musicians, actresses, and other public figures could not be "friended," only "liked" or "followed."

Prior to then, you had to be an individual to have your own Facebook page. Turning Senator Obama's page into an "entity" was a huge step forward, and would open the door for other nonindividuals (campaigns, nonprofits, businesses) to have a Facebook presence. And now that Facebook was "open for business," new tools would have to be created to support the influx of such accounts.

Facebook had no analytics just yet, so to keep track of who visited Senator Obama's page, the New Media team did it the old-fashioned way, entering the information for each person, one after the next, by hand on Excel spreadsheets; we answered Facebook messages and posts one at a time, too. We received fabulous reviews for this: people were excited to hear from Senator Obama directly, with individualized messages. It was then that I first realized that mass communication needed to be individualized to be effective—and that our data collection, however rudimentary, was profoundly important.

Back then, there was no "Newsfeed" on Facebook, and no way to advertise to or reach a particular target audience directly on the site using their data. Instead, we relied on our email account alone to receive information and materials, and our direct mailers to reach back out and engage with our supporters. I was proud of the work we were doing, despite the heavy lifting on the back end. This simple data collection allowed us to target citizens across the country with the policies most important to them and to involve them in politics in a way that increased engagement. In demographics from youth to the elderly, from the North to the South, communities across America were caring about politics again because of our careful data collection work and simple yet targeted messaging.

To reach the arts community, the campaign issued a call to action across platforms, asking artists to send their work for consideration in use in official campaign materials. I remember well the day an email arrived on my desktop from an artist named Shepard Fairey, a graduate of the Rhode Island School of Design. Independent of the campaign, Fairey had made a beautiful red-white-and-blue image of Obama's face—he originally posted it as street art—and sent it in to us gratis. That poster, which resembles the iconic Che Guevara image, would become the viral visual sensation of the campaign. That short, targeted ask calling for the assistance of artists had produced fruit beyond our wildest dreams.

The innovation that Facebook offered users at the time to help them reach people was the "like" button. When other users "liked" your page, they would then "see" your posts on their page. There were no paid ads on Facebook back then. At the time, I remember a great deal of discussion in the public sphere about whether Facebook could be a sustainable business model, given that no one had figured out yet how to monetize it. The reality was that the "like" button gave users the ability to gather basic information on their followers, but it gave Facebook even more: hundreds of thousands of new data points on each user's "likes," information that Facebook could compile and eventually turn into dollars.

Facebook, then, was an innocuous-seeming warm and fuzzy place in 2007, and the language it used was equally comforting. You "friended" people. There was no way yet to "dislike" a post—this was before Facebook introduced emojis that enabled users to be angry, sad, or shocked about something. If Google was about "information . . . Facebook was all about connecting . . . people."[2] And during the Obama campaign, even the hate speech the senator received via Facebook, however disturbing, was something we could handle on a case-by-case basis. After all, there were no algorithms yet to detect inappropriate behavior or language on the site, or to get a commenter automatically banned. Facebook hadn't yet become the polarized national and international "town hall" it would be in later years, but I still remember being shocked at some of the things that appeared on Senator Obama's page.[3] What I remember even more vividly was that the senator refused to go negative himself, and had the graciousness to turn the other cheek to the racism and vitriol spouted about him. We took turns compiling the threats and reporting them to the FBI.

Because Facebook refused to serve as an arbiter of public discourse, continuing to maintain that it was a social media platform and not a publisher, free speech ruled its internal decisions—but not ours. By late summer 2007, the New Media team had decided that there were some serious flaws in the Facebook tool, and that banning posts that incited racial hatred was something we would have to take on in-house. Our internal debate was fierce: censorship versus incitement of racial hatred. We opted to delete the offending items, which ranged from mildly negative comments, whether slung at Obama's Democratic rivals or at Republicans, to death threats aimed at the senator. In fact, our team banned negative commentary altogether, and removing it was a tedious process that required dozens of man hours every day from our unpaid volunteers, who soon became an army of censorship police.

That 2008 campaign spawned the Obama data politicos who'd later found companies such as BlueLabs and Civis Analytics and who would return to the 2012 campaign with tools to sell. These experts knew how to onboard advertising on Facebook and optimize the Democrats' use of the platform, providing a seamless experience between content creation and message delivery. What was more, BlueLabs and others like it offered predictive analytics and modeling. While, in retrospect, the modeling and segmentation might have been less complex than today's standards, these companies could help the Democrats segment beyond traditional demographics or gender or party and zero in on candidate preference, turnout possibility, partisanship, and specific issues such as health care and jobs.

I wasn't part of the 2012 Obama campaign, but I learned about Facebook's new capabilities and what enabled the second campaign to be so savvy about data and data analytics. By 2010, Facebook had found plenty of ways to monetize itself to external businesses hungry for both the wealth of data produced within the platform and the access to individuals around the world. One of the most lucrative was the development of its Friends API. For a fee, developers could build their own app on the Facebook platform, and that app would give them access, as Kogan's did, to users' private data.

This was a tremendous step forward for the Obama campaign, which developed its own apps for use on Facebook and, with the data they gathered, was able to be much more precise and strategic about its communications. The apps used by the 2012 Obama campaign weren't openly controversial, in large part because those who used them were already Obama supporters and had intentionally opted in, both to stay in the loop and to spread the word about Obama more widely. Yet no matter how creative the terms of service were in concealing the fine print, individual users should not have been able to consent on behalf of their friends to share their data, and Facebook therefore was not legally allowed to give developers access to this wider network of data. Staff from the Obama 2012 campaign have since come out to discuss how uncomfortable they felt in participating in this illegal data grab, though they believed they were doing it for a good cause, so it was less ethically dubious. The Obama campaign's director of integration and media analytics, Carol Davidsen, wrote that she "worked on all of the data integration projects at OFA (Obama for America). This [the Friends API] was the only one that felt creepy, even though we played by the rules, and didn't do anything I felt was ugly, with the data."[4]

Facebook represented an incredibly good return on investment for the 2012 campaign. Between 2010 and 2012, the platform's openness to third-party apps allowed companies to harvest ever more data. With some forty thousand third-party developers, and more and more users from those third parties spending exponentially more time on Facebook, the social media company now had the ability to provide anyone with hundreds of data points on its users. With the Federal Trade Commission admonishment of Mark Zuckerberg and Facebook in 2010 regarding use of the Friends API and "deceptive practices," the company was "now expected to plug the gaps," but it struggled to find a way to make that work in tandem with its growth strategy.[5] Would it be possible to care about both data protection and exponential profits? The two aims were at odds with each other, and Facebook began to get more daring with its murky data collection and usage.

Why the FTC failed to pay attention in 2012 is anyone's guess. It would have been hard not to notice Facebook COO Sheryl Sandberg's announcement four to five months before the social media company's IPO about its lucrative relationship with data brokerage companies, or how it was acquiring more data to add to its in-house collection, and building better and more accurate targeting tools for paid advertisers: a clear message that Facebook was more than able to monetize its database.[6] Indeed, Facebook didn't change its policy for developers using Friends API until 2015, and the FTC never followed up.[7] This was great news for the Democrats in 2012, when Obama won his second term and had the use of Facebook's massive platform to do it. It was also fantastic news for Facebook, which went public that same year with a valuation of $18 billion.[8]

By the 2014 midterms, when Cambridge Analytica began to use Facebook, it took advantage of even newer innovations. The accuracy of Facebook's advertising tools was leaps and bounds ahead of 2012. There were now two ways to use the site for advertising. Before April 2015, CA (or any other company or entity) could pay the third-party app developers for Facebook data and advertise to Facebook users anywhere online, knowing more about them than ever before. Or a company could use its own data and do something even more innovative: select from those data sets the kind of people it wanted to reach and then pay Facebook to "onboard" those lists and do a "look-alike" search. Facebook would then find ten thousand (or a hundred thousand, or even a million) "look-alikes." The company would then send its advertising over the Facebook platform directly to those "look-alikes."

Closure of the Friends API meant only one thing: no one would be able to further monetize Facebook data except for Facebook itself. No longer able to access the API, developers now had to use Facebook ad tools to reach users on the platform. No Facebook data could be used for external modeling anymore—or so most of the world thought.

By the end of 2015, when the *Guardian* story appeared and threatened to shake up Cambridge Analytica and the Cruz campaign, Facebook was still sitting pretty, fully "in control," it claimed, of all its user data. No, it insisted, there should be nothing left to worry about with regard to data security. The biggest source of scrutiny around privacy for the company had been the Friends API, but that had been closed at the end of April. No one was calling the company out in the way they had called out Aleksandr Kogan and Cambridge Analytica.

Facebook had become the world's best advertising platform. If it was unsafe or if users' privacy was being violated, the finger was pointing in another direction.

All through January 2016, Dr. Tayler worked to clear up the Facebook data "misunderstanding." As de facto head of business development, I was forwarded the weeks-long email exchange between Tayler and Allison Hendricks, Facebook's chief of policy. In one message— the subject line was "Statement of Innocence"—Tayler wondered if Hendricks was fully satisfied with the explanation he had provided her about how Cambridge had innocently come to have the unlawfully obtained data.

No, Hendricks wrote. She wasn't satisfied. Cambridge was in violation of Facebook's terms of service. Kogan had not collected the data properly, and Facebook users had not consented to their data being used for commercial or political purposes.

Alex explained that CA had contracted for the data through a third party called GSR. That contract allowed usage of the data for any purpose, and for CA to hold it in perpetuity—so, this was all a great misunderstanding. Would Facebook be willing to issue a joint press release with Cambridge to clear things up?

Hendricks didn't deign to respond to the press release query. Facebook's policy on user data was strict, she said. Had Cambridge shared the Facebook data Kogan had gathered with anyone beyond the Cruz campaign? And if Cambridge were to delete the user data, how would CA ensure Facebook that there were no backups lying around?

Tayler wrote back that Cambridge had not given any clients, not even the Cruz campaign, the Facebook data; CA had used it only internally, for modeling. Clients had received only lists of contact information, he said, with "perhaps a few tags attached," with the individuals' modeled scores, such as being 75 percent likely to vote, or 90 percent neurotic. What's more, Tayler argued, the Kogan models were virtually useless because they performed only slightly better than random during testing. Kogan had merely provided Cambridge Analytica with a basic proof of concept that personality modeling could be done and be effective, nothing more. Cambridge gathered its own data, did its own surveys, and performed its own modeling. Also, the Kogan data could be deleted, as it wasn't really of use anyway, he protested.

I was shocked to see this, as Dr. Tayler had always told me how important and valuable Facebook data was. Why, all of a sudden, was he so willing to delete it? Of course, we needed to maintain a good relationship with Facebook—getting banned from advertising on its platform would mean certain death to our business—but was it worth the loss of that data?

Luckily for Cambridge, Hendricks was somehow satisfied after Tayler wrote to her in late January that he had, "in good faith," deleted the Facebook data from Cambridge's server and had checked to make sure there were no backups, either. While Hendricks had signed her previous emails as "Allison," the final one to Tayler was signed "Alli," a gesture of friendliness and a reassurance that all was

well between the two companies and that the matter had been resolved.

By reaching out to Cambridge to ask for deletion of the Kogan data,
Facebook was able to artificially clamp down on the public controversy over the data breach, satisfying itself and the public that it had
done all it could to fix the problem. Of course, no forensic analysis
was done of Cambridge's databases, no contracts signed to confirm
legally that the user data had in fact been deleted. Rather, without
proof, legal recourse, or due diligence, Facebook took on faith that
CA had followed through on its promise.

Then, reaching for as many cosmetic fixes as it could, it banned
Dr. Aleksandr Kogan from the platform, and decried Cambridge
Analytica's obtaining the data inappropriately and against its terms
of service, as if to reassure its users, "Nothing to see here." As Hendricks wrote in the email exchange with Dr. Tayler, nothing of the
like was to ever happen again.

9

Persuasion

Even before I moved to DC, my agreement with Alexander Nix about never working with Republicans had become null and void. He and I didn't have a formal arrangement, so every day, without having planned it, there was slippage. Throughout the fall of 2015, in the months before the *Guardian* story ran, I found myself knee-deep in the GOP. I suppose I should have seen it coming: how could Cambridge Analytica Commercial get off the ground without more than one high-profile win from Cambridge Analytica Political?

But there was a great deal more to my slide down that slippery slope.

Some of it was psychological. Some of it was pure ego. Some of it was greed or, rather, the growing desire to get a paycheck that did much more than pay the bills. But some of it was that I had fallen under the spell of a charismatic man who preyed on my vulnerabilities. I take full responsibility for the choices I made while working for Alexander Nix and Cambridge Analytica. But I must also say this: I was young, and I was vulnerable. Alexander didn't know everything about me, as I hid from him, as I had from others, the truth about my family's financial situation. But he came to know just enough "data points" to be able to persuade me to do things I otherwise wouldn't have done under any circumstances.

Alexander was the brilliant inventor of a company that literally swayed voters across the world to take action, sometimes against their own best long-term interests; and I allowed him to become my very own living, breathing Cambridge Analytica: while I thought I was on the right side of the data tools, I was actually being targeted all along.

The psychological part was that, when I was a young girl, my father was a successful businessman, full of life and ideas. He had been a big personality, long on energy and short on temper. I had both loved and feared him. And so, at a time when he lay in bed nearly catatonic, unable or unwilling to act, it was not surprising that I would see in someone like Alexander the entrepreneurial male figure I had always admired.

Alexander was as mercurial as my father, if not more so. He rocket-shipped and ricocheted around any room he was in, sped up by and brimming with ideas, hard to keep up with. His joy was expansive, his enthusiasm contagious. He made people want to keep up with him, beat for beat, to be central to him, to be warmed by his approval. And it became impossible for me to imagine living outside his magnificent orbit.

Sometimes, that first summer when I was in London, I stayed late at work, in part to show that I was working hard and giving my all. Alexander would come in at twilight, just after a polo match, still wearing jodhpurs and boots and a sweat-soaked shirt with a blue blazer over it, his trouser legs covered in horse hair. He looked both ridiculous and perfect to me at the same time. He'd be slightly sloshed, red-cheeked and happy, and gilded by a victory, he'd regale me with tales of his afternoon conquests.

But there was another side to the bon vivant hero on horseback.

Sometimes I would look up from my work and see him peering out of his glass box at me and the others. His eyes narrowed, he seemed to be waiting for an instance when he could pounce, having caught us in the act of a minor infraction, an indiscretion, or an enormous mistake. Indeed, it was his habit to come out and lambaste us in public. We knew he was angriest when he called someone "Tiny Brain."

Once, early on, I passed by a computer on the screen of which a gruesome Cruz antiabortion video was playing. I laughed out loud at the video and at Cruz, making a critical remark I can't remember now. And Alexander, whose hearing must have been preternatural, burst out of his office and screamed at me. I was never to do that again, he said. What if a client heard me? I should keep my opinions to myself.

I lived in fear of those moments, and there were too many to count, but then again, his mood could turn quickly. He would yell at one moment and then suddenly turn to you as if nothing had happened and ask you pleasantly where you'd like to dine that evening.

"I don't hold grudges," Alexander explained after the first time he'd given me a tongue-lashing. "And just because I don't hold them doesn't mean my mind has changed any bit at all. It's just that I prefer to have my say and then move on. So, let's do that, shall we?"

Because Alexander saw me as a rising star, it didn't take long for him to expect too much from me and become easily disenchanted when I didn't live up to his expectations. I wasn't bringing in the kind of money he wanted. My mistake was that I had set the bar too high too early. His was that he didn't realize that my first deal had been beginner's luck.

When the second Nigerian contract (and the additional $2 million) didn't come through, Alexander had been livid. It was the first time he screamed at me, full-throated and for a long time, and even though there were plenty of reasons I could have pointed to that the contract had fallen through, I stood there and took it in silence. What about Alexander's leaving Switzerland without ever having paid the Nigerians the time of day? What about Sam Patten's failure to get traction in his crisis comms campaign on the ground in Abuja? What about the fact—I learned this from Ceris when she returned—that the company had taken so much off the top as profit and spent only $800,000 on the campaign itself?

Still, I said nothing, and tried to shrug it off.

After Nigeria, I failed to bring in any SCL social or humanitarian contracts, and then none of the elections or business contracts I had pursued came through, either. This angered Alexander, too. Even in casual conversation, his wit could turn suddenly biting. Sometimes the bite would feel premeditated.

What was worse than Alexander's sudden anger was the possibility that he might become agnostic toward you. As judgmental as he could be, it was impossibly painful to bear the thought that he might begin to find you negligible. If you could please him, bully for you, but if you failed to be noticeable, then that was the worst thing of all.

That's where my ego came in. Near the end of 2015, Alexander sent out a company-wide email announcing a restructuring of SCL. His vision included new "verticals," among them a product development team and a data-driven TV team that would work with TiVo and Rentrak to reach voters through new channels. Dr. Alex Tayler and Dr. Jack Gillett were to head up a larger analytics department, overseeing data scientists working in both London and Houston, at Cruz campaign headquarters.

Others, such as Kieran Ward and Pere Willoughby-Brown, were given more expansive responsibilities and new people to work under them. Sabhita Raju became vice president, and Alexander was relocating her to DC. Julian Wheatland, the CFO, would be far more present. Soon, in addition to the DC office, we'd be staking out space on Fifth Avenue, with Bekah Mercer's Reclaim New York firm.

And ramping up to the Republican nomination, Alexander had made two rock star hires whom I had pitched and helped interview, hire, and train. Molly Schweickert, from Targeted Victory, who had worked for Wisconsin governor Scott Walker before he dropped out of the running in September, would head up a new Digital Marketing and Strategy team. Matt Oczkowski, former chief digital officer for Governor Walker, would take over Product Development and work with SCL Canada, also known as AggregateIQ (AIQ), to develop new software for our ever-expanding list of clients. AIQ was the exclusive software development and digital partner of the SCL Group, so inextricably linked that AIQ was commonly referred to as SCL Canada, a white-label, under-the-radar brand. Employees of AIQ even used SCL and Cambridge Analytica emails for business purposes.

I wasn't mentioned at all.

Up until now, I had labored under the assumption that I was essential to the company. I had been involved in the hiring of Molly and Matt, and I had literally opened the DC office myself—scouting top consultants, hiring clerical staff, and training them all. That year, every time Alexander had asked me to do something, I had. I'd pitched Corey Lewandowski. I'd handled Brexit so he wouldn't have to. I'd traveled with him to Paris to try to convince the French to accept data science. Each of these tasks was a one-off and a distraction from my bringing in my own deals. But despite this, I had become invisible.

Now I had moved to DC for the company, and had sacrificed so much in order to do so, and I'd been neither promoted nor compensated.

That's where the greed came in, if you could call it that.

It might not be readily apparent, but I wasn't exactly cashing in on Cambridge's success. From the earliest moment, Alexander had dangled a brass ring before me, one that was the right length away, always just out of reach.

As time went on, he shifted the money conversation from salary to deferred rewards. "Equity," he said. "*That's* what you'll be wanting." We'd scrimp and save now, travel coach class, and stay in budget hotels, but because I'd come in on the ground floor, I'd get a portion of the valuation when the company went public. There was often talk of my taking Alexander's place, so he could retire and leave the company in capable hands. Or, he added gleefully, perhaps I'd even outpace him, leave the company altogether, open my own firm, and become the best-paid and most-sought-after political consultant in the world.

"Stick with me, Brits," he said.

While once I had seen myself as staying at the company for a year or two, and then had extended my thinking to five, now I was to be there indefinitely, at least until my payday came. I was twenty-eight years old. I would give 200 percent of myself, I would work myself to the bone to prove my worth, I would stay patient, and I would give up everything in order to become indispensable to Alexander and to Cambridge Analytica, even if it meant working to elect people I'd never vote for.

Also, to go to America, I had to give up my PhD. When I told Alexander that I was sorry to think I wouldn't become "Dr. Kaiser," he said, "But this is the job you were doing your PhD to get." And: "Soon, you'll have so much money you'll be able to do whatever you want." I could even go back and finish up my dissertation, he said, but this time they'd be lucky to have me and perhaps even pay me to be there.

He seemed to make so much sense.

To be able to work in America, Alexander taught me everything.

The first lesson was that one could tolerate the company of almost anyone if there were money to be made. All you had to do was hold your nose with one hand and reach for the cash with the other.

I also needn't respect the people the company worked with. And *with* was the operative word. The company didn't work *for* the Republicans or even the Brexiters. We offered them a service. And because I was only pitching them, and not working in their campaigns, I was there to close a deal and then walk away. What the operations teams did once I walked away was another story. I didn't have much oversight of the process, but from time to time, I would see some creative work used in political ads and how it was performing in the campaign process. I knew that not all the messaging was positive, and as disappointing as that was, it also wasn't surprising. I came to know negative campaigning as "business as usual," but I never saw anything too overtly offensive, and some of it was actually incredibly positive and inspiring. I was sure everything the operations team did was not only aboveboard but best in class. It kept the spring in my step to know that I was selling real products that performed well and were of high quality. Our work won elections and captured hearts and minds.

As for being a salesperson, though, that was too crude an idea. At SCL, Alexander and I had decided on the title "special advisor," for its resonance with UN work. And when I got my new stack of business cards in America, I was "director of program development" for Cambridge Analytica. I was no salesgirl. I was someone who developed ideas. I created things and connected people. With that sort of title, I could someday walk back into the United Nations or apply to work at an NGO.

In the meantime, Alexander taught me not to judge clients. There were really only a few people he couldn't stand, and he was very careful not to let it show. For me, that might be harder. Many of the people and the causes they believed in were a sick parody to me. Perhaps it would be better if I didn't see them as outrageous, but instead, outrageously entertaining.

Just as I was settled in in America, others in the company were escaping from the dark comedy. Ceris, who was British and whom I had seen as something of a mirror for me because she had come from the humanitarian sphere, gave her notice. She couldn't keep working for the company as long as it was working for Brexit. Harris, who had a boyfriend, could no longer come up with any more evangelical, antigay messaging for Ted Cruz. He was tired of sitting at his desk, red faced and muttering, "This is total bullshit! What an idiot!" while working on an ad about how marriage was meant to be between only a man and a woman.

I found it difficult to stomach, too, but I supposed I had been desensitized to the religious views of evangelicals in America, having heard the same-sex marriage argument going on endlessly my whole life. It was difficult to argue with religious folks. And although I didn't agree with them, I found that the issue was a losing argument with so many people in the evangelical community, and a staple messaging strategy for religious supporters of an American campaign. That said, the antigay messaging was still offensive to me, and I wasn't surprised when Harris jumped ship and eventually went to work for the British Cabinet Office, ironically probably dealing only with Brexit communications for years to come.

Meanwhile, I had devoted myself in the States to becoming essential to Alexander and the company, wanting to steer our work toward clients I was excited about and projects that would give me a healthy commission. In the fall of 2015, in the months leading up to the *Guardian* piece, I had worked tirelessly on Cambridge's behalf, pitching what felt like nearly every cause, conservative and nonpartisan alike, and nearly every Republican politician running for high-level office.

At the Sunshine Summit, a full-immersion Theater of the Absurd Republican event at Disney World, in Florida, I laughed when, in the Fantasia Ballroom, Dick Cheney strode onstage without irony to Darth Vader's theme music. It wasn't funny, but finally seeing someone I considered a political villain make fun of himself was kind of satisfying. Maybe they know that what they do isn't right, I thought, and that all of this is a game.

As 2015 wound down, I'd pitched without regret nearly every Republican hopeful. With glee, I'd joined as others gathered around Donald Trump to watch him autograph his own face on the cover of *Time* magazine. I'd posed for a picture with Ted Cruz. I'd traveled to Phoenix and met Sheriff Joe Arpaio, getting a collectible coin with his face on one side and the message "Don't Do Drugs" on the other, and his John Hancock on a souvenir pair of his famous pink boxer shorts, the ones he made his inmates wear. And I drank beer with and pitched a roomful of executives from the National Rifle Association, men whom I once would have considered my enemies.

In each of these cases, and in many more, I never came up short for an answer to the rhetorical question on the tip of so many people's tongues: How could you work with such people? The NRA's campaign was called Trigger the Vote, but it wasn't about guns; it was about registering voters. Yes, those voters were Republicans, but wasn't voter registration about helping Americans participate in a more truly representative democracy? And wasn't working with Senator Cruz, Ben Carson, or the RNC about leveling the playing field in an unbalanced electoral landscape? As Alexander always said, the Democrats had had the technology and know-how in the digital world since 2008; it was time to give the Republicans the same tools. *Someone* had to do it. Why not us?[1]

If this was moral relativism in the extreme, if there was a little voice in my head that told me, "Something is wrong with your thinking, Brittany," I didn't hear it. If working for Cambridge Analytica was a devil's bargain, it was neither my place, nor in my best interest, to judge the devil. After all, if I had, I would have had to judge myself as well.

It might seem strange that I experienced no crisis of conscience or cognitive dissonance. I see why now. The further away I moved from who I was, the more staunchly I became someone new: overly certain, brittle, defensive, self-righteous, and wholly unreachable.

While my logic was flawed, I took a page from my law books and thought of my human rights superhero John Jones QC, the barrister of Doughty Street in London. When defending people accused of committing war crimes, a good human rights attorney didn't judge his other clients. One upheld the principles of the law. As I did my mental gymnastics and justified my choices in those days, moving ever deeper into the world of those whom, under any other circumstances, I would have despised, I thought a great deal about my legal training and the emotional toll of the unbiased code of professional ethics.

Finding out too much about Cambridge's clients by googling them or doing any research on them would be a waste of time, I decided. It was "above my pay grade." And I was busy, I told myself. I was a pitch machine, sleepless, always traveling, always working the phones. So, I looked for everyone's best qualities.

Sheriff Joe was "hilarious."

Senator Cruz had a "good, strong handshake."

Rebekah Mercer was "gracious" and "had impeccable manners."
As for Cruz super PAC chair Kellyanne Conway, she was "resilient."

There is probably no one more difficult to like in the Republican sphere than Kellyanne. Always the most strenuous contrarian in any room, she has a nasty habit of whipping out the righteous card and speaking so condescendingly to others and with such conviction about her beliefs that sometimes it's hard not to feel that perhaps what she is saying is right, even if you know she's dead wrong.

But we had no choice as to whether to work with her. She was a close compatriot of Bekah's, so she came with the territory Bekah had laid out for us. For what it's worth, I respected Kellyanne's all-female business, the Polling Company, as I had always struggled to see much in the way of women's empowerment in politics at all, let alone conservative politics. But that just wasn't enough to win me over fully. Kellyanne was in the Cambridge office often—for what, I couldn't always tell, but always with Bekah. For a while, I would make other plans when I knew she would be there, taking a long lunch break to avoid her judging glances.

Kellyanne was never satisfied with Cambridge. She critiqued everything about the company. Nothing was ever good enough: everything we did was too expensive, and not turned in fast enough; or we weren't hitting the marks she expected. Luckily, she hardly gave me the time of day; I was irrelevant to her. Whenever I was in the New York offices during meetings of Keep the Promise (KtP1), the Ted Cruz super PAC Kellyanne ran, meetings that were sometimes held in Bekah's Reclaim New York boardroom, I'd catch a glimpse of Kellyanne here and there as she trailed Bekah from room to room like a puppy.

When she had a spare moment, Kellyanne was always up in Alexander's face, decrying the latest problem with Cambridge. He was constantly exasperated by her, but his hands were tied when fighting back: he was on Bekah's payroll, so the chain of command was slightly off balance when Kellyanne was in the office. Privately, Alexander carped to me that, at Bekah's behest, we were giving Kellyanne expensive original research and other services nearly free of charge, which was a way of saying that Bekah had sold out him and the company. In my presence, he called Kellyanne an outright bitch and wished that Bekah had another super PAC to fund that didn't have Kellyanne at the helm.

The Mercers committed millions to the Cruz campaign and KtP1. Much of that money, at least $5 million, flowed right to Cambridge Analytica, which the Mercers and Steve Bannon sat on the board of—a regular feedback loop of cash that also got the job done. Among Cambridge, the Cruz campaign, and the KtP1 super PAC, the money ebbed and flowed, but stayed within the same ecosystem. It only appeared to be distributed if you looked at the FEC filings, but really, it was coming right back into the pockets it had come out of.

Due partially to this constant injection of funding, Cruz had risen remarkably to the top of the heap throughout 2015, and Cambridge was integral in making that happen. For his part, he outlasted Rick Perry and Scott Walker, and he held his own with Marco Rubio and Donald Trump in debate after debate. He refused, mostly, to cast aspersions on others, instead sticking to policy and rousing the evangelical base in the United States like no one else had.

And in the background, according to Alexander, Cambridge Analytica took Cruz and made him more than a contender. When the senator began, he had only 5 percent name recognition in the States. And among those who knew him, most notably in the Senate, where he hadn't much time yet even to be known, he was already universally despised, with little to no supporters in Congress, let alone the American public.

While the campaign itself was shaping up to be something none of us could have predicted, one thing was clear: the magic of our secret sauce appeared to be working. Cruz was building an exponential following and a grassroots movement of small-dollar donors reminiscent of the Obama campaign. From Cruz campaign headquarters in Houston, we heard reports back about huge uplifts in engagement, more followers, and people who were committing themselves to voting for Cruz in the caucus and primaries.

In September 2015, I pitched Kellyanne CA's magical data modeling by video link from London to her offices in the United States. I was trying to win KtP1's business for another contract, one in which we'd run data analytics work for Cruz that would involve using our psychographic microtargeting and pushing more voters toward him through issues in his platform. With a small team, and thanks to an unlimited potential budget and *Citizens United* (the Supreme Court decision that held that in the case of campaign finance, the free speech clause of the First Amendment applied to corporations as well as to individuals), Cambridge's board hoped that KtP1 would be an even easier way to catapult Cruz into the mainstream and get him ready to go up against Hillary Clinton. As Kellyanne said, "Hillary Clinton woke up every morning the second most popular person in her household." If we continued to produce the great results we were seeing, we could overcome Cruz's lack of popularity and push voters toward him through issues in his platform, thus securing the nomination for him and perhaps even taking him all the way to the presidency—though I never actually thought he'd get that far. I couldn't help but think that if I succeeded in winning the KtP1 contract, Alexander would look upon me with approval and maybe even give me a healthy commission.

"Hi, Brittany. Explain to my staff why they should be working with you," Kellyanne said to me brusquely when the video link conference began. "What is it that you will do to help us? They don't know you and want to know what to expect."

She knew exactly what we did, but I supposed that by playing devil's advocate, she wanted to test one of Alexander's greener staff members to see if I was up to scratch with what she wanted, or if I would become just another Cambridge staffer to complain about.

I couldn't see her, and she couldn't see me. On the screens in each of the rooms we were in, we were both looking at the same slide deck.

I was in the Sweat Box, sweating.

First, I ran through for Kellyanne and her staff how Cambridge had been so successful in the 2014 midterms with John Bolton's super PAC. The London office had put together an impressive case study about psychographics and microtargeting—mostly friendly examples of ads about family and patriotism. Only one of the ads shocked me a bit, but it provided a stark example of how easy it is to play to people's fears, especially when it came to national security. Instead of children running happily through a field, the screen showed white flags at national monuments across America, with the inscription "We've Never Surrendered Before. We Won't Start Now." I showed the team the five different versions of these ads, which we'd used with Bolton's super PAC, each selected depending on the personality profiles of the voters and the modeling of the target audience. The data proved definitively how each ad had been effective. I had a chart with click-throughs, engagement rates, and proven uplift in voter opinion as a result of the campaign. Bolton had even used a third party to confirm our results in post-impression polling, and they were more than significant.

Cambridge's personality-based digital advertising online and on TV campaigns had succeeded in persuading voters to elect Republican Senate candidates in Arkansas, North Carolina, and New

Hampshire, and it had definitively elevated voter perceptions of the importance of national security as an election issue. In North Carolina, we'd messaged a group of younger women who tested as highly "neurotic" according to the OCEAN modeling. After microtargeting them, we found that when we compared these women with a control group, we had a 95 percent confidence rate that we had achieved a 34 percent increase in the women's concerns and had affected their voting.

I ran through a high-level summary of the services Cambridge had already provided for Senator Cruz in his campaign, and then began the big pitch: what Cambridge could do now for Cruz with even more intricate psychographics than CA had done for Bolton.

Cambridge had already done the legwork. Our data scientists had analyzed the voter base in Iowa and South Carolina, the key early primary states. In Iowa, they had identified a group of 82,184 voters who were persuadable, and in South Carolina, 360,409. Among those persuadable voters, the team found four distinct personality types in each. In Iowa, there were "Stoics," "Carers," "Traditionalists," and "Impulsives." The Stoics made up 17 percent of the total target voters and comprised 80 percent white men between the ages of forty-one and fifty-six. The Carers comprised 40 percent of the total persuadables and were almost all women between the ages of forty-five and seventy-four. The Traditionalists made up 36 percent of the total and were almost all men between the ages of forty-eight and sixty. And the remaining group, the Impulsives, were about 60 percent men and 40 percent women, predominantly white, and between the ages of eighteen and thirty-two. In South Carolina, the groups were largely the same, except that instead of Impulsives, the team had found a group they labeled "Individualists."

To determine what issues most concerned those groups, Cambridge's data scientists had used predictive models with more than four hundred demographic and commercial data points, and then had further segmented the members of each to understand what their individual needs were in terms of "mobilization," "persuasion," or "support." "Mobilization" meant getting people to interact with the campaign, volunteer, or attend a rally. Even something as simple as sharing content on social media would work. "Persuasion" meant convincing the voter about the appeal of the candidate and his or her policies, to really win them over. "Support" meant getting people to donate or become further involved.

Once we had the audience groups, then we planned the messaging. Messages were tailored to each voter and his or her needs. A Stoic who cared about national security, immigration, and traditional moral values would get messaging that used words such as *tradition*, *values*, *past*, *action*, and *results*. The message would be simplistic and patriotic; it would stick to the facts and employ nostalgic images such as the famous picture of the group of U.S. Marines planting the American flag atop Mount Suribachi on Iwo Jima.

A Carer's message was entirely different. It emphasized family, used words such as *community*, *honesty*, and *society*, and was warm in tone. Ads focused on family would be particularly effective. A message on gun ownership was "The Second Amendment. Your Family's Insurance Policy." An ad about immigration would be a little more charged and fear-based: "We Can't Take Chances with Our Families. Secure Our Borders."

The Iowa Individualist would respond best to other kinds of messaging entirely. An Individualist's messaging would contain the words (or evoke the feelings of) *resolve* and *protection*: "America Is the World's Only Superpower. It's Time We Acted Like One."

In the end, the pitch was wildly successful. Kellyanne and KtP1 signed on for the fourth quarter of 2015, looking into the first quarter of 2016 and beyond. Cambridge took the plan to Kellyanne and the team and deployed it, and Senator Cruz continued to rise in the polls in advance of the Iowa caucus.

For all her hardness on our work, Kellyanne was fiercely committed to Cruz, and she'd shown this loyalty on numerous occasions. One day, during that fall of 2015, not long after my video conference with her, I was working in the New York office when Alexander asked me to join him in the boardroom with Kellyanne, Bekah, and Steve. He wanted me to give the group an update on where we were with the Trump campaign. At that point, it had hardly been a month since Alexander and I pitched Corey Lewandowski at Trump Tower, but I went into the boardroom and began to run through what we'd done so far to pursue the Trump contract and how we planned to follow up.

Before I could get any further, Kellyanne interrupted me. She was incensed. It was immoral for Cambridge Analytica to pitch other candidates when we were representing Senator Cruz, she said. We needed to put the full force of our resources into backing Cruz, and if we weren't prepared to do so, she didn't want any part of working with us.

Alexander, trying to make peace, appealed to her sense of fair play. "But Kellyanne," he said, "we're running a business here. And," he reminded her, "you didn't have us sign a noncompete." His voice suddenly trailed off. "That's all, Brittany," he said quietly, without looking at me. He gestured to the door. "You can go now."

He must have seen what I saw: the fury in Kellyanne's eyes.

I turned to leave, but before I could make it out the door, she stormed past me in her frilly Chanel suit and her stiletto heels. Marching like a Barbie Doll in a huff, she made her way toward the elevator and disappeared into it, leaving in her wake the faint smell of hair on fire.

Alexander later told me that he and Steve were able to assuage

Kellyanne's feelings by confiding in her, as he had confided in me, that Trump wasn't *really* running to win, after all. And given that Trump posed no threat to Cruz, Kellyanne would be fine with it, she said. Apparently, that piece of information would make our potential work for both Trump and Cruz acceptable. After all, in the fall of 2015, it still felt impossible to almost everyone that Trump's campaign would amount to actual victory.

As upset as Kellyanne had been about the prospect of our working with Trump, the fallout from the *Guardian*'s splash about Cambridge Analytica, Dr. Aleksandr Kogan, the Cruz campaign, and Facebook proved even more troublesome. Kellyanne was livid. She felt that the article tainted Cruz, and it continued to haunt KtP1's relationship with Cambridge Analytica for months after.

I remember being in the Alexandria office one day when Sabhita Raju arrived and, biting her tongue, headed into a meeting to take a conference call with Kellyanne. She emerged after an hour looking as though she'd been torn to shreds emotionally by a pack of wild dogs. Indeed, it seemed as if someone at CA was always on the phone with Kellyanne having an ear chewed off, even from a distance. And at the mention of her name, Alexander would always roll his eyes.

But Kellyanne wasn't the only difficult person in the Cruz camp. She was the main voice at KtP1, but the official Cruz for President campaign officials in Houston were ornery and thuggish. Large, rough-mannered dudes, they scared the CA staff in Houston with the loaded .45s they sometimes wore. And they were complainers: They claimed that a software dashboard that Cambridge had developed especially for them was never put to use. The software may have been called Ripon, but the Cruz campaign argued that they had been ripped off. True, it had bugs, but I knew that people had it out in the field and were using it on tablets when they did door-to-door canvassing. Still, the Cruz team knew that if they broke up with Cambridge, it was possible that all the Mercers' money could disappear with us. So, they stayed on and kept complaining, all the while watching the donations roll in.

In the meantime, they made the lives of the Cambridge staff miserable. In fact, sometimes the only plus side to the relationship with the tough guys from Texas was that whenever Cambridge staff came back from Houston, they brought with them cowboy hats, leather belts with giant Lone Star buckles, and boots to show off in the office. Indeed, it became de rigueur for all of us to dress in Western wear, partly ironically but partly also to show that we were part of the yee-haw team.

Perhaps because of our cowboy hat–wearing data scientists, Cruz succeeded wildly in the Iowa caucus, taking 27.6 percent of the vote. This represented only 51,666 people, but it awarded him both 8 delegates and the first victory of the electoral season—an upset that rippled across the country.

On the evening of February 1, 2016, the night of Cruz's victory in the Iowa caucus, I finally broke loose from holding my job close to my chest. In our corporate apartments in Crystal City, Alexander, Julian Wheatland, and I drank champagne and watched the returns, celebrating late into the night. I felt crazy good for a change: I had succeeded in something. I had made something significant happen.

I pulled out my phone to look at the picture of myself with Senator Cruz from Disney World. In it, we were both smiling, our arms around each other as if we were old friends. Since coming to America, I had rarely posted anything on social media about my work, but I uploaded the picture to Facebook with the caption "WE WON IOWA!!!!!!!! Then I added the hashtags #datadrivenpolitics,

#CambridgeAnalytica, #IowaCaucus, #groundgame, #CruzControl, #winning; the emojis 🎉 🍾 ✉️ 💄 😊; and the words "Senator Cruz and I in Disney World."

When I woke up the next morning, I realized I was foolish to have done so. The hate from my progressive friends had rolled in overnight.

"You may love #winning," an old friend wrote, "But how do you sleep at night?"

I was crestfallen, and I felt entirely alone. While I had won the contract for KtP1, Alexander had never really credited me with having done so. He considered himself and Bekah to have closed the deal, not I. And I never saw a commission for the work. Yes, Cambridge had succeeded in a major win for Senator Cruz, but if you were to have asked Alexander if I truly had been a part of that, he would likely have said no. Also, by claiming the victory as my own so publicly, I had opened myself up to the harsh personal criticism I had been hoping to avoid. Up until now, if I hadn't been judging my own actions, I had at least protected myself from giving those who knew me from the liberal world the chance to judge, to write me off.

It was then that I began to see my old world truly fall away. The negative responses to my Cruz victory post weren't the last of the hate. Old friends gave up on me. And in return, I felt I had no choice but to embrace the world I'd abandoned them for.

I began not merely to be neutral to things I had once opposed, but to embrace a life of values that were very different from my old ones. I partied with new people. I cared far more about how I dressed and with whom I spent my time. I took advantage of every opportunity to rub elbows with those whose privilege might benefit me, and I began to look upon my past with disdain. What had the Democrats ever done for me? Why had I ever been so loyal?

And if I had one last hope of ever going back to that world some-day, the door to it closed forever that spring, first with the Facebook post and then with a phone call. It was my coworker Robert Murt-feld calling from London. A human-rights expert that I'd known prior to my time at CA, Robert was an extroverted German, more orga-nized than the best CRM software.

"Can you hear me?" he asked.

I was in Times Square, amid the swarming crowds of tourists, the beeping of horns. I ducked into a storefront so I could hear him.

"Either sit down or lean up against something," he said.

I looked around. I went to the back exit of the building and sat on the grimy ground. "Okay," I said.

John Jones QC of Doughty Street was dead.

I was learning of this before the story hit the news. Robert had actually introduced me to John years before and felt the duty to tell me himself. The circumstances were confusing. Rumors abounded. Robert didn't know what had happened. John had been found on the tracks of a London Tube station, but there was no CCTV footage yet to indicate how he'd gotten there.

Had he been pushed? There were plenty of people who could have wanted John dead, from those who hated any one of his controver-sial clients, who ranged from Muammar Gaddafi and Julian Assange to those who had carried out genocide in the Baltic States and those whom John had prosecuted. Had he been murdered?

John had been severely depressed, even hospitalized for a while, we later learned. He had been released too early by the NHS. Our minds raced as we imagined how burdensome his work had been, and for such poor pay. We ventured to guess that the weight of the kind of work he'd been doing and the lack of pay he received was just too burdensome. But his work was so noble, so idealistic, and so important. The United Nations repeatedly chose him to represent them in the most complicated of situations, and he was sought after worldwide for his erudition and kindness.

It haunted me. At first, I couldn't say why.

John was so significant in the human rights world that three different memorial services were held for him, and I went to each of them. The first was organized by Robert in New York, at the International Center for Transitional Justice; the second was in The Hague; and the third was in London. All the top human rights figures were there: Amal Alamuddin Clooney, John's colleague; Geoffrey Robertson QC, the founder of Doughty Street Chambers; delegations from foreign countries; untold numbers of the world's top human rights lawyers, activists, and jurists. People gave speeches, read poems, and showed videos of John at work. To see him argue cases in international court was to witness a thing of beauty and know that his passing was indeed a tragedy for the entire world. I could hardly handle it.

As I mourned John that spring, I realized that I was mourning the death of something of myself, as well. Though I hadn't admitted it, I had secretly nursed the hope that if I ever stopped working for Alexander—if I ever could—the one place that would take me back in after I'd gone over to the dark side was Doughty Street, and the one person who would welcome me with open arms would have been John Jones.

He wouldn't have judged me. He wouldn't have thought ill of me for having worked on the wrong side of things. His legacy to the world was that he had defended people who were undefendable. He would have seen me as someone who had once been committed with certainty to principles but who had lost her way. I hoped John would have looked beyond my sins and seen the sinner. I daydreamed that would have absolved me of all that I had done wrong and all I might be about to do in the name of Cambridge Analytica.

But now he was gone, and there was no one left to forgive me or take me in.

By the first week of March, Ted Cruz was one of four Republicans left standing, along with Rubio, Kasich, and Trump. We couldn't help but wonder if he really had a shot at being the GOP nominee. Of course, if he won for the GOP, Hillary was almost certain to win in the general election. In a debate Fox News sponsored in Detroit, one that devolved into ad hominem attacks, Cruz tried, and failed, to look sufficiently presidential. Although it was an interesting pipe dream—someone as unlikeable as Cruz getting the nomination with the support of our company—he simply couldn't keep up with the game Donald Trump was playing, a daily devolution of discourse and decorum that many were beginning to find delightful. Marco Rubio had recently stooped to Trump's level and disparaged the latter's inexplicably orange-tinted complexion and his noticeably small hands. In that debate, Trump defended the size of his hands and suggested that there was nothing "wrong down there, either," a reference to the size of his penis. The world shuddered at the thought.

The next day, I was at the Conservative Political Action Conference, or CPAC, the annual celebration of all things conservative. In that election year, it was held in National Harbor, Maryland, just across the river from DC. Alexander had been asked to sit on a panel entitled, "Who's Voting and Who's Not? An Analysis of the 2016 Electorate," but because he'd have to share the stage with Kellyanne Conway, he found a way to get out of it, and asked me to go in his place. He said he had an important meeting with casino magnate and Republican megadonor Sheldon Adelson. Once the panel started, he must have sneaked into the auditorium, although I didn't know this at the time.

In taking Alexander's place on the panel, I had a chance to hold my own with a slew of veteran journalists for conservative publications—and with Kellyanne. It was the most visible I'd ever been in the Republican world, and it was the biggest Republican audience I could think of: more than ten thousand people were gathered in the auditorium, and even more were watching on C-SPAN. You could say it was my coming out, or at least the first time CA was truly about to join the ranks of a real political consultancy—higher status with the GOP for being a winning organization. It was a time to celebrate for CA internally, and I was now one of the faces of this new, winning operation.

I tried to calm my nerves. I had prepared as best I could, given the short notice. I had some talking points, and my job, I felt, was to share with the audience what Cambridge Analytica brought to the table, what our added value was. Backstage, I made small talk with NRA CEO Wayne LaPierre and had my makeup done. When the panel began, I strode out in my aunt's hand-me-down cowboy boots and my mom's Enron-era cream suit (from which I had removed the 1980s shoulder pads) and tried to exude confidence. I was by far the youngest and greenest person onstage.

The moderator, American Conservative Union chairman Matt Schlapp, introduced us to the room, calling Kellyanne Conway a "pollstress," her strange but preferred moniker.

When the conversation began, it was supposed to be about how to understand the 2016 electorate, but it turned into an exercise in assessing the havoc Donald Trump was wreaking on the GOP and what to do about it. I was out of my depth.

Charles Hurst of the *Washington Times* said he wasn't sure what to do about the big divide in the Republican Party over Trump. Hurst had been in the audience in Detroit the night before, for the

Republican debate. Trump's stand on torture, he said, demonstrated the GOP split perfectly.

"In one row" in the auditorium, Hurst said, "people gasped" when Trump said he'd endorse "waterboarding plus." But two rows over, they cheered and pumped their fists.

It was a critical time.

Matt Schlapp wanted to know what would bring the party together. Fred Barnes of *The Weekly Standard*, who'd been covering politics in DC since 1976, when a Georgia peanut farmer became president, said he'd seen everything there was to see in American politics, but that there would never be a Trump White House. Trump's unlikability would give rise, Barnes predicted, to an independent Republican candidate who'd put Hillary into office the way Ross Perot had put her husband there.

I still had nothing to add.

Kellyanne jumped in and, as she is wont to do, took complete control of the conversation.

Yes, she said, a late-entry Republican spoiler would be handing Hillary the win. But there was hope, she added. She sat up straight in her little black dress, put her hands on her knees, and gazed out on the ten thousand people in the audience.

It didn't matter who the Republican presidential candidate ended up being, Kellyanne said. There was a way to get behind whoever was the ultimate GOP contender. "The fiction of electability" was gone, she said. "Electricity has replaced electability." It would be, of course, an eerily prescient statement, but it was also brilliant. And it was at that point that I could have jumped in to say something about what Cambridge could do to make a candidate electric; we had done it with Cruz, after all.

But I didn't. Indeed, during the entire panel, I spoke only once, and that was when Matt Schlapp asked me a direct question about how to reach voters.

"How do we connect?" I said. How do we find swing voters? And what was more important, I added, how do we find "their levers of persuasion?"

Later, when I saw Alexander and learned that he had been in the audience, I hoped that I had done him proud. Had I pleased him? Had I performed well? Had I found *his* levers of persuasion and convinced him that I was a person of value, worthy of praise?

But I didn't have time to ask.

"Good job," he said. He was drunk, but not with that glow he often had when coming off the polo field, inebriated half by victory. "At least," he said, "you didn't fuck it up."

And that was as good as I would get.

10

Under the Influence

SUMMER 2016

In the long run, it proved difficult to prop Senator Cruz up. His lack of popularity eventually got the better of him, so much so that not even our methods to change voter behavior could fix it. From what I heard internally, Cambridge had done an incredible job supporting the campaign and the super PAC in transforming Cruz from Congress's black sheep to a household name and well-known senator. But the Trump-induced stigma of "Lyin' Ted" stuck, and Cruz bowed out at the last hurdle.

Cambridge never considered this a loss. In fact, it was celebrated among us as a win. The long-running triumph of the Cruz machine was heralded in newspapers and TV segments across the United States, even being picked up in other places around the world that marveled at the use of data science in politics. "Could the Cruz team save print journalism?" a *Forbes* writer mused, hoping we held the secret to bringing back readers and subscribers in the digital age. "Cruz Crew Uses Psychological Profiling to Propel Elections Wins," boasted another. The incoming inquiries from companies and politicians poured in regardless of the senator's loss to Trump.

Despite the time and effort Cambridge and the Mercers had committed to Cruz, his exit didn't mean that either of us was out of the presidential race—indeed, both Cambridge and the Mercers had actually been involved with Trump for some time, much longer than was publicly known.

To some, the Mercers were pariahs. A disgruntled former colleague of Bob Mercer's said that Bob believed "that human beings have no inherent value other than how much money they make." And Mercer was quoted as stating that "a cat has value . . . because it provides pleasure to humans," whereas a person on welfare has "negative value."[1] I had nothing against Bob—it sounded like these thoughts came from the brain of an introverted data scientist, many of whom I knew to be antisocial and to love numbers more than their fellow human beings. In any case, I had been in a room with him only three times and didn't have any other frame of reference.

I first met Bob in July 2016, not long after the transition from Cruz to Trump, at our big New York City office, where he had come to check out the new digs he'd helped finance. Previously, Cambridge had been occupying one small room in Bekah's Reclaim New York space in the NewsCorp Building, just a bunch of desks and a Ping-Pong table Alexander used as his work surface—a quirky inconvenience that had its upside because, from time to time, we'd engage in impromptu matches. The new office was on the seventh floor of the Charles Scribner's Sons Building, on Fifth Avenue and Forty-Eighth Street, a quick walk from Trump Tower. The space was lean, clean, and modern, with a real boardroom with opaque windows for privacy and walls hung with uber-modern art that Bekah's sister had loaned us from her collection.

Bob, who was notoriously crowd-shy, came by before the office-christening party, to avoid the crowd. Once, in a speech—a rare event—he said he preferred "the solitude of the computer lab late at night, the air-conditioned smell of the place . . . the sound of the disks whirring and the printers clacking."[2] When we shook hands that day, we exchanged hardly a word. His handshake felt phoned-in and robotic; he was such a brilliant data scientist that I told myself that I was likely irrelevant to him.

Steve once said that because the Mercers had come to their wealth late in life, they had "very middle-class values."[3] I'm not sure I saw that in either of them, but that isn't to say it wasn't there. To each, I was just an employee of an employee, someone to whom they would pleasantly say hello.

I saw Bekah Mercer in the office. Or, if I stayed late at work and Alexander was having dinner with her, he'd phone to tell me to come by the restaurant where they were dining, so I could give Bekah an update on our clients. I was never a dinner guest; I would never have expected to be. I was an underling arriving late at the end of a meal. As I listened to Bekah, I found her mostly level-headed. She might have loathed my Democratic heroes, but she never said anything in my presence more offensive than any comment my Republican relatives made.

Whatever her politics were, the power both she and her father held inside and outside our company was considerable, something that I came to see more clearly the longer I was at Cambridge. As time passed, I never let myself forget that she was the powerhouse that made everything at Cambridge Analytica—and, eventually, Trumpworld—happen.

After I'd pitched Corey Lewandowski in September 2015, the negotiations stumbled, but they never stopped. I had drawn up the first iteration of the contract with the Trump campaign and had just handed it off to people above my pay grade when things got complicated. One of the issues was that Trump wanted the contract to be with an innocuous third party and, hence, to have no visible connection to the Mercers. At the time, he was campaigning on being able to fund his own campaign, with no strings attached to big-dollar donors. At first, Alexander and Julian suggested we use AIQ, but then they decided it was likely too obvious a connection to Cambridge, as AIQ was running all CA's digital campaigns at the time, sharing data on a daily basis. I was given to understand that, in the end, a holding company called Hatton International was chosen as the go-between. Belonging to Julian Wheatland, Hatton had been used as a contracting vehicle for the SCL Group in past campaigns.

The arm's-length removal from Trump enabled the Mercers to operate under a veil of secrecy for many months. Much later, the accepted storyline would be that the Mercers were Cruz loyalists who agreed to take on the Trump campaign only at the eleventh hour—specifically, in mid-August 2016, when the so-called Mercerization of the Trump effort took place—that is, when Steve Bannon joined the campaign as CEO and Kellyanne Conway came on as campaign manager.

In actuality, CA's transition to Trumpworld took place in spring 2016. At the time, the relationship between the Cruz campaign and the Mercers was hanging by a thread, and had been so since January, when the full impact of the first Facebook/Cambridge scandal stormed the press. Even Cruz's caucus win in February didn't fully stop that speeding train from derailing, and every day seemed to be an armed struggle between Cambridge's board and Cruz's campaign team in Houston. After one particular fight, in March, I recall Alexander whispering to me that this protest from the Texas team might be the last straw for the Cruz campaign's retaining its Mercer support. Good luck to them from there on out. This set in motion the first steps for the Mercers, and Cambridge, to take over both the Trump campaign and the rebranding of the Cruz KtP1 super PAC for Trump as well, although Alexander swore everyone in the company to secrecy.

Alexander had a green light from Bekah, and he constantly worked behind the scenes with Trump's son-in-law, Jared Kushner, to iron out a plan for the campaign. In March and April, Matt Oczkowski, who had joined us from Scott Walker's campaign, was working on the NRA's Trigger the Vote campaign and somehow had to balance bandwidth with Trump. Meanwhile, Molly Schweickert developed a tailored digital proposal. And on the super PAC side, Emily Cornell, a constantly disgruntled conservative political consultant and former RNC staffer, who in my opinion had difficulty with emotional intelligence, put together a strategy for what might have become the "Defeat Crooked Hillary" campaign—in fact, that would have been the name of the super PAC if the Federal Election Commission had allowed it. Upon rejection of the name, they ended up with Make America Number One (MAN1), which headed the anti-Hillary charge.

By late June, two teams from Cambridge Analytica were in motion, one in New York and the other in San Antonio. The Mercers were behind both of them.

San Antonio was the Trump campaign's nerve center—Paul Manafort was stationed there when he was campaign manager and not at Trump Tower, which was where the official headquarters was. That's because San Antonio was home to Brad Parscale, of Giles-Parscale. Parscale had been a longtime website designer for Trump, and Trump had picked him to run his digital operations. The problem was that Parscale had no data science or data-driven communications experience, so Bekah knew that Trump needed Cambridge.

When the early Cambridge Analytica team (which consisted of Matt Oczkowski, Molly Schweickert, and a handful of data scientists) arrived on the scene in San Antonio in June, they found Brad and the Trump campaign's digital operations in an alarming state of disarray. Oczkowski—"Oz" for short—wrote to me on June 17, when I asked him a question about a commercial client, saying he had no time to help me, as he would need all his energy for working with Brad and getting their analytics up and running. As far as I was told, they were working there for free, as a "pilot test" to prove CA's worth. That was a big bill for Alexander to swallow with a big group of his best people working 24/7 gratis . . . but I suppose he figured it would be worth it when Trump finally signed on.

When the CA team arrived, they were horrified to find that Brad had no existing voter models of his own, nor any marketing apparatus, and he had five different pollsters gathering information, all at cross purposes. At the beginning of a well-run campaign, you would expect a database to be up and running already, with a modeling program. This allows pollsters to coordinate their questions so they can be matched to the database at hand and turned into useful political models to categorize every voter in the country, with scores of zero to 100 percent for, say, how likely someone was to vote (voter propensity) or how likely someone was to be interested in a certain candidate (candidate preference). The data was such a mess that the CA team had to start over from scratch.[4]

Because I had assisted them in writing the proposal, I knew they were planning on building a database with modeled data for everyone in America, and then dividing the campaign strategy into three overlapping programs. The first part of the campaign would focus on building lists and soliciting donations from them, especially as the Trump team had not yet started any fund-raising campaign. Funds were key to our starting immediately and to scaling up the national campaign. No matter what Donald said on TV, he wasn't funding it himself.

The second program, to be started a month afterward, would focus on persuasion, also known as finding the swing voters and convincing them to like Donald somehow.

And the third program would be focused on getting out the vote, and would involve everything from voter registration to getting likely Trump supporters to the polls for early voting or on Election Day.

As everyone got down to work, there was no doubt that the Trump campaign would be spending a lot of money on social media. In fact, after the election, the final tally on the Trump campaign's social media expenditures was historically high. Through Cambridge alone, the Trump campaign spent $100 million on digital advertising, most of it on Facebook. With that kind of spend came a higher level of service—not just from Facebook but from the other social media platforms. This white-glove service was something the social media companies would frequently pitch to us, showcasing new tools and services that could help campaigns in real time.

But the social media giants offered not only new tech but also man power.

Seated beside Molly, Matt, and our data scientists were embedded employees from Facebook, Google, and Twitter, among other tech companies. Facebook called its work with the Trump campaign "customer service plus."[5] Google said it served the campaign in an "advisory capacity." Twitter called it "free labor."[6] While the Trump team welcomed this help with open arms, the Clinton campaign for some reason decided not to accept such help from Facebook, which must have given Trump a distinct advantage that cannot be easily quantified—a spare set of highly skilled hands goes a long way in a campaign, as it is expertise that does not need to be managed or taught by the campaign manager, who is already working 24/7 with little sleep.

As I would later learn, the Facebook embeds showed campaign

personnel and Cambridge staff how to aggregate look-alikes, create custom audiences, and implement so-called dark ads, content that only certain people could see on their feeds. While the Clinton campaign may have had some of these skills internally, the hands-on assistance the Trump campaign had was invaluable on a day-to-day basis, enabling it to take the utmost advantage of new tools and features the moment they came out.

After the election, I found that operations with the other social media embeds produced similar successes. Twitter had a new product called "Conversational Ads," which showed drop-down lists of suggested hashtags that, once clicked on, automatically retweeted the ad alongside the hashtag, ensuring that the Trump campaign's tweets trended over Hillary's. Snapchat also ramped up the innovation with "WebView Ads," which featured a data-capture component asking users to sign up as campaign supporters, allowing the campaign to keep harvesting data and adding to its target audience. Snapchat employees introduced the CA team to a new, inexpensive product it called "Direct Response," which targeted young people who spent all their time online. If you swiped upward on a photo, it led you to a screen where you could add your email address; the terms and conditions gave all sorts of new data as well. And Snapchat's WebView Ads and filters (such as selfies you could take that put you behind bars with Hillary) had also been big winners.

The Republican team at Google had made it easy for campaigns to bid for use of search terms in order to control users' "first impressions." On Google, the Trump campaign team had increased its ad spends for search terms, persuasion search advertising, and the controlling of first impressions. Google key word purchases had worked like crazy, too. If a user searched for "Trump," "Iraq," and "War," the top result was "Hillary Voted for the Iraq War—Donald Trump Opposed It," with a link to a super PAC website with the banner

"Crooked Hillary voted for the war on Iraq. Bad Judgment!" If a user entered the terms "Hillary" and "Trade," the top result was "lying-crookedhillary.com." The click-through rate for this was incredibly high.

Google sold inventory to Trump each day, notifying the campaign when new, exclusive ad space was available for the taking, such as the homepage of YouTube.com, the most coveted digital real estate online. Google topped that off by making it easy for the campaign to bid for use of search terms in order to control users' "first impressions." Google sold this to Trump for Election Day, November 8, and it pulled in new supporters in droves, and directed them to their local polling places.

While both the Trump super PAC and campaign teams were running behind the scenes that summer, I was pursuing ventures of interest to me. One was training for the communications team of the Slovenian prime minister. I had been shocked and humbled when the U.S. State Department called my cell phone and requested that CA be one of its partners in showing off the best of American innovation to incoming delegations. Would I host the head of state's team and run a session on political communications for them? For this ask to have come in, I thought, obviously Cambridge was becoming well known and of high profile in DC circles. I was honored. Of course, I would be happy to host the training session.

When the Slovenian prime minister's team came to our office on June 21, the meeting went swimmingly. I was saying my good-byes to them when the shyest member of the group asked about Trump. Was my company working for him? They knew, they said, that I probably couldn't answer. I gave them a smile, knowing that Matt and Molly were at that very moment staffing the campaign in San

Antonio. I told them no, that I couldn't confirm or deny, but gave a slight wink—and one of them told me before they headed out that they were so excited at the opportunity to have a Slovenian in the White House. "You know Melania is from our country, yes? We hope you are working for her husband—and we are crossing our fingers that you win!"

11

Brexit Brittany

SPRING–SUMMER 2016

While much of the company was moving full steam ahead with the Trump campaign during early summer 2016, for my part, I was moving away from politics for the first time since I'd returned to America the previous fall. By that spring, I no longer had any political pitches to make in the States—sales for the election cycle were over—which meant I was free at last to focus on commercial and social accounts in America and beyond. I'd closed Cambridge's first contracts with a law firm, a fashion company, a health care corporation, a restaurant group, and a venture capital firm, opening new verticals, aka industries to which we were applying our technology. I hardly slept, and I took poor care of myself. I was on planes most of the time, shuttling between New York, London, DC, and the offices of whichever client I was pursuing. Alexander cautioned me that I ought not to be thinking, "I fly, therefore I am," but I couldn't help but feel alive when I was in transit, making things happen. And if I found myself in any way disoriented—waking up not knowing if I was in my apartment on Upper Berkeley Street; in Tim's apartment, where I kept much more than just a toothbrush now; in the apartment in Crystal City; or in a budget hotel somewhere—I was comforted by the knowledge that I had finally found my stride.

I had vacation time in June, and I wanted to spend it with Tim, so we flew to Portugal, where he had a friend whose family owned a home there, in the sunny Algarve, a coastal area with whitewashed homes along cliffs above a perfect beach. There were ten to twelve people staying in the house, a three-story villa with room for all of us. Most of the guests were British, and we had in common that we were escaping the Brexit vote, though we weren't all fleeing from it for the same reason.

Despite my very public appearance at the press conference back in November, my professional relationship to Brexit had been short-lived. And to the best of my knowledge, so had Cambridge Analytica's.

Despite having been onstage with the Leave.EU team, following the press conference in November, I'd had only one other interaction with Leave.EU, traveling with Dr. David Wilkinson to Bristol, to visit its "official headquarters." My tasks there were to present to the campaign staff the services Cambridge would be providing to Leave.EU and to do an audit of the data the campaign was gathering and explain how to use the data analysis we had already done.

The day had a distinctly odd quality to it. I couldn't for the life of me sort out why Leave.EU's headquarters was in Bristol and not London—until we arrived at the office park where it was located. There I discovered that the plain, boxy HQ building was also the main office of Eldon Insurance, Arron Banks's company.

It was difficult, in fact, to tell the difference between the Leave.EU campaign crew and the insurance office workers as I passed by them on the way to the boardroom. There were about ten people in all, each in charge of a different department: press and PR, social media, canvassing, events, and running the call center. Mostly pale and plainly dressed, they were seated stolidly in their chairs, their ID lanyards around their necks, looking rather unenthusiastic—until they started listening to David and me speak. Once they understood what we were there to do, they were grateful that we had come.

They told us they felt like "fish out of water." None of them had ever worked on a political campaign before, and they were glad that someone with expertise in politics had come out to help. It rapidly became clear that they were nothing more than insurance company employees who had been tasked with campaign work. I thought it odd, but it also showed efficiency, if nothing else, on Arron's part.

Still, it was strange, and when David and I visited the call center, we could see at once that it was the same one used for Eldon Insurance. As I later testified to the UK parliament's Digital, Culture, Media and Sport Committee in its "Disinformation and 'fake news'" inquiry, sixty people or so manned the phones, at about five rows of desks, making outgoing calls to customers in what I was told was the Eldon database to ask questions about Brexit where they usually would be answering questions from their insurance customers.

The manager of the call center was a young woman who looked to be about my age. She generously offered to pull up on a computer screen the questions from the survey they were using, and David and I took a look at them to see if CA could refine what they were already doing.

"Do you want to leave the European Union?"

"Do you think immigration is a problem?"

"Do you think our National Health Service is underfunded?"

The questions were so biased and leading that the results would end up skewing any model. They were not doing this right, and I knew there were even more ways CA could help the campaign going forward.

When I got back to London, I wrote an email to the Bristol team, asking for as much of their data as they could send: subscriber information, info on donors, and anything else they had. David would work on the data, and the insights he gleaned would allow Cambridge to begin work on a proposal for the second phase of our work for Leave.EU.

Leave.EU's social media guru, Pierre Shepherd, gave CA access to all accounts and any other relevant data, and the CA team began to design phase two.

Only, phase two never happened. After CA had put together the follow-up proposal to the phase one work we'd done, "Banksy" and "Wiggsy" dropped off CA's radar—although, they noted on their website that they were working hand in hand with Cambridge Analytica, and they repeatedly spoke of their relationship with us in the press. Julian reached out to Arron repeatedly, and Arron continued to seem interested in phase two, but he never paid us for the phase one work we'd done. Sensitive data containing personally identifiable information on British voters had been transferred to Cambridge, matched with survey data, modeled, and transformed into useful targeted groups for Leave.EU. Where had that data gone? Why had Alexander allowed a project in his own country to be negotiated without a contract as he had in Nigeria?

The apparent end of our working relationship with Leave.EU left us in a confusing place. After all, we'd been publicly associated with them since November. In all, we'd spent three days consulting with them, two in preparation for the press conference, and one in Bristol, trying to get their team up to speed. This was in addition to the many man hours we'd spent working with the data they'd given us, to complete phase one and prepare for the news conference presentation. We'd never given them the slides, but I had talked through the findings in the slides in great detail with the Leave.EU team over

On a visit to The Hague to interview
with John Jones QC for a job at
Doughty Street International
(which I was offered, pending funds).
(*November 2014*)

Alexander Nix, at a presentation
for Ernst & Young, discussing
how audience engagement is
changing. (*London, 2015*)

On a trip to Madrid after Davos to discuss data-driven diplomatic initiatives for Libya, and to follow up on the Nigeria campaign. (*January 2015*)

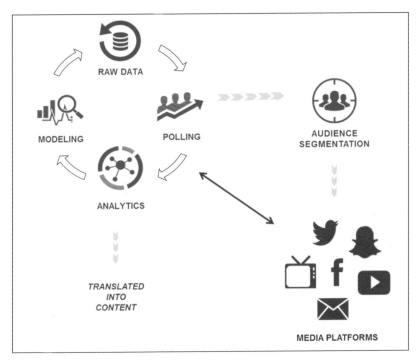

Diagram of the data analytics cycle and microtargeting process from the Trump campaign debrief case study. (*December 2016*)

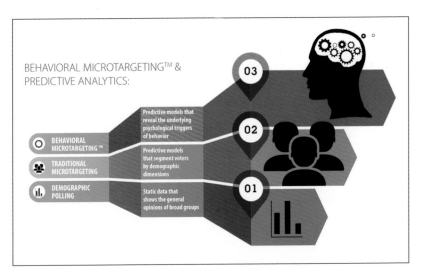

Behavioral Microtargeting and Predictive Analytics infographic from early SCL Group brochures and sales presentations, differentiating the behavioral modeling from traditional methods.

On election day in France, posters featuring Marine Le Pen show the candidate with her eyes gouged out and a Hitler-style mustache carved away. (*Calais, 2016*)

Onstage with Kellyanne Conway at the Conservative Political Action Conference (CPAC) 2016, discussing how the "myth of electability" has vanished. That year, Cambridge Analytica was a sponsor of the conference. (*February 2016*)

Donald Trump signing his own face on the cover of *Time* magazine during his entrance to the Republican Party of Florida Conference, outside the Fantasia Ballroom at Disney World. *(Orlando, Florida, November 2015)*

Mark Turnbull, former head of Global Political of SCL Group, presenting the Trump campaign case study "What We Did" at the LEAD Conference. *(Singapore, September 2017)*

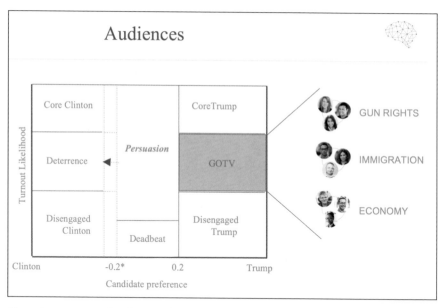

Targeting segmented audiences from the Trump campaign debrief, which included a "deterrence" group for dissuading people to vote. (*December 2016*)

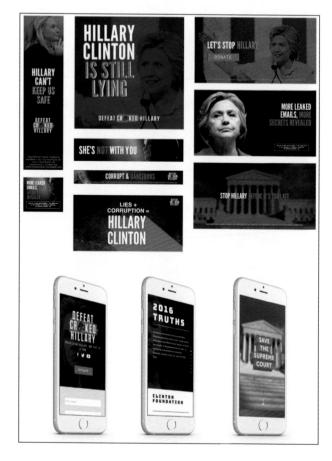

Make America Number One (MAN1) after-action report images, led by David Bossie of Citizens United and Emily Cornell of Cambridge Analytica. (*December 2016*)

View from my desk of Chris Christie at the head of the table in the boardroom of Cambridge Analytica, at our office on the seventh floor of 597 Fifth Avenue, where he met with Rebekah Mercer and Alexander Nix to complain that he was not offered a position in the Trump administration. *(New York, December 2016)*

Alexander Nix presenting data-driven commercial and political strategy at the KIO Kloud Camp. *(Mexico City, September 2017)*

Watching part of the Netflix Original documentary *The Great Hack* for the first time in the editing room with The Othrs production team at Gigantic Studios. *(New York, December 2018)*

Interview with Mark Miller, global editor of Bloomberg Live, about data surveillance and security at the Bloomberg Sooner Than You Think summit. *(Singapore, September 2018)*

the course of those days. Yet, for all that work, we never received a signed contract or payment, which made it hard for us to take credit for the work or move forward.

Because he was so unresponsive with us, we didn't know if Arron Banks planned to continue his work on the referendum, so, for a short time, Cambridge pursued Vote Leave as a client. Vote Leave was composed of Westminsterites, established and mainstream politicos from both the Tories and even the Liberal Party in England, and potentially great clients. We had approached them early on, but once they learned we were working with Leave.EU, they'd balked. To many at Cambridge, including me, our involvement in Brexit had apparently come to an end.

Throughout the winter and spring of 2016, Leave.EU appeared to be having success without our help, but while watching their campaign from the outside, I found it hard to shake the suspicion that they were leveraging at least some of the consulting and segmentation work CA had done on their behalf. Arron Banks and Leave.EU paid millions of pounds to run their own online campaign, which Banks claimed was all driven by data science, name-dropping Cambridge whenever it was convenient for him. He boasted that Leave.EU was the biggest viral political campaign in the United Kingdom, with 3.7 million engagements in one week on Facebook. "The campaign," he said, "must be doing something right to annoy all the right people consistently."

Just days before the vote, Leave.EU published an "undercover investigation" on Facebook, purporting to show how easy it was to smuggle migrants across the Channel. Andy Wigmore also posted content, which Leave.EU reposted: a series of photographs purportedly showing a woman being violently attacked by a man wearing a hooded jacket. "Migrant[s] beating up girl in Tottenham [on] Saturday," Wigmore wrote.

Mass protests and violent arguments followed hard upon such messaging—as did a murder.

On June 16, 2016, a week before the referendum, an unemployed Yorkshire gardener named Thomas Mair, who was mentally unstable and whose thinking was deeply influenced by far-right, anti-immigrant Leave messaging, National Front propaganda, and American neo-Nazi and KKK ideology he had found online, murdered Jo Cox, an MP he considered a Remainer. Using a sawed-off rifle, he shot her in the head and the chest and then stabbed her fifteen times. If there was any doubt about what had incited him, two days later, when asked to identify himself in court, Mair replied, "My name is death to traitors, freedom for Britain."

On the day of the referendum, everyone staying at the Algarve villa with us tried to make light of their political differences. Many of the guests were, by British standards, conservative, like Tim, and had voted Leave before flying that day. The others had voted Remain, because they either were liberal-leaning sorts or had significant financial interests in the stability of the euro that would be supported by Britain's remaining in the European Union. After the polls closed, we drank copious amounts of wine and huddled around the only TV in the house, monitoring the results of the once-in-a-lifetime vote that could change the course of European history.

In the end, the vote hinged on 1 percent of the British electorate. The result was 52–48 percent in favor of leaving. The effect of the vote was immediate. The value of British currency tumbled, with the pound hitting a thirty-one-year low, and global markets, including the Dow Jones, took an enormous hit.[1]

In Portugal, standing before the television set, half the Brits I was with celebrated. Others were distraught, some even crying. They couldn't imagine a Britain unhinged from Europe and now so completely unhinged from reason and sanity as well. We were divided in that moment, and I was somewhere in the middle. An American expatriate, a liberal in disguise, and a conservative in appearance, I was also a woman who had worked for a company that had worked, at least for a time, for or with, depending on how you looked at it, the Leavers.

"Oh, is that what you've gotten yourself into?" British friends had often said to me in the lead-up to both the referendum and during the Republican primaries.

"Your brand is crisis, eh?" they would say, referring to the title of a Sandra Bullock film that had come out recently in which Bullock plays a slick American political consultant whose expertise is in running political campaigns in banana republics.

I always replied with a nervous laugh.

Alexander himself refused to watch the film, as it wasn't about him. He had run more foreign elections than anyone else, he claimed. That the film was not based on him was preposterous he said. He continued to protest it.

On the day after the Brexit vote, British friends who knew both that I worked for Cambridge and that Cambridge had had a hand in the referendum, began "unfriending" me and kicking me out of their online book groups and political discussion forums. To them, I was crisis, indeed.

When I returned to England on June 27, the faces on those around me bore expressions of surprise. And at Cambridge Analytica, some people patted themselves on the back. We had assumed the Leavers would fail. In advance of the vote, we had fretted over whether to ask Arron Banks to take our name down from the Leave.EU website in order to spare ourselves the coming blow to our reputation. In the end, we chickened out. After all, it was our board of directors that had introduced us to the so-called Bad Boys of Brexit. We had been afraid we'd offend them if we didn't accept the job. Conveniently now, though, we could claim a little piece of Brexit as a CA victory, even if the actual role we had played was ambiguous at best.

Nigel Farage once said that Brexit was the "petri dish" for the Trump campaign—it was tribal, populist, and enough to tear a nation apart. It was also, in so many ways, the *technological* precursor to the 2016 U.S. presidential campaign—and just across the pond on the day of the Brexit vote, the Cambridge Analytica machine was up and running.

It wouldn't be until many months later that I would learn that my nagging feeling that some of CA's work had been used to motivate voters to cast their ballot for Leave had indeed been correct—only, as it turned out, it was Vote Leave that first confirmed having used our approach, or at least one that closely resembled it.

It was said that the head of Vote Leave, Dominic Cummings, regarded data as his religion. His plan was to carry out as much of the campaign digitally (using Facebook, in particular), a strategy at odds with the ways that campaigns in Britain had been carried out for decades. As was revealed in *The Observer*, Vote Leave had contracted with none other than AIQ, which worked for them throughout the campaign and provided help to groups connected to them, including BeLeave and Veterans for Britain.[2] AIQ became embedded in Vote Leave headquarters, maintaining a small but powerful op center there. So, while Cambridge was working with Leave.EU, AIQ, another SCL partner whose IP was owned by the Mercers, had contracted to work with its direct competitor.

When I first learned of this, I was shocked—I had thought that CA and AIQ were nearly inseparable, sharing data on a daily basis for all kinds of clients. How could they have run a rival campaign, pitching separately from CA itself? It didn't make sense.

AIQ's digital campaign bore much resemblance to Cambridge's, if not in the sophistication of its content, then in its methods. Later, the AIQ proposal would be leaked, showing that Chris Wylie had nearly copied CA proposals word for word. The strategy used focus groups, psychographic modeling, and predictive algorithms, and it harvested private user data through online quizzes and contests, using a perfectly legal opt-in. For Brexit, the campaign had matched user data to British voter logs and then it injected itself into the bloodstream of the internet, using targeted messaging to incite a nation.

The ten-week showdown had played out in the real world the biliousness of what was happening online. Vote Leave messaging delivered misinformation and fake news about countries such as Turkey, which was negotiating its accession to the European Union. They riled up swing voters by suggesting that a vote to remain was a vote to impoverish Britain's sacred National Health Service. I myself remembered being personally influenced by this messaging. As an American who had lived for more than a decade in Britain, with free health care, I could only imagine the benefits of the massive injection of funding the Leave contingent claimed the NHS would receive if the Leavers won. Now, looking back on that period, I see that such messaging was terribly flawed and even criminal: from fearmongering about funding for government services to the imagery of immigrants and terrorists storming the border, the Leave campaign was one of fear.

It would later come out through parliamentary submissions from an impressively thorough researcher named Dr. Emma Bryant that the phase one work and subsequent proposals for phase two had been used by Leave.EU as well. Andy Wigmore bragged to her about taking CA's strategy and, after hiring data scientists from the University of Mississippi, they established a CA copycat, which they called "Big Data Dolphins," and then used "AI to win it for Leave."

12

Straitjacket

AUGUST 2016–JANUARY 2017

During much of the summer of 2016, Cambridge was working on the Trump campaign largely under the radar. Up through to the Republican National Convention, our staff was working their magic across multiple offices, while many of us sat back and hoped they weren't nearly as good at persuading voters as we'd advertised.

Though knowledge of Cambridge's efforts on Trump's behalf had largely been kept secret for many months, events in August 2016 pushed the Mercers and, by extension, Cambridge, much closer to the spotlight shining on Trump. Around the office, we were wide-eyed when reading the news each day, watching our board members and business associates such as Steve, Bekah, and Kellyanne take control of the U.S. presidential race. It hadn't been too long before this that the three of them were seen as fringe elements, disruptive to conservative politics but not mainstream enough to be working with the real nominee—and having no chance at the White House.

But now the writing was on the wall: the only contender to Hillary Clinton was Donald J. Trump, and Trumpworld was fully entwined with Cambridge and its people. On a daily basis, the news cycle now featured the faces of those whom I had known to be running our company, and they were influencing not just the nation but the world.

Strangely enough, it wasn't just on TV that I saw the Trump campaign invading CA; they literally, physically, invaded our offices, too. If Trump Tower was surrounded by protestors, which it often was, or if the Trump "inner circle" just wanted some privacy, our Fifth Avenue offices became a secondary campaign office. The boardroom was now nearly unusable to our commercial team—it was always filled with Trump team spillover from HQ. And when the meetings were distinctly commercial, the potential client was usually a Mercer or Bannon introduction being placed in our boardroom for Duke Perrucci, a serious sales executive and dedicated family man, now our new chief revenue officer, and the rest of the team to "wow" into a contract. It was confusing but at the same time exhilarating. Cambridge seemed to be rising into the ranks of the powerful movers and shakers in both DC and New York, and the air was abuzz with energy.

For my part, I'd been bouncing around the United States and Mexico for much of the summer, pursuing commercial contracts. Mexico, to put it straight, was at least ten years behind the United States in data-driven decision making. I spent much of my time with the Fortune 500 companies that were known to be the lead players across the continent and the world, such as AB InBev and Coca-Cola, and I found that even the largest firms like these were hardly using analytics to reach consumers in Mexico. Data was hard to purchase there and tricky to collect, and these companies needed all the help they could get. I was impassioned as I built up our offerings across the border, and all the happier at being shielded from the virulent messaging coming out of the Trump campaign and the mass Trump rallies to the north.

I was so busy throughout the summer that I rarely spoke to my family except to chat about incoming bills and how much I could help with them. At least I was in Mexico, where the cost of living was easy—living in New York City had made it next to impossible for me to help them, even when I lived on a tight budget. When I did on occasion speak to either of my parents, the news was largely depressing, with the exception that my father had finally managed to find a job. He had gotten a gig selling insurance, which, while better than nothing, paid him only commission. And with no new family home in sight, I would need to continue to help making the payments on the storage facilities holding our belongings.

When I spoke to my father, he sounded flatter than ever.

"How are you?" I would ask.

"Okay," he would say.

"How's the job?"

"Okay" was his answer.

He was still almost monosyllabic. I tried to imagine how he could be successful working with clients, given the way he interacted with me.

At the end of September, though, it became clear that what was going on with him had nothing to do with depression or his work situation—in fact, it never had been. My father was gravely ill. He began to fall asleep unexpectedly and his lower lip had started to droop, affecting his speech. He finally took himself to a doctor, who ordered an MRI and upon viewing the shocking results, put him immediately in the hospital. Scans found two tumors, one the size of a human hand and covering one entire side of his brain and pressing upon it; the other was smaller than a dime and lodged in the other hemisphere. The tumors had been there for three, maybe five years, the doctor said, which accounted for my father's strange behavior:

his lethargy, his flat affect, his inability to make decisions while the world was falling apart around him.

When the phone rang with the news, it was also a summons to see him immediately, before the surgery; if he survived it, he still might never be the same. In a quick email, I told Alexander and everyone else I was working closely with at Cambridge that I didn't know when I would be coming back to work—and then I flew straight to Chicago.

The doctors were able to remove only the larger tumor, as his skull could not withstand a double craniotomy without collapsing. Neither tumor was cancerous, which was a relief, but each had done its damage, and with any luck, the one that remained would stay contained in size but for now could only be monitored. The surgery was invasive, and it was a while before my father awoke. My mother, sister, and I spent our hours in the ICU waiting room, occasionally going back to our rooms at the Days Inn to take a nap. The hospital was deep in the Chicago suburbs, an unfamiliar neighborhood.

With the surgery recovery, we entered new territory with my father. He had no ability to speak. He gestured helplessly, his eyes searching our faces for answers and understanding. When his hand was strong enough to hold a pen, what came out on paper were mere scribbles. We handed him his phone, thinking he might be able to peck out a message to us, but he couldn't remember the passcode. We opened his briefcase. My father had always kept all important paperwork stashed in his office, but now in the case were crumpled papers in disarray—mostly bills, some long past due.

He was largely silent, but his face was a sea of anger and frustration. He became volatile, threw fits, was unreachable—a result of the surgery, the doctor said—and the nurses warned they would have to restrain him in the bed if he would not comply with their care instructions, lest he fall and hit his still-healing head. He would need twenty-four-hour care in a nursing home indefinitely, until they could further evaluate his recovery. Luckily, he had already qualified for Medicaid, as without insurance, his care would have been in the thousands of dollars a month at a minimum, which none of us had.

Why hadn't I thought of asking him to go to a doctor sooner? Why hadn't I considered that the source of the problem was physical, not psychological? Because I hadn't been at home—none of us had—I hadn't been there to observe his further deterioration over the past two years. My guilt was overwhelming. I thought then and there of quitting Cambridge and staying to take care of him, but my mother took my hand, looked in my eyes, and told me what I already knew: I had to go back to work. Someone needed to pay the bills, even if it was only a few hundred here and there. There wasn't anywhere else I could go to get my next paycheck straightaway.

After all, hadn't my experience at CA begun so I could make money to help my family? To say I'd lost sight of that was an understatement, but in truth, I'd really just lost sight of myself.

I know only now that, from afar, my family had watched my transformation with confusion and disorientation. When I spoke with my sister, I avoided talking too much about work, in large part because I didn't want to be judged. I had changed radically, and while she was supportive of me, she was troubled by the fact that I had transitioned with such seeming ease into a world so different from the one I had previously inhabited.

My family had known me as a person who valued my moral compass above all things, and who would happily have lived in a cheap apartment on the wrong side of town if it meant taking a low-paying job at my favorite nonprofit. Now I was someone who had lost her true north, and was unrecognizable to them.

The strange thing was, though, when I looked in the mirror during that time, I really thought the person I was seeing was my true self.

As much of a stranger as I'd become from myself, my family remained one of the most important things in my life, which was why I was truly shaken when my father received his diagnosis. Cambridge was a huge opportunity for my family to have a rock, something to keep us from floating away, disintegrating, disappearing into a society that easily forgot about people like us.

I spent November 8, 2016, Election Day, in the New York City office. I didn't get much work done; no one did. Everyone else was in San Antonio or DC or in Trump Tower, so the few of us left in the Scribner Building offices rubbernecked at the screens on every wall, the volumes up and down. Some ducked out to vote and came back with I VOTED stickers on their lapels.

Perhaps most upsetting, I hadn't voted. My home state was Illinois, and I would have had to fly there. I had planned to, which is why I hadn't gotten an absentee ballot, but now I couldn't. I'd literally just come back from Chicago, and if I'd returned there to vote, it would have been heartbreaking to see my father. He had become increasingly volatile, and was being moved from the recovery unit to a psychiatric hospital. His mental condition hadn't improved at all. In fact, it had worsened. He had become more violent.

That was bad enough to keep me away, but the truth was, I was too afraid to vote. I was afraid that if Cambridge continued to do business with Trump or the Trump Organization, they'd learn things about me I'd rather they not know—they could learn that I would have voted for Hillary instead of Trump. I would be a liability to myself and to the company. I knew all too well that voter data was easy to come by.

My greatest fear was being targeted.

It was almost 5:00 p.m. when the call came in from San Antonio. The predictive models from exit polls and other compiled data now suggested that Donald Trump had a 30 percent chance of winning. This information put a wrench in my plans for the evening. I had spent the previous couple of weeks weaseling myself a ticket to the Clinton VIP victory party at the Javits Center. It was in my back pocket.

Alexander texted me. It looked like I was going to have to attend the Trump campaign party, not because he was going to win, but because it was the right thing to do, given how much better he was trending. The gathering was sure to be a consolation prize and a Hillary-bashing session, but it was important for Cambridge Analytica to show its colors, as a reminder to Trump of our worth, given the new results.

Before we headed out, my colleagues and I had a couple of drinks. We'd go to the Trump party, drink there, too, and then, as Alexander promised, we'd get out of there "before it turned ugly."

The event was invitation-only, for friends and supporters of the Trump-Pence campaign, and it was scheduled to begin at 6:30 p.m. Alexander had thrown me a last-minute invitation. I put on my cowboy hat and made my way down the five blocks from our office to the Hilton Midtown, weaving through crowds of early celebrators—Hillary supporters giddy with excitement, wearing "Hillary for President" and Planned Parenthood T-shirts and cheering and chanting about the soon-to-be "first female president."

Even on a good night, the Hilton is rather a grim place, with nothing like the gilded glamor of Trump's hotels. But if the campaign had chosen a Trump property, it would have cost them a ten-thousand-dollar fine from the Federal Election Commission. What was more, they didn't want to choose a large and gaping venue that would make what was sure to be a low turnout for the party seem ever more pitiful.

The Hilton was surrounded as though it were a fortress. Secret Service agents stood behind a phalanx of squat garbage trucks that had been set up as a bomb barrier. In the event of an act of terrorism, the police had been armed with semiautomatic weapons. Nearby, a lone protester sold homemade boxes of "Cap'n Trump" cereal, the proceeds of which, he told the gathered Trump supporters, would go not to Trump but to the city's homeless. It was an effort lost on the Trump revelers in their MAGA hats.

Donald Trump was a superstitious man: if there was even the slightest chance of a win, he didn't want to jinx it by over-celebrating. Inside the Hilton, I found a calm and nearly unnoticeable celebration. There was room in the ballroom for three thousand, but few had arrived yet, and the place was sparsely decorated, with braids of balloons near a stage and little more. The stage would serve as the site of Trump's concession speech. I guess that would happen around midnight. I hoped to be long gone by then.

The place looked like it had been set up more for a press conference than a victory party. In the press pen, journalists chomped on sandwiches they'd brought in. Nearby, boxed off and entirely empty, was a spot someone had reserved for "Trump TV." Nowhere was a morsel of real food. No Trump Steaks. No hors d'oeuvres.

In the center of the room, however, was a cake. It was about two feet tall, shaped in the likeness of Trump, with a big head of bright yellow hair and a face more sour than celebratory. It was said to have been made out of hundreds of pounds of marzipan, and the woman from New Jersey who had whipped it up from scratch stood next to it with pride.

Throughout the room was a varied display of haute couture, cheap cocktail dresses, and a sea of MAGA hats. People carried signs that read, "Women for Trump" or "Hispanics for Trump" or "Bikers for Trump." Soon, the highboy tables became littered with empty beer bottles.

VIPS such as Alexander were still at Trump Tower with Donald, the Mercers, Kellyanne, and anyone with a Trump last name, plus Jared Kushner, but in the ballroom and at the cash bar was a motley crew of high and low Trump staffers, political demi-luminaries, and big-ticket donors.

Donning a pair of aviators even indoors in the dark was the alt-right provocateur Milo Yiannopoulos. Near him were Fox News maven Jeanine Pirro and the actor Stephen Baldwin. There was pundit Scottie Nell Hughes, TV and radio host Laura Ingraham, the muscle-bound *SNL* alum Joe Piscopo, former VP candidate Sarah Palin, and even the MyPillow guy, Michael Lindell. The video-blogging duo Diamond and Silk chatted with the infamous "apprentice" Omarosa Manigault, and a bevy of billionaires (David Koch, Carl Icahn, Wilbur Ross, Harold Hamm, and Andy Beal) stood around in a huddle. Iowa congressman Steve King and Jerry Falwell Jr. kibitzed. And Trump advisers Sarah Huckabee Sanders, Rudy Giuliani, and Roger Stone, and Senator Jeff Sessions somberly drank their cocktails.

The earliest projections came in at around 7:00 p.m. No surprises there. Trump took Indiana and Kentucky, and Hillary took Vermont.

I thought longingly of what was going on at the Javits Center, that cavernous place filled with Hillary supporters. I thought of how, later that night, the indoor celebrations would spill out into the streets, into Hell's Kitchen and along the High Line; and how in Times Square, people would be drunk; and how in Central Park there would be fireworks.

As precinct by precinct, county by county, numbers from all around the country rolled in, I became transfixed by the screens. Just as our data scientists had noted, the numbers in the swing states favored Trump. I turned to my colleagues, remarking with pride that Cambridge had done a fine job, given the circumstances, and I must have said so loud enough that others heard me. People hugged us and offered high-fives when they realized who we were.

Then the media began to call states for Trump even in those places where only 10 percent of the votes had been reported. It seemed premature, but the mood in the room changed, and as time went on, each prediction proved uncannily correct.

At around 10:00 p.m., with just a scintilla of a whiff of a whiff of a possibility that Trump might triumph, the Asian financial markets plunged.

After 10:30, Trump began to break through for real. When he took Ohio, the first big swing state and the one that had picked every single U.S. president correctly since 1964, the room erupted. My Old Fashioned suddenly tasted sour. I went to get another. At the bar, a screen flashed the news that Trump had taken Florida.

Alexander called. He was coming to meet me. The Mercers were coming, too. People started to flood out of the main hall, the excitement palpable as supporters in Make America Great Again hats started to realize that their candidate might actually take the White House. I stood under one of the big screens in the lobby, waving my hands in the air so Alexander and company could see me in the crowd. In moments, I spied Alexander, who looked exasperated.

He came over to me and gave me a massive hug, while leaning in and whispering, "I've been sober all evening! God damn it, I need a drink!" I handed him my Old Fashioned. Aloud, so everyone could hear, he shouted, "It's looking to be quite a night indeed! Bekah, I've found Brittany!"

Soon, I was standing between Bob and Bekah, both of them dressed in impeccable suits. Outwardly, I tried to be cheerful.

At 11:30, Fox News declared Trump the winner in Wisconsin.

Then, at 1:35 a.m., the screen flashed red again. Trump had won Pennsylvania. Hillary hadn't spent any time or money there, assuming the state would go blue without any effort.

I focused only on the screen. At 1:35, Trump had 264 electoral votes. At 2:03, John Podesta, not Hillary, took the stage at the Javits Center. "Several states are too close to call," he announced. "We're not going to have anything more to say tonight." He looked rattled as he left the stage.

At ten minutes past 2:00 a.m., the chyron on the screen read, "The *Washington Post* Calls Race for Trump." Somehow, Bekah and Bob seemed not to have noticed. I tapped Bekah on the shoulder and pointed to the screen. Bob turned, too.

Bekah turned to look her father right in the eye. It was first a look of pleasant surprise. Then what passed between them was the inkling of an understanding: they had gone all in on black 13 and won the jackpot.

13

Postmortem

I remember the months that followed as one long phone call, but really, there were hundreds of them, incoming, outgoing. In the aftermath of Trump's victory, we were finally able to start advertising the role we'd had in the campaign—and now everyone wanted us to do the same for them.

The president of Ghana, whom Alexander had been chasing for years, wanted us to work for him in the upcoming election there. CEOs of major U.S. and foreign corporations wanted us for commercial campaigns—Unilever, MGM, Mercedes. Campaign managers and politicians on nearly every continent wanted us. Those of us in CA sales had to schedule calls in fifteen-minute intervals, and we limited each call to the essential questions: *Who are you? What do you need? How much money do you have?* and *What's your timeline? Thank you very much.* Anything beyond that was wasted.

I was exhilarated; the company had won a presidential election.

I was heartbroken; our company had helped elect Donald Trump.

I worked from 7:00 in the morning sometimes until 11:00 p.m. I hardly slept at all, and then I woke and did it all again. I ate poorly, drank too much.

The world had ended, but Cambridge Analytica's life had really just begun.

Our clients wanted to know how we had done it, but before we could tell them, we had to learn the details ourselves. Those of us on the outside had no real sense of the specifics. And those details would become our ammo as we went out and did commercial sales.

Of course, I understood the broad outlines of our capabilities, but I'd seen none of the numbers; none of the research, data collection, or modeling; none of the campaigns undertaken by each entity; nor the content, the results, or conclusions from the testing and metrics. I wasn't able to be in rooms where these were discussed. I wasn't forwarded or copied on emails. Because of the FEC firewall, just as those in the super PAC were prohibited from coordinating with the activities of the campaign, anyone outside the campaign or the super PAC had also been cut off.

Because Cambridge had been behind both, I understood the firewall to have been even more important, the training intensive, and the nondisclosure agreements stringent. I knew that the majority of the people I worked with, consummate professionals all, had observed the division. I couldn't say for certain that the same was true for others.

Now, on December 8, exactly a month after Election Day, every single individual in the company—about 120 people, including creatives, data scientists, salespeople, researchers, and managers in CA and SCL offices in New York, London, and DC—was gathered in conference rooms for a videocast. In the sleek boardroom in the Charles Scribner's Sons Building on Fifth Avenue, at the conference table beneath a big American flag, sat the now director of commercial sales Robert Murtfeld, my human-rights friend, whom I had brought into the company back in 2015; chief revenue officer Duke

Perrucci; and Christian Morato, director of business development and also new to the company; along with a group of others.

The firewall was about to come down. We had been waiting for this moment since the election.

On day one, the Trump campaign team presented. Matt Oczkowski and Molly Schweickert led us through the details. What they had done for Cruz wasn't at all what they were able to do for Trump. Whereas Cruz was a one-term senator who'd started out with extremely low favorability and name recognition, as Obama had, Trump was a wildly popular lightning rod, so it had been a very bespoke campaign. And because Trump already had a significant media presence, they had had to start with a wide-based, grassroots program that could then power a massive digital machine directed specifically to fight Hillary Clinton.

They were being terribly efficient, and proud of how lean the operation was, compared to the Hillary campaign. Hillary's headquarters team in Brooklyn was huge; the Trump team had been a lean group of only thirty when CA joined in June 2016, but they had been strategic and more thorough than the competition.

The various Trump teams worked together out of a custom ops center in San Antonio under the direction of digital operations director Brad Parscale. Because of the FEC firewalls, with the exception of the CA creative team, located across our offices in New York, DC, and London (as they were serving both the super PAC and the Trump campaign), all elements of the digital campaign were under one roof. Molly and a group of data scientists occupied a large room with workstations, with media monitoring on video walls and large interactive screens.

Upon the CA team's arrival, the need to build a database was of utmost importance. Because Brad had done no modeling of his own, establishing a functional database was a critical first step. They dubbed the operation "Project Alamo" and got it up and running in June, and started advertising in July, so they had several months to campaign leading up to November.

Brad had access to the massive RNC database, called the RNC Data Trust, comprising forty years of Republican voter history, but had no understanding of what to do with it, no infrastructure to make anything happen, and no unifying strategy. Every Republican candidate is given access to this database, and so is any vendor that has a signed contract with a candidate. But the database doesn't exactly come with a manual and requires a lot of expertise to be employed properly.

So, what other databases did Cambridge Analytica have when they began? People on the videocast wanted to know.

Matt said they had started building Project Alamo with the RNC Data Trust database. Apparently the Cambridge team had wanted to use the CA database, but the Parscale team, in charge of digital operations, had preferred to build off the RNC Data Trust. Because Matt and Molly and the rest of the Cambridge Analytica team were not the most senior people in the room, they did not feel they could push back against Parscale.

It was an interesting claim but one that left me puzzled. One of the company's main selling points had always been our database, which included data from millions of Facebook users from 2015 and before that as well as data from the various campaigns we'd worked on in which we'd been allowed to retain the data. Yet, for some reason, Matt was telling us the Trump campaign did not want to use it.

For months before heading down to San Antonio, Matt had been bragging about all the data that CA would be able to bring to the table. He talked about how valuable all the data would be from the campaigns he was managing for the NRA and for the National Shooting Sports Foundation (NSSF) especially. Matt was project manager for all three and ran both the Trump and the NSSF campaigns at the same time, all the way through Election Day, dealing with all these data sets at once. He even claimed that he still had data from the Scott Walker campaign. Besides that, he often discussed how Cambridge had even more helpful data and models, made more accurate from every campaign it had run in the United States since 2014, but most important, from the Ted Cruz and Ben Carson campaigns.

Now, though, he was saying they'd used none of that data. Instead, they'd relied only on the RNC data as a starting point. If they had had so little to start with, so late in the election cycle, why wouldn't they use our company's database? I couldn't understand the rationale, and Matt seemed to be doing a 180 from his previous frivolous comments. I tried to ignore it for a short time and kept listening.

So, he continued, they were using the RNC Data Trust as their starting point, and then built upon that with other data sets—he didn't specify where they had come from. Throughout 2016, Oz had been negotiating with a company called BridgeTree, which boasted of holding large Facebook and LinkedIn data sets. The morning of December 8, the second day of the postmortem presentations, Alex Tayler emailed Duke to confirm that CA held multiple social media data sets from Bridgetree, one of which, strangely, was the exact same format as the Kogan data set he was supposed to have deleted nearly a year before: *570 data points for thirty million individuals.* Somehow, between the two of them, they managed to beef up both the CA database and Project Alamo enough to begin the next phase; the team then began a modeling program by undertaking much more thorough and coordinated research than what Brad had been doing.

The CA team had used telephone and internet polling such as Survey Monkey. They'd polled in sixteen swing states—a lot more than Hillary's team, which had polled in only nine. They'd then segmented people into two large groups, one on the Trump side and one on the Clinton side, and then segmented those groups. The first Trump group comprised "Core Trump Voters," those you'd turn into volunteers and get to donate and attend rallies. "Get Out the Vote" targets were those who intended to vote but might forget to; CA targeted them on issues that were most important to them that they were already excited about, so they'd be certain to head to the polls. And CA spent money on the "Disengaged Trump Supporters" only if they had cash left over.

On the Clinton side, you had the "Core Clinton Voters." Then you had the "Deterrence" group: these were Clinton voters who would possibly not go out to the polls if you persuaded them not to. While the campaign did *deterrence*, a euphemism for voter suppression, depending on how you looked at it, it was the super PAC that had really focused on this group, because its raison d'être was to "Defeat Crooked Hillary."

Throughout my time in the world of human rights, I had witnessed governments and powerful individuals using the suppression of movements, free thought, and voters as a strategy to retain power, sometimes at the cost of violence. This is why in the United States, voter suppression tactics are illegal. I wondered how the Trump campaign had drawn the line between negative campaigning and voter suppression. Usually, there was a clear difference, but in the digital age it was hard to track and trace what had been done. Governments no longer needed to send the police or military out into the streets to stop protests. They could instead change people's minds simply by paying to target them on the very screens in their hands.

And so Project Alamo was at the core of the burgeoning growth of the Trump campaign strategy: they worked day and night to get it going as fast as possible. They purchased more social media data from more vendors, making the database as robust as possible. They kept it pretty vague on where all of this had come from, but I wanted to believe it was all aboveboard. When all the data was finally in one place, the modeling could start. Psychographic modeling would be too time-intensive, they said, so Molly had the scientists model supporters on predictive behaviors, such as "propensity to donate." With that, the Trump campaign's digital strategy in program one took flight. In the first month, the campaign raised $24 million online, and continued to pull in as much per month until Election Day.

In the second program, CA used models to microtarget persuadable voters in swing states. The team in San Antonio had a vast tool kit and lots of help. They were said to have had a "symbiotic relationship" with Silicon Valley, with the nation's other key tech companies, and with data brokers.[1]

The team had also been able to break down issues central to each state and each county, city, and neighborhood, and to individuals in the database. With this information, they had helped to plan Trump's travel, the focus of his rallies, and messaging on the ground. They had also produced "heat maps," a tool that used shaded colors to show concentrations of certain audience groups, which they sent daily to Laura Hilger, head of research at campaign headquarters in Trump Tower. She then interpreted them to create a set of priorities for Trump's travel plans.

The heat maps included the number of persuadable voters in the areas he needed to visit, to whom precisely the campaign should be speaking, and the top issues to cover at a rally and in the media. After a rally, the team performed "persuasion measurements," and "brand lift studies," which indicated how people had reacted to a speech or a part of a speech. They then sent that information to creative, which turned a clip from that successful speech into an ad.

The ads and the messaging were what pulled the real value from the database information and made microtargeting possible: CA's data scientists could segment individuals that were most similar to each other, and work with the creative teams to build many different types of an ad, all tailored to specific groups. There were sometimes hundreds or thousands of versions of the same basic ad concept, creating an individual journey, and altered reality for each person. Over half of the Trump campaign's expenses had gone toward digital operations, and every message had been highly targeted so that most of the population didn't see what their neighbors saw. The CA team ran more than 5,000 individual ad campaigns with 10,000 creative iterations of each ad.

"Is that why we haven't heard from you in ages?" someone joked to Oz.

Clearly.

And they'd been enormously successful. Overall, the campaign had led to an average and measurable 3 percent increase in Trump's favorability. Considering the narrow margin by which he had won in certain states, this increase had been a significant help in the general election. In the get-out-the-vote campaign, the CA team drove a 2 percent increase in voters' submission of absentee ballots. This was a huge win because a lot of voters who request absentee ballots typically never even fill them out and mail them back.

The strength of Cambridge Analytica as a company wasn't only its amazing database; it was its data scientists and its ability to build great new models. In San Antonio, Molly and the data scientists had used a dashboard Molly had built called "Siphon" for two general efforts: to ingest data and audience profiles created by the scientists, and to bid for and buy space and time across "inventory sources" ranging from Google to the *New York Times*, to Amazon, Twitter, Pandora, YouTube, Politico, and Fox News. With Siphon's dashboard, the campaign could keep track of ad performance in real time.

Working in tandem or alone, Molly in San Antonio and whoever happened to be watching the same dashboard simultaneously (from Jared to Steve to Donald himself in Trump Tower) could make decisions in real time about the effectiveness of any given digital "campaign" being run on any given platform. Dashboard users could see right in front of them such information as current costs per click, uplift, and the like, and could make strategic adjustments as to where they were spending their money based on ad performance. Contrary to public perception, the campaign strategy was not led by Donald's erratic tweets or the sweepingly vague speeches he made on TV and at rallies. Every little detail was recorded in real time, and the moment an adjustment needed to be made, an ad could be changed to perform better, reaching more people and keeping the content fresh and relevant to the millions of voters it was reaching.

The scope of what the CA team on the Trump campaign was monitoring and juggling is breathtaking even to consider: thousands of individual ad campaigns within campaigns—in other words, separate suites of content aimed again and again at millions of segmented voters in different states, regions, and even neighborhoods, all of which could be adjusted almost in real time, based on performance. The cost of a single campaign alone could be over $1 million and generate fifty-five million impressions. And testing done by the data scientists and digital strategists, such as putting money behind a controlled set of ads versus targeted issues, could show (by measuring everything from the percentage increase in viewers' favorability for Donald Trump to the percentage increase in the viewers' intention to vote for him) if that campaign was working to convert impressions into votes.

Besides Molly's sets of dashboards, the team had access to data from "sentiment analysis platforms" such as Synthesio and Crimson Hexagon, which measured the effect, positive or negative, that all the campaign's tweets, including Trump's, were having.[2] For example, if the campaign put out a video of Hillary calling Trump supporters "deplorables," it could put money behind a few different versions of the ad and watch its performance in real time to determine how many people were watching, whether they paused the video, and whether they finished watching the video. Did they click through links attached to it to learn more? Did they share the content with others? How did it make them feel?

If, for some reason, the campaign didn't see preferred behaviors, they could tweak the ad, perhaps changing the sound, the color, or the tagline, to see what performed better. Ultimately, when they started to see a video go viral, they would put more money behind it, spinning it off into the ether of the internet and spurring a string of new supporters and donations.

With Siphon's dashboard, Molly, the folks in Trump Tower, and anyone else in the campaign could see the return on the campaign's investment in real time: cost per email; costs broken down by traffic type; cost per impressions per ad; click-throughs. They could also shift the ad to a different delivery system. And if an ad wasn't returning enough on investment, the team could pull it and run it elsewhere or substitute it for another ad entirely. Someone monitored the dashboard twenty-four hours a day, seven days a week.

The CA team had also studied what it took to "convert" an audience on a given platform. Online, the average number of impressions it took were five to seven, meaning if a viewer saw an ad five to seven times, he or she was highly likely to click through to the material we wanted them to see. This had helped the team determine how long to run an ad directed at a particular group they were microtargeting and how much money to spend on it. Molly and the others could monitor that on Siphon as well.

The Siphon dashboard and the big screens in the op center also featured predictive scenarios: combinations of states required to win the electoral vote, sixteen paths to victory, and a count of 270. Polling to calculate this was done every seven days, decreasing to every three days as Election Day grew closer.

Those presenting at the videocast then gave an example of all this coming together in the state of Georgia. Georgia had 441,300 persuadable voters. They were 76 percent white, mostly female, and most interested in the national debt, wages, education, and taxes. They weren't at all interested in hearing about "the wall," so whoever was writing the speech or giving talking points was advised to drop immigration rhetoric completely. The heat map also told them where the concentrations of persuadables were, so the campaign wouldn't visit, for example, Gwinnett, Fulton, or Cobb that day. Within those groups were segments: persuasion female, persuasion African American, persuasion Hispanic, and others. These were the persuadables less likely to show up, so the messaging would cover certain topics and not others, and because these voters received their information on different platforms, the campaign would reach them differently— some on women's interest sites, local news, and the like. The team had calculated in advance how much it would cost in any particular area to get the number of desirable impressions. For this group, it would take nearly 9 million impressions to convert them.

Here's an example of a smaller segmentation: In Georgia, the best way to reach Hispanics, say, was Pandora. For 30,000 persuadable Hispanics who wanted to hear about jobs, taxes, and education, the team needed to spend $35,000 to get the 1.4 million impressions that would get that group to convert.

Another example was a group of 100,000 African Americans who had been identified as persuadable in Georgia. They had targeted them using two different ad campaigns on two different platforms. One was a display ad in their browsers: an image with text over it. And the other we delivered via video on the feeds where they spent the most time. It took more than 1 million impressions to convert the group, and it would cost $55,000 to succeed.

What was horrifying about the African American campaign was a video the Trump campaign titled "Hillary Superpredators"—the most persuasive ad of all, it converted these people into Trump voters by featuring footage from a 1996 speech in which the then-First Lady said, "Not just gangs anymore. They're the kinds of kids called Superpredators. No conscience, no empathy. We can talk about what made them that way, but first they have to be brought to heel." While Hillary had apologized for the comments—she had made the remarks twenty years before, in a campaign speech for her husband, when she subscribed to ideas in a then-widely disseminated myth about black youth—they were now being used against her.

Sitting there at the companywide videocast, I was seeing the ad for the first time, and I was gobsmacked. I had had no idea Hillary ever made such a speech—it hadn't come up in my work with Obama because we were directed never to engage in negative campaigning. More important, the comments had clearly been taken out of context, to make it look as if Hillary were inciting racial hatred, and had been used by the Trump campaign to pressure a minority community away from a Clinton vote.

Yet somehow it got worse.

In the aftermath of the release of the infamous *Access Hollywood* tape, in which Trump was recorded in 2005 giving full expression to his misogyny and entitlement, boasting about grabbing women and forcing himself upon them against their will, Cambridge Analytica's data scientists ran a model on a test group of persuadable voters in key swing states. Nicknamed the "pussy model," it was designed to determine the public's response to the tape. The results were shocking. Among "persuadables," the tape actually produced a *favorable* response—an *increase* in favorability for Donald Trump—among mostly men but also some women.

Disgusting, I thought, and tried to push this thought out of my mind.

I was amazed at how well all the various modeling efforts had aligned with the campaign's get-out-the-vote efforts. One remarkably successful technique had resulted from Trump's ground game. After the candidate gave speeches, the CA team was able to do a great deal of persuasion measurement, or "brand lift studies," and then used clips from the more-well-received speeches in online ads. Out of the voters they then targeted, the team found (through post-impression polling, i.e., asking survey questions to targeted individuals who had seen the ad) that they could achieve an 11.3 percent favorability for Trump with an online audience of 147,000 people, and an 8.3 percent increase among them in intention to vote for Trump, not to mention an increase of 18.1 percent in online searches by those same people on issues that had been brought up in the videos.

Again, those leading the companywide videocast reiterated to us the value of having Facebook, Snapchat, Google, Twitter, and others as part of the team. A new Facebook product had allowed the team to embed multiple videos in one ad. From one such ad in particular there had been as much as a 3.9 percent increase in intention to vote for Trump, and as much as a 4.9 percent decrease in intention to vote for Hillary.

Decrease in intention to vote . . .

My heart started to pump almost audibly in my chest.

Native advertising had been expensive, but the return on investment, the videocast presenters reported, had been phenomenal. An online news organization would offer anyone who could afford it the ability to put ad content on its site and design it so that it looked exactly like the news organization's content—same font, same colors, same layout. It was easy for readers to mistake the content for news, and such ads confused even the most skilled of readers into thinking that negative Hillary content was real reporting about her pitfalls. The Trump campaign had paid Politico, for example, for content on corruption at the Clinton Foundation, and the ad team at Politico had formatted this material to look like Politico's own news content. Readers encountered it as news, and the average engagement with this kind of messaging was found to be four minutes. That's an unheard-of engagement rate. No one in the modern world spent four minutes on any ad out there. It was a whole new frontier.

As Election Day approached, the team had demonstrated other strengths. Due to an agreement the RNC had with the secretaries of state in each swing state, the CA team had been provided with live ballot results, including from absentee and early voters. With this information, the team was able to refresh their lists of targetable voters they should spend the rest of their budget on. It was incredibly cost-efficient because they could also transfer money for last-minute big spends.

The popular narrative about Donald Trump and, by extension, his campaign had been that he rejected data. While that may have been true for him personally—I have no idea, but I heard that he doesn't even use a computer—the company presentation underscored just how essential data, and data-backed decision-making, had been to his campaign. Whatever he did or didn't believe about the role of data, the people around him clearly understood not just its importance, but how to deploy it. Data, metrics, measurements, carefully crafted messaging—all these and more had been deployed to great effect and efficiency during Cambridge's months of working on his behalf. The Trump campaign may have been behind the times when Cambridge arrived, but by Election Day, it had become not just an effective political machine, but a winning one. Cambridge used all the tech at its disposal, along with the new innovations being sold to it by the social media embeds, to wage a social media battle against Hillary Clinton that was unprecedented in scale.

But the battle hadn't been against only Hillary—it had been against the American people. Voter suppression and fear-mongering, I now saw, had become a part of the playbook, and I felt sick at the thought. How could Cambridge have used such offensive materials? Why hadn't I known? What else was going on around the world, or even just in my own country, that I was blind to?

On the second day of the videocast postmortem, we learned about the super PAC's strategies, which were equally, if not more, successful, and also disturbing. While Molly, Matt, and the team of data scientists were in San Antonio, Emily Cornell and her team in DC had carried out a separate but parallel persuasion campaign under David Bossie for the Trump super PAC Make America Number One. Bossie was well known as the man who'd put the "super" in super PAC. As the head of Citizens United in 2010, he oversaw the successful effort to do away entirely with caps on campaign spending, a change made infamous in the Supreme Court case *Citizens United v. the Federal Election Commission.*

Emily was in charge of presenting, but Dr. David Coombs, the chief psychologist, took a turn to explain that the team at MAN1 had been able to microtarget without doing a lot of psychographics.

Everyone watching was surprised. After all, psychographics had always been CA's calling card, but the super PAC team (like the campaign team regarding CA's database) had excuses as to why they hadn't been used widely. The psychographics they had deployed, though, had worked very well, Dr. Coombs explained. His team had performed two main psychographic tests in the run-up to the election, and the second of the two had been quite successful. The team targeted three hundred thousand people via email, the majority of whom had OCEAN scores that indicated they were "highly neurotic." The team segmented them into twenty separate groups according to issues that concerned them and then crafted different emails for them with varied subject lines.

One set of subject lines was designed to scare people. The second was designed to be "reassuring." The third group saw both "scary and reassuring" subject lines. And the fourth and final group, the control, received emails with generic subject lines. The aim was to see which subject line made neurotics click open the emails.

The combined "scary and reassuring" messages were a failure. The generic subject line's results were scattered all over the place. The "reassuring" subject line hardly worked. But the "frightening" messages were the most successful of all. They showed a 20 percent higher rate of working than the control messages.

The conclusion, Dr. Coombs said, was "If you've got a group of emotionally unstable individuals, you're going to do a heck of a lot better if you send them a frightening message."

He then gave some examples of the frightening subject lines. One was "Electing Hillary Means America's Destruction." Another was "Hillary Will Destroy America." A great number of people on the videocast broke into nervous laughter. I, though, kept quiet.

Emily, the deputy head of the super PAC, concluded by saying she was excited by the results. That would be useful for promoting Trump in 2018 and preparing for 2020.

Between August and November, Emily continued, the super PAC

had achieved 211 million impressions and drove 1.5 million users to their two websites, with 25 million actual video views. The ads, with titles such as "Corruption Is a Family Business," were most successful on Facebook. Emily played one, titled "Can't Run Her Own House," for us. While I had been shocked the day before by the "Superpredators" video, this one floored me.

It was a video of Michelle Obama from 2007, during the first Obama presidential campaign when he was running against Hillary in the primary. In the original speech, Michelle had been speaking about how the Obamas still focused on their family and their daughters' schedules even during the campaign. Michelle had said, "If you can't run your own house, you certainly can't run the White House." Perhaps not surprisingly, the quote was quickly taken out of context to be a swipe at Hillary. While the full transcript of Michelle's comments revealed the truth, it didn't matter to many media outlets that ran with the inaccurate and misleading story that she was slamming Hillary.[3]

Thanks to efforts by CA's digital team, Michelle's misrepresented comments from 2007 surfaced again, only now their distortion was in service to Trump. By using that same clip out of context, the Trump team had made it appear that Michelle had "gone low" and criticized Hillary for her husband's cheating. In repurposing and repackaging this moment, the Trump team had weaponized sexism and turned it viral, creating the appearance of pitting Democrat against Democrat, woman against woman, when in truth it was a manipulative farce.

The metrics on the ad were even more disturbing. The campaign had found, of course, that plenty of women left of center were a bit more conservative. Traditional values, CA had found, were more important to them than how much they disliked Donald Trump, and the video had decreased those women's likelihood of voting for Hillary.

As Kellyanne had said so presciently—and to much hilarity from the audience at CPAC, when she and I sat on the panel in March—yes, when she woke up in the morning, Hillary Clinton was the second-most-popular person in her household.

That day, in CA and SCL conference rooms around the globe, where my colleagues and I were gathered to see for the first time what we had done to put Trump in the White House, there were oohs and aahs, but plenty of uncomfortable laughter among the congratulations.

The work the two teams had done was technically fantastic, but in two days, I had seen nothing less than the darkness I knew existed in politics—the appeals to our basest instincts, the fearmongering, the manipulation, the way we had turned against one another, and how I had had no idea.

Something horrible had been growing while I wasn't watching. Something horrible had attacked the central nervous system of our country; had overtaken it; had altered its thinking, its behavior, its ability to function. The tumors in my father's brain had been benign, but they had caused lasting damage. This technology had seemed so benign in the confines of a PowerPoint presentation, and now I could see it had ruined us.

I wished at that moment that I could go back in time and un-take so many decisions. I somehow had become a part of a monstrous windfall of negative messaging that had stoked the fires of division and hate among people across the country. It was a reality I could barely swallow. I had sat idly by while this was happening under my watch. This was my crisis-of-conscience moment: how could something so seemingly commonplace turn so dark?

I wanted to run, but my hands were tied. Because of my father's situation, I felt I couldn't abandon the job. I had nothing else to go to. I had had a successful year. The company for which I was working was on the rise. There'd be more business coming in. How could I leave now?

I was in a straitjacket.

Just like my father.

And, wearing that straitjacket, I went on.

This is what my calendar says of the time that immediately followed: two days before the inauguration, Cambridge opened its new DC office. We needed a headquarters to prepare for upcoming senatorial and gubernatorial campaigns, ballot initiatives, and of course the 2018 midterms. It was smart as well to hold a place for 2020. It was a small space, but it was strategically located, right on Pennsylvania Avenue.

I was there on the nineteenth for the office-christening cocktails, but the calendar says that I left early, with Julian Wheatland, for a party thrown by Nigel Farage and Arron Banks on the penthouse floor of the Hay-Adams Hotel, also in Washington. It was odd to see them again, but their friendship with Trump and Steve Bannon made it ever more important for CA to attend, for me to attend, and with enough champagne, I not only found it bearable, but allowed myself to enjoy it. Nigel signed a fresh copy of the new book for me, *The Bad Boys of Brexit*, a runaway best seller, with the inscription "2016 was the year that changed everything! Thank you for being a part of it." I posed for a picture holding the book up, partially with pride and partially to add to the ongoing jokes running inside my head.

When I look at pictures of myself during the period of the Trump inauguration, what I see is a woman wearing the most offensive of outfits: On the night of the Breitbart-sponsored "DeploraBall," I donned an NRA hat and a bright red dress, my lipstick also bright red. The next night, I wore a chinchilla coat over a black ball gown; tied around my neck were several long strings of pearls.

There are the photos, and there is my calendar. On Inauguration Day itself, my calendar says that I was on the rooftop of the W Hotel, at a party hosted by Politico. It says that the Forbes family was there, and my friend Chester and the Central Asian men I was with at that first sushi lunch meeting with Alexander in early 2014. There were apparently CA colleagues beside me, and a Swedish princess. It was cold, and it was raining. I peered over the balcony to watch the inauguration ceremonies below. I saw the sparse crowd and knew that, in it, right up front, were Alexander and Bekah and Steve, their faces likely beaming. For the first few up-close shots, I watched the events on a big screen: the oath, the pomp and circumstance. The rest of the ceremony is a blur.

The world was filled with the ghosts and ghouls of my two past years; Kellyanne walking by in her red hat, white dress, and blue military-style coat; Gerry Gunster, the pollster who worked on the Leave.EU campaign stopped to say hello. That night, I ate something with Alexander, Chester, and Bekah at the Four Seasons. And at some point, Alexander and I went to a casino to wait for our flight somewhere with a bar that was still serving. It was exhilarating to take what I had and bet it all. That's what all of this had been about: putting down your money in the crazy hope of winning.

The memories of that night get fuzzier and fuzzier. For the most part. I drank myself into oblivion at the Heritage Society Ball and then stumbled over to the Trump-Forbes Inaugural Afterglow Ball, where I danced among the Trumps, the Forbeses, and an array of less run-of-the-mill conservative donors—the kind who likely were still nervous about being labeled Trump supporters and who had avoided the main Inaugural Ball to keep a low profile.

As fuzzy as my memory of that night is, I do recall one particular image with the clarity of crystal: it was of Bekah Mercer, America's greatest gambler. She was beautiful and dressed in a long, green ball gown, with her ginger hair shining. She looked to me like a mermaid afloat upon a sea of mortals. She danced with us until 2:30 a.m., celebrating her hard-won victory, spinning in circles, drunk with the concept that we had just seen the close of Donald's first day as President Trump.

It was a theatrical enactment of the Mercers' accomplishments. In many ways, they had become a stand-in for the Koch brothers, also big, bad billionaires, but whereas the Koch brothers had created a grassroots network and a basic data company called i360, the Mercers had done something far more powerful, and perhaps more disturbing: they had engineered a victory using a philosophy grounded in very advanced computer science, far more advanced than anything else on offer in the Republican Party. Bob and Bekah Mercer now represented a very new kind of force in American politics: wealthy donors with the money and the wherewithal to use their dollars in measurable, provable ways to make sure their expenditures produced some kind of return on investment. The end result was the creation of a political tool that was ruthless, effective, and, most dangerous of all for democracy, scalable.

14

Bombs

If I was traumatized by what I had learned at the Trump campaign postmortem, I was further shaken by events that followed hard upon it in the first half of 2017.

An article about Cambridge Analytica appeared in *Das Magazin* and went viral in Germany and Switzerland. It was then translated into English by *Vice* and went viral again.[1] The piece was in some ways reminiscent of the *Guardian*'s Facebook takedown from late 2015 in that it introduced into the Cambridge Analytica storyline a character much like Dr. Aleksandr Kogan.

The man's name was Michal Kosinski. Currently a professor at Stanford, he had started out at Cambridge University, at the Psychometrics Centre. In the article, he claimed to have created the psychographic testing that Cambridge Analytica had used in the Trump campaign, and he suggested that Dr. Kogan had stolen it and sold it illicitly to Cambridge. What was worse, Kosinski described the technology itself as a devastating weapon of mass destruction.

Kosinski's story was that he had arrived at the Centre in 2008 from Poland and, as a PhD candidate, had used the Facebook app My Personality (developed, he said, by a colleague named David

Stillwell) to build the first precise models of millions of Facebook users. By 2012, he claimed to have proved that these models could predict quite specific information about people based on only sixty-eight Facebook "likes" an individual user might have garnered. According to the article, he could use those few "likes" to predict skin color, sexual orientation, political party affiliation, drug and alcohol use, and even whether a person had come from an intact or a divorced household. "Seventy 'likes' were enough to outdo what a person's friends knew [about them]; 150 'likes' [and he] 'knew' [about users] what their parents knew; 300 'likes' what their partner knew. More 'likes' could even surpass what a person thought they knew about themselves."

Kosinski's story was a very different version of the one Dr. Aleksandr Kogan had told. Kogan had come to Kosinski in 2014 not with an academic purpose, but with commercial intentions and on behalf of the SCL Group to use Kosinski's database. Kosinski said he'd turned Kogan down because he suspected the request wasn't kosher in some way, and now he'd been proven right: Kogan had procured the data set through underhand and possibly illegal means, and Kosinski's work had been deployed to push both the United Kingdom and the United States to the far right, to sway votes and suppress voting.

Kogan had since slunk off to Singapore, where he was living under an assumed name pulled straight from a bad movie: Dr. Aleksandr Spectre. The bottom line was that Spectre was a criminal and that Cambridge Analytica had dropped an atom bomb on an unsuspecting world.

Once again, as we had done the year before, we at Cambridge tried to brush the article off. Alexander Nix and Alex Tayler seemed unruffled. Who was this Michal Kosinski? They hadn't heard of him, they said, which I found strange, as here he was claiming to be the godfather of psychographics and of the "behavioral microtargeting" work that CA had apparently copyrighted.

In response to the article, the company issued a statement reminiscent of the one from the year before: "Cambridge Analytica does not use data from Facebook," the release said. It also said that Cambridge had had no dealings with Dr. Michal Kosinski. Cambridge "does not subcontract research," we said. "It does not use the same methodology." Furthermore, the company claimed, we had hardly used psychographics in the Trump campaign. What was more, we hadn't done anything at all to suppress voting. Our efforts, the press release said, "were solely directed toward increasing the number of voters."

I was told to think about Kosinski the way I'd been told to think about Kogan: that he was an outlier, a liar, an unaffiliated unknown trying to take credit for CA's "achievements." Perhaps he had done some similar work and was using Trump's victory as a PR opportunity to promote his PhD thesis. I was told to explain to clients that CA had no affiliation to the man, and to leave it at that.

Something didn't feel right to me. Out of all Cambridge Analytica's claims, its "hardly" using psychographics was the biggest stretch for me, as we had done testing in the campaign. The voter suppression denial was yet another problem. After all, some of the Trump super PAC's most disturbing messaging—the "Can't Run Her Own House" and "Superpredators" videos, the latter of which had specifically targeted African American voters in vulnerable areas like rural Georgia and, it would turn out, Little Haiti, in Miami—could be argued to have been suppressive. The idea that all CA had done was aim to "increase" voters was pure bullshit. I'd seen the evidence with my own eyes in the companywide postmortem. After all, they even had target groups they'd labeled "Deterrence."

And Kosinski's claim that Cambridge Analytica had weaponized data? This disturbed me deeply.

I had to figure out what to do. I needed either to find a way to stay at the company and make use of data for the common good, which had been my intention in joining SCL in the first place, or get out somehow.

In this tumultuous moment, I pursued the former idea quietly, by reaching out to social justice and human rights contacts. I saw more clearly than ever that CA might be able to use Big Data to help diplomats manage crises in conflict zones. I brainstormed ways that AI and new language recognition and sentiment analyses could assist us in processing massive amounts of war crimes testimony, finding patterns in it. Perhaps psychographic modeling, which had been deployed on the U.S. population—to, I felt, disastrous effect—could be used to create regime change where it was most needed. I worked with Robert Murtfeld to reach out to Fatou Bensouda, the prosecutor of the International Criminal Court, and the U.S. ambassador-at-large for war crimes, Stephen Rapp, and we began to explore some options.

I tried to take refuge in the bittersweet memory of John Jones, now gone for nearly a year, wishing that I could seek his counsel. Perhaps that's why, in mid-February 2017, when the opportunity to visit with Julian Assange of WikiLeaks arose, I didn't hesitate. Julian, who had been one of John's last clients, was still holed up in the Ecuadorian embassy in London, where he had sought political asylum some five and a half years before. John would often visit him, riding over there on his bike and leaving it unlocked outside; he always joked that there was so much security around the embassy that it was the one place in London where you could leave something without getting it stolen. He would make the joke and then tell me I should go visit Julian with him one day, as he never got enough human contact. Upon John's passing, I thought I would never get to go.

So, when I was extended the coveted invitation, I didn't regard my decision to see Assange as anything close to paradoxical; it was intuitive and deeply personal. While I fully acknowledged that he had a complicated backstory, I had long respected him the way I respected other whistleblowers in recent history. In high school, I'd studied the history of the Vietnam War and learned about and come to respect Daniel Ellsberg, who leaked the Pentagon Papers. And I found Assange's choice to leak documents on the U.S. military's involvement in war crimes in Iraq heroic—in fact, as I've mentioned, I had written my graduate thesis for my LLM (or "master of laws") on war crimes using WikiLeaks's data dumps as my primary source material. And in 2011, when WikiLeaks donations were blocked by major credit card companies, the nonprofit had launched a widget to donate using Bitcoin instead—I donated a couple of hundred dollars' worth in recognition of the research the organization had allowed me to do.

While I was incredibly skeptical of Wikileaks' choice to leak Hillary Clinton's emails during the election, at first I felt there had to have been a reason for the organization to do so. But after there were no explosive revelations, it seemed that this had been done to affect voter perception. I struggled to find a real reason that this had been done. I had now spent almost two years surrounded by anti-Hillary messaging (at every conference I went to, jokingly pasted on the inside of people's cubicles, on the buttons I was handed at Trump speeches), and I was starting to be persuaded. I was becoming numb to the targeted content on my phone, at conferences, and on the screens of my colleagues' computers. As for Assange, I saw him the way I saw Chelsea Manning, another whistleblower, and someone who had suffered for her beliefs in the name of government transparency.

The invitation to see Assange came through a friend of a friend—he told me during a birthday party that Julian was mourning John, as I was, and perhaps it would be good, emotionally, for the two of us to meet. In some way, I saw meeting with him was a way to reach out to someone else who cared about John's legacy and to open, if only for a moment, a portal into the world of human rights that had absolutely been closed to me, it seemed, when John died.

I didn't tell a soul I was going, but I wasn't so naïve that I didn't understand that merely walking in the door of that embassy could put me on any number of watch lists. Still, I felt that my reasons for going were personal, and nobody's business but my own.

The meeting was a mere twenty minutes long, and it took place in a blank-walled room with just white chairs and a table. I was put in the room first, and as I waited for Julian to join me, my mind raced with everything I wanted to tell him. How could I express my gratitude for his bravery?

As he came down the stairs and entered the room, my heart dropped. Sorrow welled up inside me as I realized that he had become a desperate shut-in. He was pure white, almost see-through, as white-haired and white-skinned as he appeared in pictures at the time: clean shaven, but with the life bleached out of him. The sun hadn't touched his skin in more than six years.

He longed for an ear, an audience, at least a friendly one. In our twenty minutes, he did most of the talking. We spoke briefly about John and how we both mourned him, but Julian used the meeting for more of a diatribe than a conversation. He waxed on about the European Union, its strengths and weaknesses, about the Transatlantic Trade and Investment Partnership.

He had been deeply disappointed in Obama, for whom he had once had high hopes but who, Assange said, had surrounded himself with people who'd made poor choices, such as the increase in drone use and actions that had led to civilian casualties abroad. As for Hillary Clinton, he had no love for her at all; Benghazi had been an avoidable tragedy. I agreed with him on this, as I'd had colleagues who died there that day: during my time in Libya, I was preparing to work with Ambassador Christopher Stevens and his team; Stevens and three of them did not survive the attacks. I recalled flying to DC on September 11, 2012, and seeing all the flags at half-staff, and attending memorial ceremonies instead of briefings at the State Department for the remainder of my trip.

None of Assange's opinions about what had happened in Benghazi surprised me, but what did was what he had to say about Trump: he had been, Julian insisted, the right candidate, not Hillary, and the only one without blood on his hands.

Given the direction in which the Trump administration seemed to be going then—Trump's stand on torture, his position on immigration and the wall—this wasn't likely to be true (if it was true at all) for much longer, but at the time of my meeting with Julian, I was relieved to hear him say something good about Trump. The person more likely to start wars and end lives had lost the election, Julian said, and as desperate a reach as it might seem in retrospect now, this gave me some weird feeling of affirmation. I loathed the idea of Trump at the helm of my country, but my ultimate goal was to prevent war. Julian's words were a relief, however fleeting, that I and my choices were possibly moral, still on the side of peace. Perhaps the tone of the campaign would differ from the new president's behavior. Only time would tell.

Whatever the fallout was from Kosinski's attacks on Cambridge in *Das Magazin* and *Vice*, it was minimal. Business was booming for us from the moment Donald Trump was announced as the next U.S. president.

Alexander and Bekah seized the moment to reorganize and re-brand the company. With the Cambridge Analytica name instantly the most visible part of the business, Cambridge absorbed the SCL Group. Under the Cambridge umbrella, Alexander and Bekah created a new division, SCL Gov, which consisted of a tight team of only those with high-level U.S. government security clearance— and to make their intentions even clearer, they took up residence in a brand-new office, around the corner from the Pentagon, in Arlington, from which they would be bent on securing only government and military contracts.

SCL Gov hired two seasoned professionals to run the new division: Josh Weerasinghe, appointed CEO, had an impressive résumé. Among other places, he had worked as director of intelligence for the U.S. Department of Defense in Baghdad; had been deputy policy director for the House Committee on Homeland Security; and had served as the staff director of the House Homeland Security Sub-committee on Prevention of Nuclear and Biological Attack. Chris Dailey became SCL Gov's chief data scientist. He had a background with the navy, working with fleet-level Tomahawk land-attack cruise missile operations and Big Data analytics. The two men were perfectly positioned now to secure contracts with every federal agency, from Defense to HUD.

Meanwhile, Emily Cornell, who had run the MAN1 super PAC during the campaign, took over "CA Political," which she ran out of the office at 1900 Pennsylvania Avenue, spitting distance from the White House and, ironically, sharing a wall with the Mexican embassy. Emily would work with legislators on upcoming bills; begin to cultivate contracts for senatorial, gubernatorial, and congressional campaigns in the 2018 midterms; and hold our spot for the 2020 Trump reelection.

To aid in global expansion, Alexander and Bekah sought out new investors worldwide, individuals who'd bring an influx of cash to the company and also provide SCL Gov with footholds in new countries such as the United Arab Emirates and Hong Kong. Alexander wined and dined billionaires, and as quickly as he could secure their involvement, Julian Wheatland filed documents in the United Kingdom that added them to the company's board of directors.

As Bekah and Alexander were working to put our rapidly expanding company in proximity to the White House, our ties with the young administration were being strengthened elsewhere. While the press focused on how inept the Trump administration seemed in appointing cabinet members, reporters failed to notice the lean, clean, under-the-radar HR machine Bekah was running half out of our New York offices. As she and her team interviewed people for cabinet jobs and negotiated contracts, the Charles Scribner's Sons Building provided cover for those who didn't wish to be seen coming and going from the White House or Trump Tower. In those days, I would often look up from my desk to see a swarm of beefy, heat-packing security guys enter the room and case the office before the arrival of people seeking succor, such as Rick Santorum, or disgruntled rejects such as Chris Christie, who came in to complain that he hadn't gotten the appointment to which he felt entitled for having switched his allegiance so publicly to Trump.

For my part, I wanted out of the States now. Particularly, I hoped to be able to go to Mexico to continue the work I'd begun the year before when I cultivated business deals with both commercial and political clients. I'd closed deals for a number of Mexican gubernatorial elections, and the presidential election in that country was upcoming. Alexander had his eyes on that as well, and I was hopeful that I'd be able to convince him to allow me to open a proper office in Mexico City once I came back from an early January business trip in 2017.

But it wasn't to be. Alexander wanted me in London, where I could help out, he said, with incoming SCL Commercial and SCL Political contracts. They were understaffed there in sales. A new head of SCL Global had come in: a fellow by the name of Mark Turnbull, and I'd be working under him—though I certainly wished that if I were going to be making another move, Alexander had considered promoting me.

Mark was less posh than Alexander, older, clearly of a different social class than he, rougher hewn. I quite liked him, though. He had spent decades running elections, including the first democratic elections in Iraq after the fall of Saddam Hussein, and he knew a lot about defense operations and conducting communications in the face of adversity for both the military and political party elections. As much as I resented not having been promoted, I was looking forward to working under Mark and learning from him. And moving back to London at least represented an out from the nastiness of the United States. It also gave me an opportunity to reconnect with Tim, whom I was still dating. In other words, I looked on the sunny side of things, and though I still dreamed every night of Mexico and occasionally traveled back there to train the new people Alexander had hired to run my contracts without me, it looked like London would be home for the time being.

It was in those busy early weeks of Trump's presidency that Russia became a more frequent topic among us at CA. Though the press was focused on Russia even before Trump had a chance to take a seat in the Oval Office, our group had largely dismissed the early reporting. In the Cambridge office, it wasn't unusual to hear the term *fake news* invoked, in part, I think, because we Cambridge employees felt that the Russians' efforts either had been made up by those who couldn't accept Hillary's crushing defeat or, perhaps, had been negligible when compared with our own. Cambridge Analytica, and not some outside government, had secured Trump's presidency, we believed, and the focus on Russia was considered disruptive to the new administration in whose success the company was deeply invested.

Of course, Russian influence on the election was of great concern in intelligence circles, and quickly this "fake news" grew harder to ignore. Mere weeks after Trump took office, it became clear that the actions of Trump's national security adviser, Michael Flynn, had led to a much higher level of scrutiny of the Trump-Russia relationship. Flynn, who had contacted Russian ambassador to the United States Sergey Kislyak during the transition to discuss the sanctions Obama had put in place in response to Russia's election interference in 2016, was eventually revealed to have lied to the FBI about his conversations with the Russians. And Trump campaign chairman Paul Manafort's ties to Ukrainian oligarchs and, potentially, to Russia had led in part to the decision to replace him with Steve Bannon in August of the year before. Soon, Flynn was out, a departure that would have ripple effects far bigger than anyone could have foreseen.

In mid-February 2017, not long after Flynn was removed as national security adviser, I was in the UK office—we had a new and bigger one now, on New Oxford Street. Alexander wasn't in that day, and I was retrieving something from his office when I spied a book on his shelf of so-called fascist literature, the one he'd pointed to jokingly during my interview with him back in 2014. Nestled in with books by Ann Coulter and Nigel Farage was one by Michael Flynn. I hadn't known Flynn had put out a book. It was recent, published in 2016, and was titled *Field of Fight: How We Can Win the Global War Against Radical Islam and Its Allies.*

Given that Flynn's name had been in the headlines just days before, I picked it up. My intention was to leaf through it, but I stopped short at the title page, which was covered with Flynn's handwriting: it was an inscription to Alexander, a voluminous and clearly personal dedication explaining the importance of what they had just done together. My eyes were drawn to the bottom of what Flynn had written in enormous, loopy letters:

We Made America Great Again Together!

I froze.

We? What had Flynn meant by that? Had he and Alexander or Cambridge Analytica worked together more than I thought? From what I understood, he was consulting to SCL, as Alexander celebrated his appointment (an obvious direct route to government and military contracts) and mourned his firing. The very recent firing of Flynn and this inscription made the hair on the back of my neck stand up. I didn't want to be seen standing there reading it, so I contemplated taking a snapshot of the page, but then thought better of it. Doing so would have made me look suspicious. Still shaking, and not bothering to read any of the contents, I put the book back on the shelf and made my way out of the room as fast as I could.

How much did I not know? How much was Alexander hiding? How much had I chosen not to see?

Quite a bit, as it would turn out.

In late February, Julian and Alexander called me into the office. The Information Commissioner's Office (ICO), a public body that deals with how information and data are handled in the United Kingdom, had launched a criminal investigation into Cambridge Analytica's involvement in Brexit. Leave.EU had filed its campaign spending report, and in it was no mention of payment made to Cambridge

Analytica for its services. Such reporting was required by British law, and the ICO wanted to know precisely what CA's involvement had been.

For me, Cambridge's involvement with Leave.EU had been very clear. I had had numerous meetings with Arron Banks and his motley team. With Arron's blessing and with the agreement of Matthew Richardson (the UKIP secretary who also strangely acted as our legal counsel), I had procured both membership data and survey answers from UKIP, and our data scientists had modeled them to come up with target audience segmentation. While I hadn't handed over the physical results of that work to Leave.EU, I had presented them in a briefing with Leave.EU's executive team and then in a televised panel. This was followed by another day of work with the team in London. Dr. David Wilkinson, one of our senior data scientists, and I had then traveled to Bristol to meet with and brief UKIP's campaign staff (aka employees at the offices of Eldon Insurance) about our work and begin an audit of their on-the-ground operation. That had been phase one of our work for Leave.EU, and as far as I knew, no, Arron Banks had neither paid Cambridge Analytica for it nor continued to work with us after that.

Alexander and Julian explained to me the problem as they saw it: We, and others, had spoken about our work in public. Alexander had directed one of our in-house people to craft a press release announcing the work, that press release had been covered in the news, and Leave.EU itself had posted about our working together on its website—and that information was still online. Arron Banks had even written about the partnership in his recently published book, *The Bad Boys of Brexit*. Also, I had discussed it in interviews with Bloomberg, PR Newswire, and other news services.

All that, Alexander said, had just been overzealousness on our part. We, and Leave.EU, had been so excited about potentially working together that we'd all jumped the gun. We had benefited from the press, but now it was time to walk it back.

"And, well, luckily," Alexander added, "no work was done."

What? I thought. "But we *did* do work," I said. "We did work but just never got paid for it."

"Well," Alexander said, "we never got paid because it was all over-glorified. You," he said, "spent too much time and money pitching."

I turned to Julian. "But you sent them an invoice. For work we did." Julian had even offered to keep the money in escrow, if Leave.EU preferred, but Arron had never ponied up.

I turned to Alexander. "We *did work*," I said.

"No," Alexander said, "because we didn't give them data."

"We did *orally*," I said. We'd shared it with them; we'd delivered it orally.

"But we didn't *physically* give them the data," Alexander said. "We didn't even do much work. We didn't change the world or anything."

"Technically, we didn't do the work," Julian added, "because we never signed a contract, and the work wasn't usable."

"It *was* usable," I said. The segmentation had shown impressive insights from the UKIP data, and I had no reason to think that Leave.EU hadn't gone on to take the audience groups we'd provided them orally, at the very least, and use much of the advice we'd given after working with them for three days in a row at such an important time in the campaign.

"But we didn't give them anything, really," Alexander insisted. "Maybe they *took* it. But we didn't *give* it."

I thought I was going insane. Why were they protecting Leave.EU? Why would they try to cover this up? We could get hit up for an electoral spending violation ourselves.

"A questionnaire has come in from the ICO," they told me, on Google Docs. They wanted me to fill it out. And they'd "collaborate" on it, making sure my answers were correct.

They wanted me to lie.

"There are not any laws against lying," Alexander said. "And, besides, what we're doing is *correcting the narrative*."

It's an old saw: it's not the crime, it's the coverup. By covering up the fact that we'd done any work at all for Leave.EU, however small, I knew we'd be making a complicated situation far worse.

I wanted to tell the truth. So, in the questionnaire, I told the story as I had experienced it, but I also told it as Alexander and Julian directed me. I explained that when we were in contact with Leave.EU, we were hoping to get a bigger contract but hadn't. That, at least, was true.

I felt shitty about prevaricating, but I didn't want to lose my job, so I didn't tell a soul. What was behind their insistence that I change the narrative? Something bigger than I was, and even bigger than Alexander. Something, perhaps, to do with Steve Bannon and his relationship to Arron and Nigel? I could only guess. As it was, the ICO's investigation determined there was "no evidence of a working relationship between [Cambridge Analytica] and Leave.EU proceeding beyond this initial phase."[2]

A few days later, on a Saturday, an investigative journalist named Carole Cadwalladr published an article in the *Guardian* that took a long, hard look at what she alleged was a connection between Cambridge Analytica, Leave.EU, and Robert Mercer. Coming hot on the heels of the *Das Magazin* piece, which had slightly rattled Cambridge's cage with claims that we had stolen user data and weaponized it to unethical ends, the Cadwalladr article was a hard blow.

Cadwalladr's article focused on campaign spending issues in general, including a potential violation even by Vote Leave, the Brexit

campaign that had won the designation over Leave.EU. But she la-
sered in particularly on Cambridge and Leave.EU.

Unfortunately, Andy Wigmore, who presented himself as communications director of Leave.EU, had granted Cadwalladr an
interview and discussed what seemed like even more nefarious connections: While in June 2016, in the days leading up to the vote, he
had said that Leave.EU hadn't used Cambridge Analytica, now he
was doing an about-face. Why was anyone's guess. Nigel Farage and
the Mercer family, Wigmore now said, had had "shared goals." What
the Mercers were interested in doing in the United States was parallel to what Farage wanted to do in the United Kingdom. Wigmore
had introduced Farage to Cambridge Analytica. "They were happy
to help," he said, "because Nigel is a good friend of the Mercers."
Cambridge and Leave.EU, Wigmore said, had "shared a lot of information."

In response to the article, Alexander issued a company statement:
"We are in touch with the ICO," the statement read, "and are happy
to demonstrate that we are completely compliant with UK and EU
data law."

But not everyone was satisfied. The Brexit vote had been the most
consequential in British history, and Parliament now wanted Cambridge Analytica to offer better answers as to how an American billionaire had gotten his fingerprints all over it.

I wasn't happy, either. In her article, Cadwalladr freely mentioned
me, attributing me with far more authority and power in the company than I actually had. The article suddenly made me once again
the face of Cambridge Analytica and Brexit—exactly what I'd never
intended to happen.

"You take Britain, and I'll take the Americans," Alexander had
said to me when he'd asked me to do him the favor of presenting at
Leave.EU's public panel on Brexit, and it had seemed at the time like

old friends splitting the check at lunch. I'd agreed to pay my half, as it were, but when you stopped to look at the outcome, it seemed that I was the one now accountable for the entire cost of the meal. In the article, Alexander's name wasn't even mentioned, and Cadwalladr attributed the statement he'd issued to her to merely a "company spokesman."

By April, the problem still hadn't died down, and the Electoral Commission announced that it was going to make a thorough inquiry into campaign spending during Brexit. Vote Leave would be looked at as well, but the real focus would be on an invoice for £41,500 that Arron Banks had apparently still not paid Cambridge for work we had—or, according to Alexander, *had not*—done.

Alexander sent out a curious email to Julian Wheatland; our head of global PR, Nick Fievet; Kieran, our director of communications; and me. It was copied to UKIP secretary Matthew Richardson. The subject line read, "Electoral Commission Investigation."

"Dear All," it began, and then laid out the sticky situation for us once more. The launch of the investigation had put us in a pickle. Things had moved beyond the ICO's simple little questionnaire. Still, we hadn't done any work for Leave.EU, Alexander wrote, so we had nothing to worry about. However, he said, there was a great deal of press out there, including some of which we'd generated ourselves in-house, that indicated that we *had* worked for Leave.EU. He pointed to the unfortunate press release he had directed Harris McCloud to send out:

Recently, Cambridge Analytica has teamed up with Leave.EU—
the UK's largest group advocating for a British exit (or "Brexit") from the
European Union—to help them better understand and communicate
with UK voters. We have already helped supercharge Leave.EU's
social media campaign by ensuring the right messages are getting to

the right voters online, and the campaign's Facebook page is growing in support to the tune of about 3,000 people per day. And we're just getting started!

He also once again referenced the interview I'd given to PR Newswire right after the public panel on Brexit in November 2015. "She said the firm's team of data scientists and analysts, some of whom were based full-time in the UK, would be enabling targeted messaging."

And again, Alexander broached the prospect of lying. He felt we ought to "establish the narrative" in order to "mitigate loss of credibility." There were three "facts" we needed to assert: "(1) We were in discussions with Leave.EU about the possibility of working for them; (2) Whilst these discussions were underway we agreed to share a platform with them / issue a press release—on the assumption, that we would indeed start working together" and "(3) We did not end up working together."

He wondered if we might be able to get control of the situation by saying that we had somehow "got ahead of ourselves," or that "our PR division had received mis-information from the operations team about the status of the project." And then he asked us all for feedback, which it didn't seem he really wanted, considering what he'd just laid out.

He added a postscript, wondering if we might be able to consider anything we'd done for the Leave.EU campaign not as a donation but as something he referred to as "goodwill," which I was pretty certain didn't exist in politics.

Meanwhile, Carole Cadwalladr of the *Guardian* continued to beat the bushes for a conspiracy. She was determined to find a smoking gun somewhere, and she became ever more focused on me, continuing to believe, erroneously, that I was the person who'd pulled its trigger.

In early May, she emailed me directly. (Why she hadn't gotten in touch directly before was beyond me, but now I assumed she'd finally guessed at my email address and sent a shot in the dark.) The subject line of her email was "Press Inquiry." We'd never met before, so she introduced herself—as if it were possible that I'd never heard of her, even though she had been starting to ruin my life for several months by that point. "Leave.EU is now saying that Cambridge Analytica did no work for it during the referendum campaign. I would like to give you the opportunity to explain your presence on the panel at the Leave.EU launch event on November 18, 2015."

I was beyond angry.

So, now either Andy Wigmore or Arron Banks (or both) was denying that Cambridge Analytica had worked with them. Nigel Farage might have been in on it, too. And because everyone was denying it, it had become a problem. I was angry that Alexander and Julian had insisted that we skirt around the details in our response to the ICO. I forwarded Cadwalladr's email to our PR guy Nick.

"Please take this one and advise me," I asked bluntly, knowing that all this had been avoidable.

But Nick didn't have anything useful to say. And when Carole Cadwalladr didn't hear back from me, she teamed up with an American freelance journalist named Ann Marlowe, who'd written pieces for the *Village Voice* and who had also begun to look at Cambridge Analytica's role in elections on the U.S. side of the pond. In August 2016, Marlowe had done an investigative piece for *Tablet* magazine in which she went on a fishing expedition to find some sort of connection between SCL and Paul Manafort's Ukrainian business dealings. What she came up with in her research (a former SCL shareholder with ties to Ukraine) had made more smoke than fire.[3] Her only conclusion was that the world ought to be "paying closer attention to who owns companies collecting data on American voters."

Now, Carole and Ann began to tweet back and forth with each other, and what they said in 140 characters was accusatory and damning about me, spreading misinformation. Alexander did nothing to help. I pleaded with him to get a PR firm to come in to handle the situation, but he wouldn't do it. For a man whose bread and butter was crafting messaging strategies for a living, he was horrible at laying out money to pay someone else to do it for him, even when he needed it desperately. He was cocky, believing that he himself, through his infinite charm, could solve any PR problem that might arise, but he failed with this one. The messenger had lost control of his own message.

I was deeply unhappy, and I felt betrayed. Now even my British friends either looked askance at me or considered me a pariah. And I felt like a pariah sometimes.

Alexander had brought me back to the United Kingdom to do global commercial work, but meetings with potential clients were often distasteful. One, for example, was with an international tobacco company. They wanted very much to pivot and get their addicted smokers to discover their newest product, vape pens, but the challenge was finding how legally (or extralegally) to promote them. As in America, the advertisement of cigarettes is illegal on many platforms. So, the company wanted us to find a workaround, some way to strategically veil the true purpose of the ad and lead potential customers to their site and messaging via click-throughs that started with something more innocuous than tobacco or nicotine.

Shortly after I was asked to strategically edit my response to the ICO, I'd gotten a message on LinkedIn from someone named Paul Hilder. Paul had an impressive résumé. He was a writer, a political organizer, and a social entrepreneur who believed that Big Data could be used to power grassroots movements. Though British born, he had spent much of 2016 embedded in the Bernie Sanders campaign, and he had found me, strangely enough, via a video in which I made a brief and impromptu cameo and which someone at Cambridge had posted online.

The video was part of a strange phenomenon: one of our data scientists had been keeping a vlog on YouTube, chronicling his life, including his work at Cambridge, for 365 days. One of his videos was of a company party that took place in the summer of 2015 at a dog track in London. The video would later become rather infamous because, in it, one of my colleagues toasted Alexander, saying of him that he was the sort of person "who could sell an anchor to a drowning man," a less-than-complimentary comment that would outlive even the company, but what Paul had noticed was something else.

The video was filmed during the company's involvement in the Cruz campaign, and at one point that afternoon someone on the Cambridge Cruz team had yelled out, "Who's going to win the election?" and I had been the lone voice that called out Bernie Sanders's name.

That's how Paul had found me.

He'd likely googled the SCL Group, because he was in the midst, like so many other people, of trying to understand what had happened in the United Kingdom and the States and to chart a way forward. He had long been an advocate of the left's use of social media as a means to organize and had founded something called Crowdpac, a grassroots alternative to super PACs. He'd also been involved in founding Avaaz, an organization I had paid attention to and admired because it was one of the most widely used petition platforms in the campaigning world. What was more, he had worked as a campaign director for a UK peace party during the Iraq War; had been a candidate for general secretary of the Labour Party; and, in 2016, had called for a new English Labour Party altogether.

I wasn't quite sure what Paul wanted with me. We spoke on the phone while I was in Mexico doing a hand-off of contracts. While turning the projects over to the two people Alexander had chosen to do that work, I found both of them profoundly unprepared. One was Laura Hilger, whose primary experience in elections had been while working in Trump Tower. She had little idea what it was like to work in politics on the ground in rural Mexico. The other was Christian Morato, who had claimed to speak Spanish but couldn't really and who had even less election experience than Laura. But he was a former Green Beret, so Alexander had taken a liking to him.

What I was turning over to them was something in which I'd been invested for a year. One contract was for the gubernatorial elections in the state of Mexico and three other states; the other was for potential work with one of the biggest media companies in the Spanish-speaking world, Cultura Colectiva. I had been cultivating the company, and the plan was for CA to partner with it, undertake OCEAN surveys in Spanish, and do content creation.

My phone call with Paul Hilder while in Mexico was a breath of fresh air because I was so distrustful of Laura and Christian's ability to handle the work and also because I had grown so bitter about so much at Cambridge over the past months. I couldn't tell what Paul wanted, but I liked him very much. He seemed smart and interesting, and we agreed to meet up when I was back in London.

At our first lunch, at a restaurant a few minutes away from the London office, I learned that he wanted a variety of things. One was to learn what Cambridge did. He wanted this in part so that he could finish writing an article for *Prospect* magazine about Big Data, Brexit, and Trump, and in part to see how what CA did might be applicable both to the new Labour Party he wanted to form and to other liberal endeavors. His third interest was in me: how could a Bernie supporter have ended up at a place like Cambridge Analytica?

I wasn't terribly careful about what I shared with Paul. I didn't violate the company's NDA, but I treated him as though he were a client inquiring about our services, which, in part, he was—at least potentially. I shared with him the same kinds of things I'd have shared in any normal pitch: what our capacities were, what our analytics and psychographics could do and had done. And I explained to him why I had originally come to work at Cambridge, the social programs I'd seen myself being a part of, and how that dream had slipped away.

He wondered if I could imagine a life beyond SCL and Cambridge. Whenever I was ready to take the leap, he said, there were progressive causes waiting.

I saw him for several dinners after that. He was interested in what the company had done in Nigeria and Kenya, about Buhari and the Kenyatta family, and if CA's work in Africa had been as aboveboard as it seemed on the surface—the same concerns I had.

Soon, I no longer saw him as a potential client. I knew he likely didn't have the need for or interest in Cambridge's services, and even though I told myself that perhaps he knew someone who might become a client, and that I ought to keep cultivating the contact for business purposes, in truth, I thought that I might someday have a chance to work with him.

He reminded me of John Jones. And he seemed an ally, a compatriot, and just possibly my first liberal friend in years.

Otherwise, England felt like a trap. Carole Cadwalladr of the *Guardian* simply wouldn't let the subject of me and Brexit go. Still, the American scene was no better.

In April, Cambridge won a prestigious advertising award for the very video the super PAC had made that I hated, the "Can't Run Her

Own House" campaign with Michelle Obama. The very idea of it was perverse to me. In May, Special Counsel Robert Mueller began his investigation of Russian meddling in the 2016 election, and at the beginning of June, when I told Alexander that I was supposed to go to a friend's wedding, which happened to be in Russia, he freaked out. While no one at Cambridge had seemed bothered before by anything to do with Russia, something about it was clearly rattling Alexander.

Upon finding out about my impending trip, he sent me an email, copying Mark Turnbull. I wasn't to take any Cambridge Analytica business cards with me, he warned. As if that wasn't enough, he called me and commanded: "Don't do any meetings, either. Just go there. Just drink your champagne. Have a dance. Have a nice time. And come home." I did just that, but of course I began to wonder why he seemed so shaken.

When I returned, Alexander had gotten bad news from Mexico. While the candidate we had supported in one of the gubernatorial races had won, Laura and Christian had badly mismanaged the campaign and CA's involvement in it.

Alexander told me I had to go down there and sort it out.

I was curious how long I'd be there.

"Until you've fixed it," he said.

15

Quake

The previous two and a half years had exhausted me. I wasn't even thirty yet, and I felt ancient. I hadn't slept or eaten properly in ages; I'd stopped exercising and had gone up three or four dress sizes; and the endless plane travel had exacerbated my scoliosis, a lifelong condition for which I'd had life-altering surgery and which, when badly managed, brought me endless pain. Now I was in Mexico City, and for the first time in a long time, things slowed down. In the mornings, I awoke to sunshine; and in the evenings, as the city cooled down, so did I. I was away from the United States, where I'd burned my bridges, away from the United Kingdom, where I'd been burned. And I was in one of the most beautiful places on earth.

Alexander had sent me to Mexico to secure a contract in the up-coming presidential elections and to get control over CA's other commercial business there, so I was living in a corporate apartment in Polanco, the fanciest neighborhood in Mexico City, on a peaceful street. The place had floor-to-ceiling windows and a wrought iron balcony that looked out upon a row of palm trees. For the first time in a long while, I was truly happy.

Being in Mexico, catching my breath even for a moment, helped bring things into stark relief for me. I knew I wanted out; that much was clear. But I wasn't about to up and leave with no plan. For one thing, I couldn't. I'd been sending money home to help my parents, mostly for the multiple units storing what was left of our family home, but also to help make ends meet when needed. My sister shared her salary; indeed, our parents had come to appreciate the helping hand. With my father's health deteriorating, none of us could afford to have that security disappear.

More than just the paycheck, something larger was preventing me from quitting Cambridge, despite my increasing disgust with the work we'd done, the manner in which we'd done it, and how I was now being asked to account for my role in that work. As much as the work had come to disturb me, Cambridge was a company that I'd helped to build—for better or, at this point, for worse. I'd been undercompensated for much of what I'd done, with the understanding that one day, after the company had reached a new threshold of success, there would be equity in it for me. From my earliest time with SCL, Alexander had talked about the company as though it were a Silicon Valley start-up—it was his unicorn.

And after the 2016 election, it seemed that that rhetoric was becoming a reality. Despite the investigations and the negative press, we were now sought after the world over. As much as I was prepared to leave, I wasn't about to jump ship right as the company was coming to realize the kind of success I'd been envisioning since first coming aboard. I'd already sacrificed so many of my values for Cambridge; to walk away empty-handed would be the worst insult of all.

But just because I was biding my time until the company's larger success was realized, it didn't mean I wasn't plotting my exit. In fact, in the weeks immediately following the 2016 election postmortem, I'd been working on an idea with my old friend Chester, one that would allow me to leave Cambridge behind for good while still building on my experience in the data economy. He, too, had grown tired of affiliating with Alexander after he had made multiple successful introductions to clients and investors—and Alexander paid him a grand total of $0.

So in early 2017, Chester and I made strong efforts to be introduced into the "blockchain technology" crowd, a group of wide-eyed and optimistic technologists, cryptographers, libertarians, and anarchists who saw data security, ownership of one's own assets and information, and even the management of one's own currencies outside a bank as of ultimate importance. It was an exciting time in that industry, which involved an emerging and disruptive technology that, in addition to many other uses, enabled people to take control over their own data with ethical technology built on transparency, consent, and trust.

A "blockchain" is a public database or ledger, decentralized across hundreds or thousands of computers around the world that validate transactions and record them, so that no one central authority can edit or delete any data. Among other things, users can store and encrypt data safely and track its transfer transparently. Every transaction is recorded publicly, and once enough transactions are gathered, they are put into one "block" of data that is "chained" to every other block of data since the platform's inception. In order to edit a transaction, someone would need to hack every block ever made before that transaction, which has never been done.

My eyes were open, and I was listening.

I had known about the underlying technology of blockchain for a while; the earliest solution was Bitcoin. I'd first heard about Bitcoin in 2009—some of my human rights friends were tipping one another with it (sending Bitcoin as a thank-you for work or information) when running underground operations to move North Korean refugees out of harm's way and to a place that would give them asylum. What made blockchain so revolutionary was that it was a completely new "electronic cash system that was fully peer-to-peer, with no trusted third party," so, at the time, it was an ideal way to provide value without being tracked by governments.[1]

Now, so many years later, I had seen Big Data exploit users; I'd seen how it could be toxic enough to alter the very basis of democracy in both the United States and Britain. Blockchain appealed to me as a way to redemocratize information and turn the old models upside down. As Chester and I began talking about using data science and connectivity-focused blockchain technology, we knew we would need a lot more expertise than we both currently had.

So, we got started on our global networking spree, looking for the best and the brightest minds around. Luckily, a group of the top technologists in the field were gathering for the wedding of Brock Pierce, one of the industry's titans, and Crystal Rose, a data sovereignty thought leader, in Ibiza. We were told by a new friend, Wiley Matthews, also a former savant of data-driven advertising, that if we flew there, we were sure to meet some of them. We did, and within the first twelve hours on land, we met many of the top people in the industry, most notably, Craig Sellars, one of the founders of Tether, the first stable coin pegged to the U.S. dollar; and Matt McKibbin, cofounder of both D10E, a blockchain conference series, and DecentraNet, one of the first blockchain advisory firms. We also met a slew of fascinating people involved in everything from blockchain-funded space projects to digital banking services for the unbanked rural populations.

Chester and I walked away from the experience on a high. The potential in the field was vast, but even more invigorating was how blockchain seemed to represent the perfect off-ramp for my time at Cambridge. Tech-driven, built around ideas of data security, it was an ideal next step, an act of both personal and professional penance.

If I figured out how to make it work, I could, once the Mexican presidential campaign was secured, I told myself, be gone from Cambridge for good. I'd secure a lucrative contract for the company, make a good commission, and then say *adios* to Cambridge Analytica and hello to a technology based on principles I had forgotten about for far too long.

Mexican presidential elections are different from those in the United States. I had learned about them back in 2015, when my friends and business partners in Mexico City began contacting me to help them with the 2018 elections. I had a team do some research to prepare me to make a pitch one day soon. In Mexico, the elections start early and are a huge deal, because presidents serve only one six-year term. Potential candidates for the next term compete in a primary-like process that involves the voting not of the general populace but, instead, of party insiders. And the political scene in Mexico is made more complex by the fact that there are multiple parties of note, not just two.

When I first arrived in Mexico City, I began productive meetings with PRI (Partido Revolucionario Institucional), the party of Mexico's sitting president, Enrique Peña Nieto. PRI was known as the most powerful force both within and outside Mexico. It was still early in the primary season, and I had time to secure the contract and create a solid infrastructure at SCL Mexico to carry out a consequential national campaign.

Despite the fact that we had backed candidates in the gubernatorial races in Mexico, we didn't have the infrastructure in place. Our two team members had been able to query focus groups and do basic research, but they hadn't built a database of any helpful size or relevance, and they'd been unable to do any proper modeling or targeting.

When I arrived, I set out to assemble the database and create a dream team of young professionals, from both inside Mexico and out—researchers and creatives, pollsters and data scientists, radio and television producers, and social media influencers—to support a winning effort.

As a U.S. citizen, I found it a fraught time to do business in Mexico, commercial or governmental—never mind at the presidential level. Trump had demonized the very people with whom I was going to work, and my success with clients required caution, humility, apology, diplomacy, and patience. That I was able to make any progress at all was surprising because not only was Trump a challenge, but so was Alexander.

Since Trump's win, Alexander had developed an inflated ego and a swagger and confidence that didn't do him any favors abroad. He had always, I felt, lacked basic respect for those from non-English-speaking countries, had always viewed work in those places as something to which he and SCL were entitled. And for him, Mexico seemed yet another territory to conquer, its people exploitable. He fashioned himself a white savior whose means of rescuing Mexicans from the morass of their underdevelopment was, of course, the technology his company could provide them. Data would elevate them. Data would bring them into the modern world. And it was his job to conquer, convert, and colonize them.

Even though I always had fun with him, I was more nervous than excited whenever he visited. His trips to Mexico were infrequent but memorable, as they often left clients with the impression that he was an elite stooping to work with them. What was distasteful to me as well was the wink-wink, nudge-nudge attitude with which he ingratiated himself with the locals, an approach that seemed to suggest that he understood the way things in Mexico *really* worked, and he often intimated that he was more than comfortable with the under-the-table dealings, corruption, and corner-cutting that he presumed were rampant there.

This was his modus operandi throughout his career, though; something I first discovered in a meeting with Mexican nationals whom we were pitching for a campaign. Alexander had come to Mexico with his laptop and his usual PowerPoint presentation, but when he got to the part where he covered case studies of the campaigns he had run in other countries, I was horrified to hear how he described them. Indeed, many of his accounts were profoundly different from those I had heard before, and deeply troubling.

His slide show began with Indonesia. The narrative of SCL's campaign in that country in 1999 no longer included the empowerment of students but, rather, the manipulation of them. While before I had heard him use language describing how SCL had *helped* to bring about a prodemocracy movement in Jakarta, now SCL had effectively *created* that movement. From SCL's high-tech op center in Jakarta, the company, he claimed, had spent eighteen months orchestrating massive student rallies that otherwise wouldn't have occurred and had incited demonstrations that spilled out into the streets and had led to the resignation of the long-ruling dictator, Suharto.

It had been a crafty and complex operation, Alexander boasted. Indonesia was a massive country, the seventh-largest in the world, an archipelago spread out among more than three hundred islands. Given the challenge of messaging across those islands, and the backdrop of the 1999 Asian financial crisis, SCL had had to work to calm an entire population of Indonesians who were terribly anxious when the only leader they had known for years stepped down. People feared the instability that Suharto's resignation would bring to the country, and SCL had anticipated this as it carried out the second phase of its operation: a propaganda campaign that reassured the nation that life without Suharto was "a positive development." Finally, in SCL's third phase, it had run the election campaign for Abdurrah-man Wahid, who, Alexander said, in an uncomfortably light and un-apologetic aside, turned out to be far more corrupt than Suharto.[2]

The next set of slides covered SCL's first presidential election cam-paign in Nigeria, one that preceded the 2015 debacle. In the earlier 2007 campaign, Umaru Musa Yar'Adua, the incumbent, was so fear-ful of losing the election that he planned to steal it. "In Nigeria, the presidency is meant to be handed around," Alexander said, so stealing the election would have been widely unpopular had Nigerians discov-ered it. SCL therefore convinced Yar'Adua to be proactive. He would indeed steal the election, but SCL would leak his plan intentionally, and far in advance of Voting Day, so that by the time he was reelected, the illegitimacy of the election wouldn't bother anyone anymore. In other words, SCL "inoculated" the public against their own concerns by allowing them to process the information over a long period.

I had never heard Alexander say anything like this before, and I was shocked. One of my dream jobs had been to be an election monitor at the United Nations or the Carter Center, precisely to prevent this type of underhanded behavior. Indeed, Jimmy Carter himself had been part of overseeing that particular election. Elec-tion observers from the European Union described that election as the worst they had ever seen anywhere in the world, but by the time both they and Carter publicly declared the election process not to have been free and fair, Yar'Adua was already in office, and no one in Nigeria cared any longer, Alexander said, smiling broadly.

"You know," he explained to the men in the room—and they were always men—and using that condescending and complicit wink-wink I found so distasteful, "if you walk in on your wife fucking an-other man, you'll blow his head off." But, he went on, if you learn slowly over time that she's having an affair, you're far less likely to resort to violence.

SCL had been able to do this very thing in Nigeria: parse out the information early to dull its effect. "We put the information out through rumors and social media," he explained. Through YouTube and Myspace. "It was also the first year of Facebook," he said, implying that it had finally gone global and was useful in foreign elections. And one of the great successes about the campaign was that there was "minimal violence" leading up to and after Voting Day.

The next slides were about a mayoral race in Bogotá, Colombia, in 2011. Every candidate running for mayor was absolutely corrupt. Hated, in fact, Alexander explained. They were "all cheats, all stealers, all liars," in the public's opinion, according to the polling SCL had done. Most Colombians had already decided they weren't going to vote for anyone, they were so disgusted with them all, so SCL had used a clever strategy in that country as well.

"We persuaded our candidate," Alexander said, "to run a campaign that didn't feature him at all."

Colombians have huge egos, he said, "so it was difficult to convince" the candidate to play along, but eventually he did. And "instead of putting up a thousand pictures of the candidate that were thirty feet high that said 'Vote for Me,'" Alexander explained, SCL went to every neighborhood in every *barrio* and found respected people who we were able to convince to endorse the man. Speaking to "doctors, teachers, restaurant owners, shopkeepers," SCL convinced them to give a quote and their photograph. The company then put up three thousand different posters of three thousand different people, with their photos and their words of support for the corrupt candidate, within a five-block radius.

"People change people," Alexander said. That's how influence works. Each of these three thousand trusted individuals, pillars of their community, became the campaign's spokespeople. "It was a really good campaign. Really effective," he said.

The next slides were about Kenya, 2013. That's where Alexander had lived with his family and had done the work himself. SCL's client, presidential candidate Uhuru Kenyatta, wanted to disassociate himself from the Kenya African National Union, or KANU, the party of his father, former president Jomo Kenyatta, because his father "had arrived in office poor and left with a million dollars." The Kenyan people had therefore associated KANU with corruption, so SCL had to create an entirely new party under whose umbrella the son could run.

It wasn't a simple process. SCL couldn't be seen to be behind it; nor could the candidate. "So, we did research," Alexander said. Kenya was "very tribal"—at least Kenyan elders were. The youth were not; they were rebellious against the old ways and felt disenfranchised.

"So, we made it a youth movement." The new party was called the TNA, or the National Alliance.

In an operation similar to the one in Indonesia but beginning in a way that wasn't overtly connected to anything political, SCL spent eight months creating massive events to bring together Kenya's youth—"Football matches, music festivals, initiatives to clean up villages," Alexander said. By the time they were finished, the TNA "movement" had two million followers.

Next, SCL orchestrated a youth rally, the largest rally in the history of East Africa, Alexander claimed. And at it, SCL seeded the crowd with the chant "We want Kenyatta. We want Kenyatta." Kenyatta, Alexander said, feigned surprise at the youth support. He left his father's party, KANU, for the TNA, and when he did, the youth supported him, but so did his father's supporters from KANU.

SCL then staged a de facto election, and Kenyatta ran as the TNA candidate and won.

"So, we created that party," Alexander explained. "We created everything. We created a need that didn't exist," and we provided

Kenyatta as the solution. "We were down there for sixteen months or something," he said. "That party still exists today," he added proudly.

The pièce de résistance of the case studies Alexander presented in Mexico was Trinidad and Tobago. I had heard the story on the very first day I visited the SCL offices in London, in October 2014. Back then, the story was about the creation of a youth movement, the empowerment of young people to make choices. But now, in Mexico, the story took a sinister turn.

"Trinidad," Alexander told the potential clients, is a tiny country, only 1.3 million people. He pulled up an image of the country on the screen. What SCL did there, he said, would give the Mexican clients an idea of the company's innovative thinking.

He then gave a blow-by-blow account of the work, moving in and out of the past and present tense, as if narrating a sporting event.

"There are two main parties. One for the blacks and one for the Indians," he said. "And all the Indians vote for the Indian party and the blacks . . . well, you know. And when the Indians are in power, the blacks don't get anything, and when the blacks are in power, it's vice versa. They screw each other," he said.

SCL was working for the Indian Party.

He continued: "So, we say to our candidate, we only want to do one thing—wanted to target the youth—*all* the youth, the blacks and all the Indians, and we try to increase apathy." He explained that the candidate didn't really understand why, but went ahead and allowed SCL to work its magic.

You see, "we had done research," Alexander said, "out of which two important insights arose. The first was that *all* the youth in the country felt disenfranchised—the Indians and the blacks alike." The second insight was that only among the Indians, but not the blacks, were "family hierarchies strong." And that, he added, "was enough information to inform the entire campaign."

He paused and pulled up another slide.

As in Nigeria, the campaign had to be nonpolitical because "kids didn't care about politics," Alexander said. "It had to be reactive . . . exciting, bottom up, and make them stakeholders, which means nontraditional means."

SCL therefore came up with a campaign called "Do So," which was all about "being part of the gang." It was really simple. "Do So" meant don't vote, that voting was uncool.

He pulled up a slide that showed youth dancing, painting, laughing. A poster in the slide presentation, being held up by a young woman in a headscarf, read, "Do So."

"So, we targeted the youth. We targeted *all* the youth," he said again. Not just the blacks but the Indians as well.

"It was putting up posters like this," he said, pointing to the screen, "and graffiti, yellow paint with stencils, and a mop, and we'd give them to the kids, and they'd get in their cars at night, you know, smoke a joint"—he brought his fingers up to his lips and mimed inhaling—"And they'd race around the country, putting up these posters and being chased by the police, and their friends were doing it. It was brilliant. Great fun. There was five months of just chaos," he said, laughing.

"It was like a sign of resistance against not the government but against politics and voting, and very soon . . . they're making their own YouTube videos, and the minister's house is being graffitied. It was carnage." He laughed, as if it had all been just good fun.

He pulled up a slide that showed the minister's house. Years later, it was still covered in yellow graffiti.

"And the reason why this was such a good strategy is because we knew, we really, really knew that when it came to voting, all the black kids wouldn't vote, but all the Indian kids would, because the Indians do whatever their parents told them to do, which was 'go out and vote.'

"And so," he concluded, "even though all the young Indian people had participated in the fun of 'Do So,' in the end, they all voted in the election for the Indian candidate, and the difference in the eighteen-to-thirty-five-year-old turnout was, like, forty percent. And that swung the election about six percent, which was all we needed." The Indian candidate prevailed.

SCL, he continued, wasn't just about psychographics. It was about "gathering information at a number of different levels, not just demographics or situational information, but also sociodynamic, like what groups people belonged to, what are people's locus of control, whether they believe they control their own destiny," he said.

"What social networks do people belong to? What power structures? What common enemies do they have, and how can we use that to drive behavior? We look at culture and beliefs and religiosity.

"But you also ask questions about the individual. We're not interested in what you think about the president. We're interested in *you*. What are *your* buttons? We believe that people change people. Not messages. We want the people to do the talking for us."

He pointed to me. "I've got to convert her," he said.

Now he pointed at the men in the room. "And she's got to convert you, you see?"

The presentation, like so much about Cambridge, was evolving, and leaving me increasingly unsettled. And I became more so after I noticed that Alexander had been negligent about an important matter.

In Mexico, data compliance was becoming a significant issue for me, as I was trying to build a company and a database that were fit for the purpose of all the projects I was pitching, both political and commercial. In point of fact, SCL and CA's compliance with applicable laws in the countries in which it operated, from Lithuania to the

United States, had always been lax, but it was becoming ever more worrisome to me now.

I had begun building strategies with Mexican data firms and polling companies such as Parametria and Mitofsky, but in building a database in a country with no local data infrastructure, I wanted to make sure we obeyed all Mexican laws. Early on, I reached out to SCL's lawyer in New York, Larry Levy, the same attorney who had handled the Trump contract and who had been a colleague of Rudy Giuliani's at his firm before switching. I had spoken with Larry about data compliance many times, but most memorably in 2015, while preparing a proposal for Caesars Palace, in Las Vegas. I'd inquired about Nevada data laws, and about how to handle gambling data, to figure out what kind of services I could offer—and I'd angered Alexander: apparently, I'd generated too many legal invoices for us with Levy.

Alexander constantly admonished me about asking for outside legal advice on data. It was too expensive, he said. We had all the expertise we needed in-house, with Dr. Alexander Tayler and with Kyriakos Klosidis, who was trained in human rights law and had begun to take all our in-house legal contract work, even though it wasn't his expertise. He complained to me that he had come on as a Project Manager and that SCL should be using barred lawyers for this "admin work."

When I spoke to Dr. Tayler about the Nevada laws in 2015, I had been unsatisfied with his answers. "Yes, we're fine," he said, and waved me away. He was similarly dismissive other times as well.

One of my greatest concerns was how and where the Mexicans' data was going to be modeled. I had heard from many of my local colleagues that it would need to be processed in-country, and I had to find out if it was kosher for our London- or New York–based data scientists to touch it. I had discussed international data compliance with Alex Tayler back in March 2017, to find out how data, especially political data, could be used for commercial clients in the rest of the world. He had been vague then, and he was vague again about Mexico, and seemed unfussed about any potential legal problems. So, once again, I reached out to Larry Levy.

My ignorance of the local laws was making it difficult for me to proceed with the pitch for the presidential contract, and I wasn't able to come to a deal with President Peña Nieto and the PRI. When Alexander saw the invoices from Larry, he yelled at me, but now he became even angrier. He was losing faith in me. Maddeningly, to me, he couldn't understand what was taking me so long, and he insisted on coming down to close the deal himself.

On the date scheduled for a meeting with President Peña Nieto and the wealthy and powerful Mexican national Carlos Slim, the owner of the *New York Times*, I made a terrible mistake, one that didn't do anything to improve my relationship with Alexander or renew his faith in me. Days before the Peña Nieto and Slim meetings, scheduled to take place in the president's office and Slim's firm, respectively, I took a vacation to the States and, while there, lost my passport. I was supposed to be back in Mexico City in time for the meeting on Tuesday morning with Alexander, but it was a long weekend, with the Monday a federal holiday in the States, and no passport office would be open until Tuesday morning. I wouldn't be able to get the replacement travel documents in time to fly back to Mexico City for the meeting.

It didn't help that my vacation had been at Burning Man. I had never been to anything like it. Begun as a summer solstice event in San Francisco in the late '80s, Burning Man had since grown into a global phenomenon in which tens of thousands of people came together to form a massive, idealistic, money-free impromptu "city" of tents and campers. The celebration went on for a week and culminated in the torching of a forty-foot-tall effigy made of wood. The event was a revelation to me, wild revelry and relaxation, like nothing I had ever experienced before and certainly nothing like my job at Cambridge Analytica. "Black Rock City" was full of people who survived in the desert by *giving* (their water, time, skills) to others—not taking or expecting anything in return—the opposite of the data business I was caught up in. The experience of participating in a society that reimagined an ethical way for people to interact with each other was so transformational that many "Burners" tend to call it home.

Alexander would never understand.

I was shaking when I called to tell him what had happened. He was still in London, and he fumed. The fact that I had been at Burning Man, something he saw as "frivolous," and that I had been so thoughtless as to misplace my passport, made him even angrier. I had been irresponsible, he said, childish and selfish.

When we finally met up on Wednesday morning in the Polanco office, he had already met, unsuccessfully, with Peña Nieto and Slim—the day before, and this had further enraged him. Now he took me into a tiny unfurnished room out of hearing range of the rest of the Mexico team and told me he wanted to fire me.

I knew I deserved to be disciplined for having missed the meeting, but I wasn't expecting to be threatened with being let go.

I'd been threatened with dismissal once before, in 2016, when he, Bekah, and Steve were unhappy with an interview I'd done on Facebook Live. While discussing SCL's background in defense work, I said something that *The Hill* later used in a print article. Taken out of context, my words implied that Cambridge was using "military-grade tactics" to defeat Donald Trump on behalf of Ted Cruz. During that mini-PR crisis, Alexander had been in my corner, and able to stand between me and Bekah and Steve and "save my job," as he said. I'd had to write a letter of apology to Senator Cruz and his team, and eventually, after *The Hill* issued a correction, the whole thing blew over.

But now felt very different from then.

He wasn't going to fire me, he said, but he clearly felt no obligation to me nor gratitude for anything I'd done for the company. He told me that if he had someone in front of him who could replace me, he would do it right then and there. The only reason he was keeping me on, he said, was because I was *of use* to him. Precisely what that *use* was, I had no idea.

As time went on, Alexander became so frustrated with how long the PRI contract was taking that he did something unsettling. Instead of waiting for the contract to come through, he began to pitch other parties in Mexico, taking meetings with representatives of parties that were keenly opposed to one another.

I tried to tell him that he was playing with fire. Mexico simply didn't work the same way that the United States did. Unlike in the States, loyalty in all things was paramount. In America, it might be possible to get someone like Ted Cruz to forgo signing a noncompete contract, so that you could work for more than one candidate at a time. In Mexico, though, the powerful people all knew one another, and word traveled fast. Negotiating with or working for competing parties was simply not done. While one might have been able to be relatively cavalier about party loyalty in the States, in Mexico, fidelity meant everything. I had learned this quickly. Indeed, it doesn't take long to understand these things if you pay attention to a culture's dynamics instead of trying to foist your own worldview on it. In some countries, what Alexander was doing might have led to leverage in business, but in Mexico, as I had come to understand, it could mean death. Alexander's joke about the cuckolded husband shooting his romantic rival was all too real in Mexican politics as well as in love.

While Alexander had lived in Mexico before, it had been, by his own admission, a time of youthful frivolity. He seemed not to understand how business there worked, the customs and norms involved, or the very serious implications of failing to observe those norms. On the contrary, he saw Mexico as his playground. No matter how much I tried to reason with him on this, he wouldn't listen. And every day that he interfered in the work I was doing, I stood on shakier and shakier ground.

On the morning of September 19, the ground in Mexico shook for real. I was in the midst of an early afternoon business meeting in downtown Mexico City. I had been pursuing a contract for SCL with the Institute of Cement Manufacturers, a group of Mexico's largest cement producers. It was 1:14 p.m., and I was standing in a conference room full of executives, making my pitch for SCL to take over their external communications, when I was thrown off my feet. They, too, were tossed from their chairs and onto the linoleum floor.

It took me a few minutes to realize what was happening, but those around me knew right away what it was. That very day marked the thirty-two-year anniversary of the great Mexico City earthquake that in 1985 killed ten thousand people. In fact, just two hours before, the nation had paused to commemorate the quake and to practice an earthquake drill. So, with horrid irony, when the earth shook again now, it was to some all too real and to others unimaginable.

The building swayed. Somehow each of us managed to get up and out of the third-floor room. We quickly descended the shaking stairwell, grabbing the railing as tightly as we could as we were tossed back and forth. I thought I would die on those marble stairs, and was shocked to finally get to the ground and see sunlight. Once outside, we ran into the middle of the street and stood watching the trees and lampposts sway. On the near horizon, just blocks down the road, a massive cloud of dust formed as building after building around us crumbled.

When the earth finally stopped shaking, there was a quick moment of quiet, and then screams and moans emerged from under the wreckage. Everywhere, gas leaks were causing buildings to explode. Asbestos filled the air.

That day, in a matter of twenty seconds, the 7.1 temblor killed 361 people and injured as many as 6,000.

I quickly took photos of my surroundings and put out my first-ever public Facebook post, to let my family and friends know where I was and that I had survived. I was shaking and in shock, but at least I was alive. We all were trying to contact our loved ones, and I somehow managed to get a message out to my family that I had gotten out of the building in one piece.

When I finally got to the neighborhood where I was staying, not too far from my office, I found that the walls were cracked and the façade had tumbled to the street. According to experts, until the building was checked for stability, the place was uninhabitable.

I did my best to locate as many SCL employees as I could, but there was no cell service. We got information by word of mouth, slowly. Finally, everyone was accounted for. Their homes were still standing, but one of my employees was engaged to a man whose brother was missing, and she and her fiancé proceeded to pick through the rubble of a building trying to find him.

On the evening of the nineteenth, many people were still missing. The bodies of students and teachers were being pulled from the rubble, and survivors in rural areas were stuck without food or water. I headed down to the Red Cross to see how I could help.

Most streets were blocked, and there was no power, no lights, so people were without necessary equipment, food, and medication. I helped pack motorcycles with supplies. One of my employees got on a motorcycle herself and began making deliveries. We were not alone—the entire population of Mexico City had dropped everything and made themselves available to volunteer. The Red Cross was having trouble managing them without any communications and started to turn people away.

When the lines of communication finally began to open up, Alexander called to check in with me. When I picked up the phone and said hello, I heard him say "So, you're alive, eh?" in such a jovial way that I was put off. He then joked that I was using the earthquake as a good excuse to take some holiday time.

It wasn't funny. By this point, little he said was.

16

Breakup

In the aftermath of the earthquake, I did my best to get the office back up and running—not for Alexander, but because I knew that the faster I returned to business as usual, the faster I'd be able to finish my job and leave the company. I couldn't move on until I'd secured the contract with PRI and received my commission.

A couple of months after the earthquake, I attended a large, several-day political thought leadership conference held at Centro Fox, the estate of Vicente Fox, former president of Mexico. Some eight hours by car from Mexico City, in San Cristóbal de las Casas, Centro Fox is a sprawling ranch, home to a vast conference center where, in mid-November, some five hundred politicos had gathered, in part to hear from the two most prominent potential PRI candidates, Aurelio Nuño Morales and José Antonio Meade Kuribreña. PRI needed a candidate who could formidably stand against its main rival, the liberal Partido Acción Nacional, or PAN.[1]

One purpose of mine at the conference was to pitch former President Fox and his wife, Marta Sahagún. The two were involved in voter registration efforts and ran a training program for political activists. I sought them out as partners for SCL, and on the second day of the conference, we met in a boardroom in their home to talk about what the company might be able to do to help them mobilize voters, especially the youth.

The boardroom was the length of a small ship, and featured one of the longest conference tables I'd ever seen. I stood at one end, by a large screen on the wall, where I had put up my PowerPoint presentation. President Fox and the former First Lady sat far down the table in what struck me as an almost comical distance. The possibility that the president planned the absurdity of the moment wasn't lost on me: he was known worldwide as a man with a wacky sense of humor. Fox was also Mexico's most comical and acerbic Trump critic, so, in my presentation, I steered as clear as possible of the work Cambridge Analytica had done for Trump, preferring to have a positive conversation on youth leadership and voter registration.

In addition to pitching, I shared with President Fox and his wife my hope of becoming the PRI campaign's embedded communications adviser. At Los Pinos, the Mexican presidential office (similar in stature to the White House), my name had been put up on a chart listing the high-level communications team. I was proud of this, and received congratulations from the Foxes, but also words of caution: when President Fox left the room, Marta made her way down the length of the conference table and over to me.

She was a stunning woman of late middle age, wiry of build with impeccably penciled eyebrows, dark eye shadow, and a head of cropped dark honey–colored hair. Her face wore a look of genuine concern.

"You seem to have it all figured out," she said. She paused and took a breath. "But do you have your security sorted?" she asked. "Not that you would have put that in your presentation," she added, but "I couldn't help but wonder if you've addressed this issue?"

Security. No, I said. I wasn't sure yet what I'd need. My team wasn't fully assembled; we were still negotiating the size of the campaign contract.

She looked alarmed. "If you're already meeting with these people," she said in a dark tone, "then you're already in danger. If you're not already being driven around in an armored car, I would highly suggest that you start."

I must have looked stunned.

In Mexico, she went on to explain, politics is deadly. I knew that, of course. That's the very thing that I had told Alexander.

But I didn't fully understand, Marta said. When someone in Mexico wanted their candidate to win, they didn't go after the opposition directly. That would be too obvious. Instead, they hurt the people around them.

And "Often," Marta said softly, "it is the person *running* the campaign that they target."

Many years ago, she said, during Vicente's presidential campaign—before they were married—she was his communications director.

"It's a high-profile position. Everything political, especially anything presidential, is high profile in Mexico," she said. "And I, of course, . . . I was closest to Vicente."

On the eve of one of the presidential debates, the opposition kidnapped Marta. They blindfolded her and drove her far out into the desert, where they stripped her naked and left her for dead. That they didn't kill her was fortunate, of course. They didn't need to. During the time she was missing, Vicente was shaken to his core. His fear of what had happened to her made him stumble during the debate. The kidnapping was intended to rattle him, and send a warning. That's how far these people were willing to go.

Recently, she told me, her own ex-daughter-in-law had been kidnapped.[2] After seven months, she had still not been freed.[3]

I told Marta I was sorry.

Don't be sorry, she said. "It could happen just as easily to you."

She gave me the names of a security person and a driver she

trusted. I had to choose these people carefully, she explained. "Even the driver can kidnap you or work with kidnappers. There's always someone in Mexico willing to be paid more by someone else who wants to hurt you than you have paid them to protect you," she said flatly.

I had already felt endangered by the possibility of Alexander angering a rival party; now I realized that I ought to have been afraid for my safety from the beginning. I remembered then seeing regular businessmen in Mexico, and even some of my Mexican friends who were unpolitical, with personal security. How had I not realized how essential it was?

After the conference, I set about researching how much it would cost to get the security I needed—the bodyguard, the armored car, the driver—and planned a move to an apartment with an alarm system in addition to a doorman. In early December, I sent a spreadsheet to Alexander, but he wasn't interested in looking at it. These were unnecessary expenses. Besides, he said clueless, security might be needed only once the campaign began.

I told him what Marta Fox had said. "People disappear here," I said.

I was foolish to think so, he said. He felt perfectly safe in Mexico. And without a contract yet, how could he justify laying out the expense? I was being ridiculous.

Didn't he remember Nigeria? With some countries, you never knew if you even *had* a contract. He should know that in many foreign countries, including Mexico, nothing was ever in writing. Maybe we were already obligated to Peña Nieto.

He wouldn't listen. "We're only obligated and in business with someone when the money comes in," he said. If I wanted security, he told me, "Take it out of your own paycheck."

I thought that was unreasonable, and told him so. But he was immovable.

He was quiet for a moment. Finally, he said, "You're afraid?"

Yes, I said. "That's what I've been trying to tell you."

"Well," he said. He'd have someone else come down to Mexico, then. That was all. He was sending me back to New York. I'd be useful there. Julian needed help.

I needn't worry myself about Mexico any longer.

Davos, that tiny mountain town where the world's power brokers meet annually to do a year's worth of business in a week, had been the site of much chaos and misery for me three years earlier. I had been twenty-six years old and still wet behind the ears—stupid, overzealous, hopeful—when I'd taken on so much, when I thought I could, like an expert juggler, spin twenty dinner plates above my head at once. The fire-spewing bartenders, the deep-pocketed asteroid miners, the Nigerian billionaires, the precipitous ice-covered streets— Davos was the start of the slippery slope I had been on ever since.

I had also attended in 2017, right before Trump's inauguration, where Chester had to protect me from attacks by people who were not pleased at the appointment of "The Donald"—especially in meetings with outspoken Hollywood stars such as Matt Damon, who rightly took issue with Trump's disgusting choice of a climate-change denier to run the Environmental Protection Agency (EPA).

Now it was 2018 and I was returning, but this time I was older, wiser; my feet were more firmly on the ground; and those feet were in boots with better treads.

I had just turned thirty. I could be the captain of my own ship now, the architect of my destiny.

I spent the week before Davos in Miami, at the North American Bitcoin Conference, where I helped throw an event on data ownership, a launch for Siglo, the new company of my friends, the brilliant entrepreneurial brothers Isaac and Joel Phillips. The company was helping people in Mexico and Colombia own and control their data, and be rewarded for sharing it: the token rewards they received paid their phone bills in a place where many people normally couldn't afford connectivity without such assistance. We were going to celebrate the launch of Siglo at Davos, putting data ownership up on the world stage.

I was also helping to organize a conference, the start of my future in a whole new field. Though the planning had been last-minute, I'd made the event occur by partnering with my new friend Matt McKibbin, the blockchain veteran who'd introduced me to the industry back in July 2017, after I met him at Brock and Crystal's wedding in Ibiza. Matt's firm DecentraNet had stepped in to help scale up a global conference to take Davos by storm: the first time that a major blockchain event had been held during the World Economic Forum. The technology to digitize both money and governance could be the greatest innovation to come out of tech in decades, but because it was a threat to governments and banks around the world, and given that the audience in Davos comprised the world's wealthiest people and top government officials, we had to get this one right.

Between Matt's contacts in the blockchain industry, my own, and Chester's contacts around the world, we'd been able to put together a weeklong event called "CryptoHQ," featuring panels, keynote addresses, and social gatherings of entrepreneurs and thought leaders. Guests included U.S. Treasury Secretary Steve Mnuchin (one of the officials in charge of blockchain policy for the U.S. government); the CEOs of many of the top blockchain companies at the time; mixed with powerful policy leaders such as the head of the European Commission's FinTech and blockchain strategy.

In Davos, Matt and I cochaired the conference with his colleagues from DecentraNet, and we ran the events out of our CryptoHQ "Blockchain Lounge," a massive three-story affair with a restaurant, après-ski bar, and conference venue, set up on Promenade 67, the main street running through the middle of the World Economic Forum.

I had every desire to make the event a success, and in my enthusiasm to do so, I swallowed my pride and anger and invited Alexander and Dr. Tayler to come speak on a panel about data and predictive algorithms. I wanted to support their interest in blockchain and help the company network in the industry. I envisioned Cambridge as having its own blockchain solution, which was in the works at the time, for transparency in data management and advertising, a design that would allow the user to own his or her own data and receive compensation for keeping it updated, and would let advertisers confirm that they were actually reaching the people they were paying to put their message in front of. I thought that the company might be headed in a better direction, and could reform the industry by choosing a more ethical technology as the backbone of its operations. I saw a light at the end of the tunnel.

I had already been in Davos for a week when Alexander and Dr. Tayler arrived, and they seemed surprised, particularly Alexander. I hadn't told either that I had organized the conference, and they appeared shocked when I stood up to speak to the crowd. Everyone in the blockchain community had begun to recognize me. It felt so empowering. I wasn't just a random, obsessive blockchain enthusiast. In a short time, after attending and speaking at just a few conferences myself, I had already established myself as a voice in the movement. I considered it both the best statement I could make to Alexander about my feelings and, perhaps, a bit of revenge for how he had treated me.

All the events at CryptoHQ were packed, including Alexander and Dr. Tayler's panel. After the talk, which I had arranged, Alexander met up with me in the bar. He looked a little sheepish. He also seemed to understand that I was moving on.

With a drink in his hand, he leaned in and shouted over the music and the loud, enthusiastic voices blaring around us. There were hundreds of people in the venue, most of them my friends or new colleagues in the blockchain industry.

"So," he said, "I can see you're really busy with other projects." He didn't seem angry, as if he'd caught me cheating on Cambridge; rather, he appeared to be peacefully acknowledging that I had found another way forward in life.

"So, you really just want to do blockchain, yeah?" he asked. "You think there's money there, that this is where everything is going?" he asked.

"Yes," I said.

He thought for a moment. "Would you prefer to leave your permanent job and come back on with us as a consultant? Doing blockchain?" I could have more autonomy, he said, work on developing the blockchain data solution with Cambridge, but be free to do my own projects at the same time.

This interested me. An arrangement like that would allow me to remain in the Cambridge fold while pursuing blockchain full time. I could stay under the company umbrella until CA's success finally rewarded my patience and I at long last received compensation for my part in building a juggernaut. More than that, I would be coming full circle—after all, it was the same arrangement I'd had when I first joined the company in December 2014.

I took a sip of my drink.

It was clear we were in a negotiation now. I could see a future in which advertising for blockchain companies was a big business, and Cambridge could be a part of that. If Cambridge wanted a piece of that market, it had an opportunity to build technology for the industry, perhaps even create its own blockchain technology ecosystem, for full transparency in the data-brokering business and advertising, allowing consumers to control their own data. Through blockchain, Cambridge could use its data scientists and tech background for good, with actual data protections in place, an idea with echoes of my original sense of purpose when I joined Alexander three years before.

Between us was the recognition that what we had been doing until now hadn't been working. It felt for the first time like a negotiation between equals. He wasn't firing me; I wasn't quitting. We were resetting the rules. It wasn't a bitter divorce, but rather, a kind of uncoupling and reconfiguration—if not with great goodwill then with an amicable change of status.

I smiled. I'd consider it, I said. His suggestion made me think for the first time about whether I ought to reconsider breaking with Cambridge entirely, as I'd been planning. But there seemed to be some benefit to the loose affiliation. As long as I could set the rules, it was appealing. But I wasn't ready to commit to anything yet. If Alexander wanted my expertise and connections within the blockchain industry, I felt I had the upper hand, and could at least get a much better daily rate and commission structure for the work I helped him with.

Perhaps we'd talk about it after Davos, Alexander offered over the noise of the crowd.

"Yes," I said.

We'd make time, he said. First, I should talk with Julian Wheatland about what the arrangement would look like.

After nearly two weeks in Switzerland, I flew to New York to speak with Julian about a future working *with*, not *for*, Cambridge Analytica. For any number of reasons, it felt strange to walk into that office at the Charles Scribner's Sons Building again, not the least because in order even to walk in, I had to be beeped in, through bulletproof security doors.

Julian had had to have them installed recently. There had been threats against the company because of new revelations about its role in the Trump campaign.

While I'd been in Mexico, focused on the presidential elections there, to the north of me, investigations into the Trump presidency had been heating up. Both Paul Manafort, former chairman of the campaign, and political consultant and lobbyist Rick Gates, a Trump adviser, had been indicted on charges of money laundering and tax evasion related to their work with Ukrainians linked to Russia. On the first day of December 2017, Michael Flynn pleaded guilty to lying to the FBI about his relationship to the Russian ambassador to the United States Sergey Kislyak. Meanwhile, Facebook was beginning to acknowledge how its platform had been used to spread division and fake news. After an internal audit, the company revealed that some 3,000 politically related attack ads were connected to 470 fake Russian-linked accounts.[4]

Investigations in the United States had also been coming closer to Cambridge. Not much later, it would become clear that Sam Patten, whom Alexander had hired to work for SCL in Nigeria, and whom he was considering as my replacement in Mexico, had once been boss to Konstantin Kilimnik, a suspected Russian spy who had worked with Paul Manafort. Terrible news—that and the fact that in October, the *Guardian* revealed that Alexander himself had reached out to WikiLeaks during the campaign to try to obtain Hillary Clinton's hacked emails. This had probably been enough to spark Congress's interest in Cambridge's relationship with the Trump campaign. Both Alexander Nix and Julian Assange had come out in public saying that the former's attempt to get Hillary's emails had been unsuccessful. Assange hadn't even bothered to respond to him. Neither of these revelations surprised me. As far as I knew, Julian Assange had no reason to help out a man like Alexander Nix, and he wasn't exactly a man to accept cold calls, either.

In December, the House Judiciary Committee had interviewed Alexander by Skype and requested that he turn over all the emails between Cambridge and the Trump campaign. While Alexander told the company that the request was all part of the "fake news" Russia conspiracy, the request, and the threats, had concerned the company enough for it to take added measures to protect itself.

Given the investigations going on that touched Cambridge, it was a relief that I was returning to the New York office with a tentative exit strategy in hand. It seemed that with each passing day, new, disturbing details surfaced about the work we'd done and the boundaries that had been crossed. Rumors that had started surfacing during the companywide campaign postmortem had grown louder in the year since. New, concerning details trickled out here and there, each more troubling than the last, and it was hard to shake the feeling that there were worse revelations lying in wait. By meeting with Julian Wheatland, I was hoping to bring myself one step closer to the door and to a future that I actually believed in.

Julian was happy to see me and welcomed me like an old friend. So much had changed, including the office itself. While the walls were still hung with Mercer art, the place looked a bit barer. And seated at the sleek desks were unfamiliar faces. Many of the people I'd worked with during 2016 had been offered huge salaries elsewhere. Others, such as Matt Oczkowski—who took credit for all the work CA had done on the campaign—started their own firms.

It wasn't just personnel; the very foundation underneath the company seemed to have shifted. Steve Bannon had been forced out of the White House back in August, which had struck me, and others at Cambridge, as disturbing. He had clashed with Jared Kushner, Ivanka, and White House chief of staff John Kelly, and his leaving represented a decided and unexpected schism. Indeed, it had been so abrupt that by the time a friend and colleague I'd sent to Washington to meet with Bannon (to discuss his becoming U.S. ambassador to Mexico) arrived for the scheduled meeting at the White House on August 18, Steve was already out on the street. The two ended up having the conversation (which went nowhere) in a DC coffeeshop. So much for my White House connections.

At first, it seemed that Steve would be headed back to the star-carpeted Breitbart "Embassy" to run that empire again. I even wondered if we'd begin to see him back at Cambridge. I hoped we would get something out of having associated with such controversial figures for so long, but that risk was beginning to look like it would bear little reward.

Steve hadn't just clashed with the White House team; he had offended the Mercers—and they were the set of hands you didn't want to bite. Revelations from Michael Wolff in his incendiary book *Fire and Fury*, in which he makes unflattering comments about Trump's family, made Steve persona non grata beginning in early January 2018. Bannon had also alienated Bekah and Bob with private, unattractive boasts that had leaked out: to whoever would listen, Steve had said that Bekah and Bob would back him if he himself were to run for president. Bekah responded with a statement that read in part, "My family and I have not communicated with Steve Bannon in many months and have provided no financial support to his political agenda, nor do we support his recent actions and statements." Steve was out—not just from the White House but from Breitbart and Cambridge as well.

In the aftermath of the tumult, morale was low at Cambridge, Julian told me, gesturing to the young people working so diligently and quietly at their laptops nearby. They looked so lifeless.

"It's just not as fun as it used to be," he said, as if he'd read my mind. The old company spirit, the late nights and morning hangovers—it was all gone.

Julian missed the fun, and said he hoped I'd come back to New York and "spread a little of the cheer." Anyhow, he said, there was plenty coming up to be cheerful about.

Alexander had established a new holding company, called Emerdata, which would now own all of SCL and CA's assets and intellectual property. He had apparently led an investment round of $36 million in order to scale the company globally, and with strategic investors in Mexico, Hong Kong, Saudi Arabia, and elsewhere, there were huge opportunities coming up for CA. Perhaps I wanted to help grow Hong Kong, given that I had lived there and spoke some Mandarin?

I didn't know what to say. The only condition under which I'd stay, I told Julian, was if CA let me take the lead on the blockchain business. I'd stay if I could create my own team, do my own thing. I didn't want to be full time, either. And I was through with politics all over the world. It was too dodgy and too dangerous.

We parted as friends, but Julian could tell he hadn't fully won me over. He asked me to follow up with emails to Brendan Johns, our HR person in London, to confirm a daily rate, terms, and the conditions of my consultancy.

I waited to do so. In the meantime, I headed down to Mexico to pick up my belongings and get my commission for the presidential contract. After years of work in Mexico, I was hell-bent on getting that commission.

In Mexico City, I met up with Alexander and a team he'd brought down to talk about the strategy for the Mexican presidential election. My job was to hand over the election completely. I understood it also as my transitional moment, from Cambridge employee to possible blockchain consultant.

The group included Mark Turnbull and three or four other employees, most of whom had been flown in at great expense. Even though he had taken me off the project, Alexander clearly expected me to have closed the deal already when he arrived. At times that day, the conversation was tense, the air full of silent recriminations over why the PRI talks had stalled.

That evening, I was anxious about not only the contract and the handover, but also my forthcoming commission from the presidential deal. The group of us was seated at a large table at a steak house. As we ate, we discussed plans for the election contract, talked about staffing, about salaries. We tried to cover the issue of safety—a fraught topic, of course, and one that Alexander tried to skirt. We still couldn't talk about security for anyone until the first payment was completed, he said.

Then he turned to me and said, "You're dragging your heels."

The others had begun to engage in a conversation of their own. This was between Alexander and me.

I hadn't given the contract my full attention, he continued.

The accusation simply wasn't true, I thought, but no matter what I said, he blamed me: It had been essential for me to close the deal, and I hadn't done it. The company was losing money.

I was silent for a second. *Losing money?* I asked how that could be possible, given all the business we had.

Much of the work that Cambridge had done thus far, Alexander explained, had been either for free or at cost, as pilot projects (also known as "favors" to the friends of board members). Even for the Cruz campaign and much of the Trump campaign, lawyers had warned us to price our services "fairly," for fear of the Federal Election Commission coming down hard. There were rules about charging "fair market rates" for services; otherwise, the work could be deemed a "donation in kind" and subject to scrutiny or perhaps even considered a violation.

But what about the millions of dollars that had flowed to Cambridge from the campaign? The millions of dollars that had paid for the campaign and the super PAC?

Despite the public perception of Cambridge's income, almost all the money, especially Trump money—$95.5 million—had flowed *through* CA or one of the holding companies Cambridge used to hide the link between its board members and Trump; in other words, the money never stayed with us. Instead, it had paid for all the data analytics and advertising we'd done on Facebook. Facebook had made the profit. There had never been enough for the salaries of the 120 people Alexander and I had hired to scale up his global empire. We'd always been short, and had relied on Mercer money to fill in the gaps. That's why paychecks had sometimes been late. That's why Alexander hadn't been able to afford security for me, he explained.

My mind raced. I myself had brought millions of dollars into the company that had nothing to do with Cruz or Trump. Where had all that money gone if we couldn't even afford our basic costs?

It was a stunning revelation. Ever since I came on board more than three years earlier, I'd worked on the assumption that this was an expanding empire, the beginning of something magnificent, and that I was getting in on the ground floor. Alexander was a lot of things, but above all else he was a salesman, and I'd bought everything he sold. I'd tolerated a lot in service to the idea that my grand payout, my due for all my hard work, toil, and, perhaps worst of all, compromises, was coming. Perhaps I might not receive it today or tomorrow, but soon.

Now, as I struggled to process Alexander's speech, I finally saw things not as I wanted them to be, but as they really were. For years, I'd held on to hopes that had been wholly unjustified. This wasn't a unicorn. We weren't in Silicon Valley. This was a company that would apparently succeed or fail thanks to the patronage of the Mercers— there was no larger vision or plan. The huge round of fund-raising that had been announced wasn't going to result in equity stakes; it was going to keep the company afloat. Without that money, the company was failing; the situation had been dire before that infusion, and in many ways, it apparently still was. The fact was I remained a long way from some grand payday such as an IPO or a sale to a media conglomerate.

"By the way, Brittany," Alexander said then, snapping me out of my head and back to the table, "I'm hoping you'll be able to help Mark and Sam out as they make the transition to Mexico." He meant continuing to serve as an adviser to them, to mentor them as they took over my deals and contacts. And he was clearly thinking I would do it for free, on the side—one of those extra things he asked people to do to show they were part of the team.

The thought of it infuriated me. It was typical Alexander. And it was typically unfair.

Seeing no reason to hold back, I asked him about my commission for the Mexican presidential campaign.

He lowered his voice so that what he said would be out of hearing range of our colleagues, at the end of the table.

"Now that there are others involved," he began, "the commissions are obviously not going to be the same." I was no longer closing the deal, so the money coming in would have to be split up appropriately.

Split up appropriately. In what universe was splitting it up appropriate at all? I had initiated the contract, been pursuing it for a year.

"You must be joking," I said.

"No," he said. "Not at all." He pointed out that now that so many other team members were involved, I shouldn't expect what I had before.

As I stared at him, it occurred to me for the first time that regardless of what he had told me, and what I had told myself, I was just a glorified salesgirl. It had been my job, after all, in each pitch to "sell myself" as much as the company's services. Time and again, I'd sold myself and the company—to the Nigerian billionaires, to Corey Lewandowski and the Trump campaign, to the NRA, to PRI. This list went on. And time and again, Alexander had refused to give me credit for many of those sales I'd brokered. He always managed to swoop in himself to close the deal or to send in someone else, Julian or Oz, to wrap things up and walk away with the commission. It usually went to whichever man had "supported me" and "closed the deal" despite my having done most of the work.

Often, I would approach Alexander with a list of the deals I'd worked on and point out those I'd initiated (for which I'd written up the proposal and the contract) and massaged to closure. I advocated for myself and defended my role in the success of those deals, but Alexander would always look at the list and tick off each item, pointing and saying, "No, that one's Matt's. That one was mine. Robert closed that. Matt. Duke. Matt, Matt. Mine. Me. Mine. Me. None of these is yours," he would say, and that would be that. He even had the nerve to tell me that some of the deals were Bekah's, as if she were in sales! And I'd walk away fuming, and empty-handed. I had managed to convince him to give me a commission for the first Mexico deal, but he made me split it with multiple people who were not even at the company when I started working on the project.

For years, I'd sat back and tolerated these slights, in the hope that something grander was imminent. Now, as I tried to walk the tightrope between leaving the company and maintaining my claim to the work I'd done, I had far less patience for this kind of treatment. I'd already compromised too much of myself for that.

I thought of my father, now handicapped and penniless. I'd made a quick trip to see him a while back. He looked sweet and innocent, with a soft face and a full head of hair grown back over his massive scar, but he was heavily sedated. We'd had to move him from one psychiatric hospital to another because of his erratic and sometimes violent behavior, as his brain struggled to cope with the massive trauma he had experienced. The cost of moving him anywhere else besides the Medicaid-financed facility he was in was prohibitive and unsustainable. I thought of my mother, a flight attendant who shuttled back and forth from Ohio to Chicago, where she looked in on my father; to Tennessee, where she'd been tending to her own father.

And I thought of myself, how for years I'd been unwilling to share with anyone any details about my family that would have revealed their more-than-modest circumstances, their fall from grace, and by association, my nearness to a kind of life that those who were wealthy and well-heeled could never have imagined. Whom could I have shared my secret with? Concealing these things had been a strategic choice on my part. The rich and powerful people I knew at Cambridge and in the Republican Party—our donors and backers, our clients and our partners—saw poverty as a personal weakness, financial failure as a measure of character and competence, and I'd been hell-bent on never showing them mine.

I pushed my chair back and stood up. "You're putting me through hell," I screamed at Alexander. I'd suffered a lot for Cambridge's cause, perhaps most of all because I'd pretended it was mine, too. But I couldn't suffer this.

I was crying now, tears streaming down my face and onto my shirt. I wasn't done with him, not yet, at least. The round of fund-raising had produced money, and I wanted what was mine, either through a payout or the consulting work. It wasn't just what I'd earned; it was what I deserved.

"I have a family to take care of!" I screamed.

Alexander looked up at me, at my tear-streaked face and my misery. He seemed perfectly unruffled. He neither shifted his position nor changed his expression.

"Everyone has a family to take care of, darling," he said, coldly and blankly.

I shook my head. There was only one thing left for me to say.

"Fuck you," I said, pushing back my chair from the table and grabbing my belongings as I stormed out of the restaurant—not even turning to look back at what I was leaving behind.

17

Inquiry

Nothing was ever straightforward with Alexander. I'd have thought a good "fuck you" would have meant good-bye forever. Then again, Alexander had always said that anger was temporary; he could yell, have his say, and then it could be over. Maybe he thought the same was true for me.

Not long after I stormed out of the steak house in Mexico, he called me as if nothing at all had happened, asking me to help with the DC office. I didn't know where my next paycheck was coming from so I agreed, thinking that closing DC lobbying deals for passing blockchain legislation was a good way to earn commissions without doing too much work. Then, in early February, Brendan Johns, in London HR, sent me Julian's, and obviously Alexander's, proposal for my ongoing work with the company. If I were to come on as a consultant, my per diem would be precisely the same as when I had contracted with the SCL Group part time back at the beginning, in 2014.

I was insulted by the terms, even more so when Brendan wrote again to say that the company wanted an official resignation. He said that in order for me to move forward as a consultant for Cambridge, I would first have to stop being a full-time employee. And while that might have made business sense for the company, I found the very idea of it offensive.

I was still fuming when I got back to the New York office to see Julian Wheatland later that month. We met to discuss the offer he and Alexander had made to me, but we didn't come to terms. Instead, I spent time looking over CA's new blockchain plans.

It seemed that Alexander had seen the light regarding blockchain, which meant that his thinking on data and privacy had evolved. Cambridge Analytica, the proposal read, "passionately believes that consumer data belongs to the consumer . . . and wants to develop a mechanism to give back control to the individual." Cambridge wished to "leverage off the openness and transparency inherent in blockchain technology."

It was precisely the kind of mission statement that kept my hopes alive about Cambridge, albeit fleetingly. For a brief moment, I felt as if the tide at the company might turn. I had seen Cambridge behave as a less-than-stellar actor with regard to user data. Now it seemed to be repenting, aiming to change its entire business model and its very relationship to data to become a champion of data privacy. Of course, I could not have been more wrong.

As soon as I started to calm down and concentrate on my new tasks at hand, there was another sign of trouble from Julian: the ICO still had questions for Cambridge Analytica about its role in Brexit. The commission clearly hadn't been satisfied with the answers CA had provided the year before—the half-truths that Alexander and Julian had had us submit, edited by them in a shared document. Sometimes I couldn't sleep at night thinking about how much more to the story there was that they wouldn't let me tell.

In the past year, the former features writer from the *Guardian* had continued to dig into Brexit and Cambridge Analytica. Her articles suggested that she had been speaking to former employees. She gave them pseudonyms, so it was hard to tell who they were. Carole Cadwalladr was at the head of the pack, dogged in seeking evidence of a grand conspiracy: between the Trump campaign and the Russians; between Brexit and the Russians; between Vote Leave and Leave.EU and AIQ; between the right-wing nutjobs and billionaires like the Mercers, who, Carole contended, were using Cambridge Analytica and Facebook to take power in both the United States and Britain. It had all struck me as "fake news," in large part because a lot of what she had written about me I knew to be entirely untrue. Hence, why should I believe anything else she had to say?

But others had paid close attention: everyone from the Electoral Commission to the ICO.

The ICO was beginning to laser in on particulars. Had anyone from CA met with the UKIP data team between November 2 and 19, 2015? Was data shared at any meeting or meetings, or subsequently? What kind of data was it, and for what purposes was it shared?

Clearly, they'd done some footwork, spoken to sources.

As I'd warned them, Julian and Alexander's insistence on subterfuge had backfired. Trying to hide the full truth never goes well. I had taken a day to craft my answer. I didn't lie, but afraid of losing my job, I had committed the sin of omission.

I knew that Dr. David Wilkinson had visited UKIP headquarters on November 3, 2015. I shared that he had met with many members of the UKIP team to explore what data they had, and I included the information that someone from UKIP had delivered a hard drive to our office—in fact, entirely unnecessarily, they had delivered an entire desktop computer tower. I included my November 18 panel appearance. And I wrote that I had participated on the assumption that Leave.EU was planning to hire us, although we never signed a contract and never carried out modeling work for them.

Because the ICO wasn't asking about any work we had done with the UKIP data on the hard drive, I made no mention of the rough modeling and segmentation the data scientists had done between November 3 and 18, and I did not say that we had shared that data, as I'd only summarized it for Leave.EU at our meetings before and after the panel, and in person at Leave.EU headquarters. I included the trip that Dr. Wilkinson and I had taken together to Bristol, to the Eldon Insurance office.

Six days later, a curious all-company email from Julian crossed my desk. This was entirely separate from the ICO. It was about a completely new inquiry, on "fake news," that the House of Commons Digital, Culture, Media, and Sport Committee (DCMS) had been carrying out for a year. Alexander had been "invited" to speak before the committee on February 27, to "help" its members understand data-driven marketing. He didn't anticipate any adverse publicity from the appearance, but he wanted the staff to be aware. Our company didn't have any experience with fake news, he said, so we were "delighted to help," Julian wrote. Alexander was among many experts who had been invited, including major news organizations such as CNN and CBS and executives from Facebook, Twitter, Google, and YouTube.

It all sounded quite reasonable. In fact, the email was so upbeat and so very British that I didn't realize the real reason he had received an invitation was to be grilled in the hot seat.

When the day of Alexander's appearance before Parliament arrived, I was at a blockchain event in San Francisco. As the day progressed in England, my phone began to blow up. Friends texted me that my name had been mentioned in Parliament—more than once. Robert Murtfeld texted me every quote, word for word. The committee's inquiry into fake news wasn't an academic exercise designed to swing the Brexit vote using propaganda to force a new revote, or "people's vote," as so many Brexiteers claimed. Alexander hadn't been invited to share his insights about the dissemination of fake news. He had been summoned there to account for Cambridge Analytica's complicity in it.

The DCMS comprised eleven members, nine of whom were present that day. Its chair was Damian Collins, a no-nonsense, conservative Remainer with a background in advertising. Collins, seated across from Alexander at the center of a U-shaped table and surrounded by eight of the committee's other members, all MPs, called the meeting to order and dug right in.

Why, he wanted to know, if it was insisting now that it had done no work for Leave.EU, had Cambridge Analytica claimed again and again, and very publicly, that it had?

Alexander, dressed in his usual crisp navy outfit and designer glasses, primly read an opening statement in which he said he found it ironic that the DCMS had itself been the victim of fake news on Cambridge. The unfortunate problem had begun when an overzealous PR consultant had sent out an erroneous statement. As soon as Cambridge became aware of the mistake, the company had made it "absolutely crystal clear to all the media outlets that we were not involved" with Brexit.

Collins made it crystal clear that he didn't buy Alexander's explanation.

In his experience in the ad world—albeit, a very traditional *Mad Men* experience, the kind that Alexander claimed was dead—there certainly were overzealous PR people. But the material in question wasn't just a press release. It was an article in *Campaign* magazine. Collins had the issue in front of him. The piece, entitled, "How Big Data Got the Better of Donald Trump: A View from Alexander Nix," had been published in February 2016, just after Ted Cruz bested Trump in the Iowa caucus and before Brexit.

In it, Alexander had written that Cambridge had recently "teamed up with Leave.EU" and supercharged its social media campaign so successfully that it was getting three thousand new Facebook "likes" per day.[1]

It was quite odd, Collins said, that a leading figure in a company would allow something like that, if it was erroneous, to go out, with his name on it, in the first place, and once he had discovered that it was out there in public, why hadn't Alexander worked harder to retract it? Why was it still up on the magazine's website?

Alexander coolly responded that he hadn't any idea. Nor did he know why, when Collins asked him, similar statements were still out there in various other places, nor why he hadn't responded to them publicly or asked their authors to correct them. Leave.EU still claimed on *its* website that it had worked with Cambridge. Indeed, Andy Wigmore had tweeted, "You should use Cambridge Analytics [*sic*] . . . We did apparently . . . Can highly recommend them."

Ian Lucas, a cheerful-faced Labour MP with a double chin and a broad Gateshead accent, held up a copy of Arron Banks's book, *The Bad Boys of Brexit*. Did Alexander have a copy? he asked sarcastically. If he didn't, he ought to get one and read it. In it, Mr. Banks writes that he hired Cambridge, a "big data and advanced psychographics" firm, "in order to influence people."

Unfortunately, Alexander said glibly, he had no control over Mr. Banks. He said he'd tried time and again to get Arron to correct the statement. Banks was clearly a man who was difficult to control.

"You could have sued, couldn't ya?" Lucas asked wryly. "So, that's not true," he said. "So, he's a liar," then?

Alexander sighed. He clearly wasn't willing to call Arron Banks a liar in front of Parliament. "It's not *true*," he said irritably.

Collins moved the conversation in a different direction. In his experience in his very antiquated form of advertising work, he said, he recalled that in pitching potential clients, firms often presented fresh examples, or "draft campaigns," using the client's materials to demonstrate the kind of work the ad firm was capable of producing for them. Had Cambridge produced something like that?

Alexander dismissed the idea. To prepare an example of its work in advance of signing a contract would require intense data analysis that was far too sophisticated and labor-intensive.

"Look," he said, clearly annoyed, his brow furrowed. "Whilst your point is valid, the facts of the matter are that we *did no work*"—he knocked the tabletop with one knuckle for emphasis—"on that campaign or any campaigns. We *were not involved* in the referendum." He continued: "Whilst we could dwell on this, I think we should probably look at the facts of the matter, which are that we were not"—he knocked on the table again—"involved, period."

As emphatic as he had been, he looked weary. He licked his lips. His face shone with just the merest mist of perspiration.

There was blood in the water.

Simon Hart, a gaunt, narrow-chinned Conservative MP from Carmarthen West and South Pembrokeshire, leaned in. An outdoorsman, when he was not politicking he hunted badgers.

Cambridge "preyed on the fears of vulnerable sections of the electorate in order to influence their voting," he said pointedly. Did Alexander think that what he did for a living made a positive contribution to society? Did he have any sort of "moral compass," or was he merely out to pay the bills? Did he ever ask himself where his social responsibility was in all this?

Others piled on.

Wasn't OCEAN modeling a less-than-subtle form of understanding people's personalities in order to manipulate them into doing what you wanted them to do? Did Alexander fancy himself an "all-powerful presence"?

The company claimed it had up to five thousand data points on every adult in the United States, the entire voting population. Did every adult in the United States know that?

It seemed odd that Cambridge worked in the United States and not the United Kingdom. Was it collecting data on the British public as well?

What was Cambridge's relationship to Facebook? What about Dr. Aleksandr Kogan?

Did the company obey relevant laws in foreign countries? Had Cambridge Analytica or the SCL Group carried out political campaigns in a third country on behalf of someone else?

What *was* the difference between the SCL Group and Cambridge Analytica? Did they share information and resources?

Why was a controversial American figure like Steve Bannon on the company's board?

Alexander took each question and fumbled it.

The company wasn't fear-based. It presented the clients it represented in the best light possible. It didn't single out voters; it was selective to whom it sent messaging, in order not to be wasteful. It had an in-house legal team that was thorough in making certain the company observed laws in other countries. Steve Bannon had advised the company on how to work in America. Alexander then likened the circumstances with Leave.EU as a series of dates that hadn't resulted in a "value proposition" leading to a marriage. He had no idea why Leave.EU hadn't decided to work with Cambridge. No, he didn't see himself as all-powerful. No, he couldn't give an example of any material the company sent out that he had ethical qualms about, but he'd look into it and get back to the committee if he found anything relevant.

All the while, he stumbled, stuttered, knocked on the table, grew red in the face, and minced his words.

When Alexander tried to explain the difference between *hoping* to work for a client, *planning* to work for one, working *with* a client, and working *for* them, one committee member complained that he felt as if he were "hearing the English language changing in my ears."

The work with Leave.EU had simply never happened, Alexander insisted again. "I do not know how to explain this to you more clearly.... However you look at this or however it appears to you or whatever tweets other people have said about the situation, we ... had no formalized relationship with them. We did not work on the EU referendum with that organization or any other organization."

But nothing worked.

The man behind the greatest influence machine in the history of the world failed to sway his audience. They had turned out to be classic "unpersuadables," most especially when they turned to the subject of me.

What about this Brittany Kaiser? they asked. What exactly was she doing on that panel in November when she declared that CA was "working on running large-scale research for Leave.EU"? Who was this Brittany Kaiser?

Alexander licked his lips. "Brittany Kaiser," he said, "was an employee of Cambridge Analytica."

To me, that statement was particularly important. It was hard to miss that it was decidedly in the past tense.

I didn't watch Alexander's questioning live. I read it after the fact—and somehow that was worse.

I'd been with Cambridge for over three years, and during the last year, I'd been working hard to contort myself so that I could justify what the company had become. Even as more and more red flags were raised regarding Cambridge's and Alexander's behavior, I'd been able to rationalize my choices through the lens of my family's need for money or my need to plot my career on a more sustainable course.

As I sat there reading Alexander's words to Parliament, I couldn't help but think back to the dilemma that had weighed on me when I first agreed to work for Cambridge. In the years since, the story of my time with Alexander had been one of compromise. I had made one compromise after another in the service of moving ahead and succeeding, so much so that, for a time, I'd lost track of the values that were most important to me. And now, by working with block-chain, by plotting a different future for personal data, I'd been trying to right that ship, to use my experience with Cambridge as a small form of atonement, while holding out the hope that the company would compensate me for all I'd put into it.

But seeing my name in print from that parliamentary hearing finally broke through all the noise and rationalization: my time at Cambridge was over. There would be no blockchain consultancy future for me there. No keeping one foot in the company while making my name in the larger data economy. No big equity payout. No pot of gold at the end of the rainbow.

There was no coming back now. Brittany Kaiser was clearly a liability to Alexander Nix and Cambridge Analytica.

I was still thinking about the ramifications of all this when a communication from the company arrived in my in-box on March 9. It was from Brendan in HR. "Dear Brittany," he began:

> As you are aware the HR team have made several requests for you to provide documentation confirming your conversation with Alexander Nix regarding your wish to end your employment with the company on January 31, 2018.

As you have not provided this documentation please find a letter confirming the end of your employment with the Company as per your agreement with Alexander Nix.

If you have any questions regarding the attached letter, please contact me by phone or email.

Terminated. The email was backdated to the evening I told Alexander to fuck off.

I dashed off an email, addressed to Brendan, Alexander, and Julian, explaining that I had not quit the company. I wouldn't have done that to them, I said. So many other people had jumped ship. That wasn't me. Yes, it had been a roller-coaster ride, but my intention was not to leave them high and dry.

Six days later, Alexander wrote. It was the Ides of March.

He was sorry to have had to send the dismissal letter. "Clearly this is not a workable relationship," he wrote. And as for the future, if I wanted to talk to him about anything, I could make an appointment with his secretary.

Nothing could have been clearer.

He "hoped I was well."

He signed it "A."

I put my phone away and stood up onstage at the conference, no longer wondering why I had asked its organizers to print "DATA"— for Digital Asset Trade Association, the blockchain lobbying non-profit I'd recently cofounded—instead of "Cambridge Analytica" on my nametag.

18

Restart

I will always wonder if Alexander saw it coming, the first swing of the wrecking ball, the impact of its repetitive strikes, or how soon his company would crumble.

On Friday, March 16, less than twenty-four hours after Alexander sent me his farewell letter, my phone lit up with notifications and texts from my friends and former colleagues. Late in the day, Facebook's vice president and deputy general counsel, Paul Grewal, had released a statement that Facebook was suspending Cambridge Analytica from its platform. Facebook had recently received information—the statement didn't say from where—that Cambridge had not acted in good faith in 2015 when it told the social media company that it had deleted all the data bought from Dr. Aleksandr Kogan. Facebook had been told that Cambridge was still in possession of that data, and, Grewal wrote, in addition to CA, Facebook was suspending its parent company, the SCL Group, Dr. Kogan, and an individual named Christopher Wylie of Eunoia Technologies.

According to Facebook, Cambridge, Kogan, and Wylie had certified to Facebook that they were not in possession of illicitly gathered data. If these new allegations were true, they would represent

Cambridge's second, and unacceptable, violation of Facebook's trust and its terms of use.[1]

Grewal had posted the statement on Facebook's website, and the news had spread across the world like wildfire.

I read the statement and the reports, and wondered how CA could still be in possession of the data that had prompted the late 2015 article in the *Guardian*. Alex Tayler had assured Facebook that he had deleted it. If someone from CA had it, who was it? Why did they have it, and what did Christopher Wylie and Eunoia Technologies have to do with any of this?

I had never met Wylie in person, but I had spoken to him once, on the phone in early 2015. I was a new employee then, and Alexander had given me the task of calling around to all SCL's branches and affiliates to introduce myself. As I was seeking new leads, I was to check with each branch to see what ideas and business they might be drumming up.

When I called SCL Canada, our partner company in Victoria, British Columbia, which I would later learn was called AIQ, the person who answered was Chris.

I knew a little bit about him. It was said that he had worked at SCL before I did, leaving sometime in 2014 to move to what then became SCL Canada. Other SCL employees shared a little office gossip: Chris, they told me, had been some kind of technical project manager in Alex Tayler's domain, but his work hadn't been high level. He wasn't a data scientist, but he had passed himself off as one. He had been difficult to work with, and when he left the company, he'd been disgruntled about something, but no one shared with me what they thought was the source of his resentment.

The call with Chris in early 2015 wasn't particularly successful. He was neither friendly nor forthcoming, and he sounded impatient, as if he were in the middle of something and wanted to get back to it. Perhaps I had been off-putting. Perhaps I had been unpol-ished or overeager. I didn't understand what Christopher Wylie was doing working for SCL Canada when he had left the company so unhappily—perhaps he had merely relocated—but when I hung up the phone, it never occurred to me to ask anyone about it. And that was the last I heard of Christopher Wylie—until now.

The evening of the Facebook announcement, I was far away from England and far away from Cambridge Analytica. The news found me in Puerto Rico, where I had traveled to attend "Restart Week," an effort by the blockchain industry to reinvigorate the island's economy in the wake of the devastating hurricane of September 2017. Maria, a deadly Category 5 storm, with winds as strong as 175 miles per hour, had destroyed the island's infrastructure and caused a humanitar-ian crisis of unprecedented proportions. It had left thousands upon thousands of people without shelter and had nearly wiped out Puerto Rico's electricity grid. Storm damage made access to medicine, clean water, food, and fuel nearly impossible, and between the storm itself and its aftereffects, nearly three thousand American citizens were dead. Restart Week was a way for the blockchain industry to invest in the island by making it a center for innovation, commerce, and technology—and to infuse Puerto Rico with tourism dollars, thou-sands of entrepreneurs, thought leaders, lobbyists, and newly curi-ous followers had converged there. Restart was also a means to give a positive public profile to an industry whose complexities made it opaque to many; and the service portion of the week was intended to make clear that blockchain was not about anarchical disruption, but literally building and rebuilding communities.

I wasn't sure what to make of the Facebook announcement. If Facebook didn't restore Cambridge's privilege and its access, CA's entire business model would be upended. It was hard to imagine the company surviving beyond this. Its, and its clients', reliance on the platform was so complete as to be almost symbiotic. Without Facebook, CA was nothing; nearly 90 percent of all advertising CA spent for each campaign went to Facebook. Even though I was finished at the company myself, I couldn't help but feel a sense of loss, that this was how a company whose future had been so bright might finally come to an end—not through governmental hearings and oversight, but through the power of Facebook.

The next day, Saturday, March 17, I headed out early with others from Restart to help with the recovery effort in rural areas of the island. I had no connectivity through most of the day as we worked with a group called Off Grid Relief to set up retractable solar panels in the countryside. For months upon months, people there had lived without electricity, and therefore no refrigeration or lights, let alone internet and phone service. It felt good to get my hands dirty again, to put my shoulder to an effort that directly helped others. It was gratifying to watch as families turned on the lights and appliances in their homes and began the business of establishing a new normal after the disaster.

As connectivity returned, my phone, which I had completely and blissfully forgotten about, began to light up, as it had the day before, with text after text. Early that day, Cambridge had issued a statement in response to the Facebook suspension, but what it said—that it had fully complied with Facebook's terms of service and was working with the company to "resolve the issue"—was lost in a raging storm of new, more confusing, and more catastrophic news than the day before.

Carole Cadwalladr and the *New York Times* had coordinated and simultaneously published related investigative pieces about CA and Facebook, and Christopher Wylie's role in events had expanded. Each piece was a damning and highly detailed exposé. Chris had cast himself as the keeper of CA's long-held dark secrets and the hero now of a story in which he revealed those secrets to the world.

Carole's article was entitled "Revealed: 50 Million Facebook Profiles Harvested for Cambridge Analytica in Major Data Breach." A subhead read, "'I Made Steve Bannon's Psychological Warfare Tool': Meet the Data War Whistleblower."

Chris's allegations, if true, were mind blowing for most of the world's population, especially in the UK and the United States, and, unfortunately for me, confusing. In juxtaposition with so much I had been told over and over by my former colleagues at Cambridge, so many of the accusations were hard to digest.

For one thing, Chris said he had emails that proved that CA had, in fact, had direct dealings with Professor Michal Kosinski at Cambridge University—he of the 2016 *Das Magazin* article and the originator of the My Personality quiz app. For another, Chris said he had evidence that Aleksandr Kogan had eventually taken on the work that SCL had wanted Cambridge University's Psychometrics Centre to take on, and that the company had never bothered to vet the work to see if it was even legal or in compliance with Facebook's terms.

But far more damning, Chris also had a copy of the executed contract between Kogan and CA, which spelled out the work Kogan had been contracted to do—which was not, as Kogan had claimed, designed for academic purposes, but explicitly for commercial ones. Chris also had copies of receipts, invoices, wire transfers, and bank records that showed that CA had paid Kogan's company, GSR, a whopping $1 million for the Facebook data scraping; other records showed that CA had spent $7 million on the entire Facebook harvesting and modeling project.

Kogan, Chris said, had been able to scrape the data of fifty million people from Facebook in a matter of weeks, thanks to the Friends

API. Chris said he knew that both the swiftness and the enormity of Kogan's extraction had triggered alarms at Facebook, but for some reason, the company had chosen to ignore them—a sign of clear negligence in how Facebook guarded its users' privacy and data.

The figure of 50 million was nearly twice the number of users whose data was stolen, and was what Cambridge had used to model some 240 million Americans. With that single, prodigious harvest, and personality profiling, Cambridge had been able to categorize, through predictive algorithms and the other data it had purchased, every single American over the age of eighteen according to many different models, including OCEAN scoring; that's how it knew which individual Americans were "open," "conscientious," "neurotic," and so on. And that's what had made its microtargeting so precise and effective. It was one of the main ingredients in Cambridge's secret sauce.

More shockingly, Chris also alleged that CA was still in possession of that raw data it had more than likely used during the Trump campaign to target Americans to sway the general election. In short, CA's illicit Facebook harvest had changed the course of history forever.

Cadwalladr's article raised the question of where that data was now. A Facebook executive who testified before Damian Collins and the DCMS prior to Alexander asserted that CA couldn't possibly still have the data. And in his testimony before the DCMS on February 27, Alexander had stated forcefully that CA hadn't *any* Facebook data at all. In the pages of the *Observer*, Chris Wylie wondered aloud why Cambridge would ever have deleted the data, as it formed the basis of the company's business, was the source of its signature psychographics, and had been so expensive to acquire.

Wylie himself had received a letter from Facebook in 2016 asking if he had deleted anything of which he was aware. All that had been required of him was a signed certification, nothing more—no other proof. Wylie had sent the certification, but Facebook had never followed up, had done no due diligence. If he had kept the data of 87 million users, Wylie wondered, how would Facebook even have known?[2] Surely Cambridge had the data, he said. And if Cambridge indeed possessed it now, Alexander had lied to Parliament and Facebook had been negligent beyond belief.

The *New York Times* article went further than Cadwalladr's piece to find the answer to this enormous question. And the answer was that Cambridge did indeed knowingly and at that moment have in its possession the scraped data. It had apparently never deleted it.

In a story headlined, "How Trump Consultants Exploited the Facebook Data of Millions," writers Matthew Rosenberg and Nick Confessore, with an additional byline from Carole, who had apparently received the byline for connecting the *Times* to Wylie as a source, reported that copies of the data still existed and that the *Times* had viewed a set of raw data from the Facebook profiles Cambridge Analytica obtained. A former CA employee—it was unclear if it was Wylie—said that he had *recently* seen hundreds of gigabytes of Facebook data on Cambridge's servers.[3]

If true, the implications of both articles were disconcerting and the consequences far-reaching. Cambridge had lied to Facebook over and over again, and Facebook had accepted reassurances from a simple email chain.

If these allegations were true, Alex Tayler must have been lying in his email exchange with Facebook when he told them he had deleted the data, all its copies, and any trace of it on CA's servers back in 2015. He had possibly also lied when he said that Kogan's modeling had been largely useless and merely a proof of concept. All this meant that Cambridge was a part of an enormous cover-up, the center of both the biggest data breach in the history of modern technology and one of the biggest scandals of our time.

People were calling it Datagate.

I was reeling as I read the texts and articles. And even as I read, more texts poured in:

"Is this true?"

"Did you know about this?"

"What the hell is going on?"

What had I been a part of? What had gone on behind my back while I acted as a face of CA?

A friend and I were setting up for a party that evening when he asked me what was going on. I myself didn't know the answer. I'd been forwarded the emails between Alexander Tayler and Allison Hendricks of Facebook, I started to say, then stopped myself.

I'd been forwarded those emails in January 2016, so many months before Project Alamo, the building of the database for the Trump campaign. I had thought that this particular data set was long gone before CA went to work on that campaign.

My heart raced. I grabbed my phone and searched my emails.

I found it: the weeks-long exchange with the subject line "Statement of Innocence." There it was, in black and white: Alex Tayler's affirmation of compliance and Allison Hendricks's grateful response.

How could I have believed Dr. Tayler's assertions? I had believed him because I had absolutely no reason back then to doubt him. I wasn't a data scientist. I had never had access to the CA database myself, never peered into its contents. I boasted to clients of what we had, knowing we had Facebook data, but Tayler had assured me and everyone else that it had been properly obtained. I had boasted hundreds of times of SCL's and CA's capabilities in modeling and reaching audiences, and possibly all those boasts had been based on subterfuge and lies.

It was a confusing moment for me. The *Times* reporting seemed reliable and I knew it had been fact-checked—although, the *Times*, too, had been shown to be the purveyor of some inaccurate news about both me and Cambridge over the past year, issuing corrections on many occasions. But Carole Cadwalladr's article was more dubious to me.

I looked back at it. I had never believed a thing she'd reported because every single thing she'd ever written about me had been so inaccurate and speculative, to say the least. Later that year, Carole would cite an anonymous source stating that I was "funneling" Bitcoin to fund Wikileaks (I guess she's referring to my student-budget donation in 2011) and had gone to visit Julian Assange to discuss the U.S. elections. Her theory and inference that I could be Guccifer 2.0, the conduit between Russia, the DNC hack, and Wikileaks, was a bit much to take in. Her allegations against me had real collateral damage: I was subpoenaed by Mueller the next day, which she then printed nine months later, conveniently leaving out the date and touting it as though it had just happened, further confusing the world and obfuscating the truth.

Even before those "articles," in my opinion, Carole's spread of disinformation was beyond shocking—especially on Twitter—let alone her lack of journalistic ethics, constantly leaving me without any right to comment before publication. Because this was typical of her behavior, I thought, why should I believe her now?

Furthermore, it was hard to see Chris Wylie as reliable: he was a disgruntled employee whose current access to information had to have been limited, unless he had someone on the inside at SCL or CA serving as a kind of mole.

Also, his description of himself as the architect of psychographic modeling was so out of keeping with the way my colleagues had described him. Chris put himself at center stage of CA's creation myth, in a story at odds with so much I had heard. He said that he'd jetted around with Alexander, had chummed around with Steve Bannon; that Steve had introduced him and Alexander to the Mercers in Bekah's New York City apartment. How did that square with the stories others had told me?

Even Cadwalladr described him as an odd sort: He was a pink-haired high school dropout who had somehow, without a degree, gone on to study at the London School of Economics. He was a punked-out Canadian from Victoria, British Columbia, with serious learning disabilities who was supposedly a savant at coding and claimed to have been "research director" at Cambridge Analytica. He even described himself as a difficult-to-grok figure: a gay vegan who ended up creating "Steve Bannon's psychological warfare mindfuck tool."[4]

How, as a doctoral candidate in fashion industry forecasting, of all things, had he been able to come up with the idea of using Facebook profiles, OCEAN scoring, and predictive algorithms to model users and microtarget audiences *for elections*? He also claimed to be familiar with Kosinski's academic work and to have been the point person at SCL who had reached and found Kogan. To hear him tell it, Chris Wylie was Dr. Frankenstein, and CA's technology his out-of-control monster.

Alexander had told me at a company party once that he was in active litigation with multiple former employees. "They all think they can leave SCL and create their own version of my company!" he said, and described the pillaging of his contacts, the pitching of clients that were definitely his. Chris Wylie had been one of these people, and Alexander was suing the pants off him for contravention of his contractual obligations. Wylie, Alexander said, had committed crimes against him and wasn't to be trusted as far as he could be thrown.

So, I wondered, how much truth was there to each of these sides? So much of the rest of Cadwalladr's article was filled with conspiracy theories about CA that seemed improbable to me. Apropos of an article she had written a year before, using Chris Wylie, it was now clear, as an anonymous source, she again wondered aloud if CA and the Russians were somehow involved with each other in the Trump win and in Brexit. She justified this speculation with a proposal she'd come across for Cambridge to work with a Russian company called Lukoil, whose CEO was a former Soviet oil minister and an associate of Vladimir Putin's. While Cambridge, she allowed, had never officially worked for Lukoil—Wylie had a copy of that proposal, which I myself had seen in my early days at SCL—Cadwalladr wanted to tie it all together, despite having no causal evidence. This features writer posing as an investigator wanted to connect CA with WikiLeaks, with the downfall of Hillary and the rise of Trump, and she presumed that both Julian Assange and Alexander Nix had been lying when each said that they had not in fact ended up working together when Alexander reached out to WikiLeaks in search of Hillary Clinton's emails. Carole wanted so desperately to find a smoking gun that she blew smoke everywhere, with larger-than-life characters such as Chris Wylie and villainous companies such as Cambridge Analytica, which she described as deploying psyops and operating much like MI6.

My head spun. I didn't know whom to believe or what to think, and that night I hardly slept. Among the things that kept me up were that Chris Wylie, whose fashion industry experience seemed to make him uniquely unqualified to be an authority on any of this, had said something quite observant. His comment about what Cambridge had been, in part, able to do with Ted Cruz and in the general election rang true. He'd said that Donald Trump was "like a pair of Uggs," those shapeless, shearling-lined Australian boots that, inexplicably, had become popular in recent years. The trick to getting people to like Trump, Chris said, was the same as the one that changed people's minds, making them think that Uggs weren't ugly. They *were* ugly, but all you had to do was convert the world into thinking they weren't, and suddenly everyone was wearing them.

Eclectic as his background was, Chris's account of how he came to work for SCL and Alexander, as reported in Cadwalladr's article, was so eerily reminiscent of my own. He was such an unlikely candidate for a job there. A lifelong liberal, he had worked for Democratic causes. But Alexander had convinced him to work for him by telling him that SCL was a place that could support his interests, offer him infrastructure and funding for what he was passionate about doing. And in that way, Chris said, Alexander had made him an offer "he couldn't resist."

Why be out on your own when you could be working here? Alexander had said to me. He had said much the same to Chris. "We'll give you total freedom. Experiment. Come and test out all your crazy ideas," he'd told him. And however different Chris and I might be from one another, each of us had said that we would. Neither of us could turn Alexander down. We'd both said yes.

I felt for Chris for a moment, but I couldn't help but wonder if there was more to this story than met the eye. Was Wylie using this chance to get back at Alexander for suing him? Was he retaliating for having lost business to his former boss? How could he even know about half the things he spoke of with so much authority? He hadn't even been at the company during Brexit or the Trump campaigns. He had pitched for both with his own data company in opposition to CA. A whistleblower or anyone giving legal evidence should never repeat unverifiable hearsay. I was angry and tearful all at once, and preparing myself for what was to come next.

On Sunday, March 18, I gave a talk on blockchain and data ownership on a stage in old San Juan. Just days before, I had arrived in Puerto Rico feeling as though I were part of a new community, the blockchain community. Now I looked out on the audience and wondered how much they saw me as part of them, too. Everyone had read the news, and as I made my way around the conference, people approached me again and again to ask what I knew about the Cambridge/Facebook debacle.

It was hard to explain with any credibility that I didn't know what to say about all the accusations—that I had pitched CA's services and touted what we could do with data, but had never peered into the database, wouldn't even have known how to, and had none of the passwords to access its intricate contents. I knew only what I'd been told, and that sounded like a convenient, even damning thing to say.

I might have seemed even less credible when saying these things because, in joining the blockchain community, I had freely capitalized, and quickly built my image and my reputation, on the foundation of my association with Cambridge Analytica. Just as my Obama campaign experience had once been my *carte de visite* with CA, now I had used CA in much the same way with blockchain. So, when I told people that I no longer worked for Cambridge, it probably rang false, and it was hard to explain myself in a sentence or two, or even in one conversation, however long.

As that day went on, I felt worse and worse. There I was at a conference of professionals committed to a new vision of data privacy and data ownership, and who I was and what I was doing there just didn't add up, at least not to others. That evening, at a party, a major blockchain entrepreneur who had previously told me he was interested in my serving on his board of advisers approached me, drink in hand, took me aside, and said, "Um . . . about that meeting . . ." and withdrew his interest.

I don't remember much more about the rest of the night. I drank until the news headlines disappeared, and when I woke the next morning, I was hungover and even more miserable. I had been disinvited from an exclusive, all-day outing a group of high-level investors was going on. In just two days, thousands of articles had appeared in the news across the world, and I spent the day catching up on them, sick at heart. Facebook had been strangely silent since March 17, when Grewal amended his public statement to say that Facebook wanted to reframe the story from the evening before: what had happened was egregious on the part of CA and the others, but it didn't constitute a data breach on Facebook's part. The message was clearly damage control, but there was no public statement of any sort from Mark Zuckerberg, and the silence felt heavy and ominous.

On March 18, I went to my in-box and discovered that my Cambridge email account had not been shut down yet, despite my having received a termination letter. I was ecstatic—hidden in nearly four years of communications and documents, there might be something that would help me understand better what had happened. I scrolled through my emails and found an email from Julian, an announcement of a companywide meeting, written in classic Julian style: "A short session . . . to brief you on some recent inquiries we have had from the press." All employees were to gather in conference rooms in London, DC, and New York at 3:00 p.m., UK time.

I also had a message on LinkedIn that I hadn't noticed before. It was from my friend Paul Hilder, the writer and activist I'd met in London in March and April 2016, with whom I'd discussed my future and my concerns about data. We had gotten together several more times after that, but we hadn't been in touch for a while. He was responding to an update I'd posted on my LinkedIn profile: I'd changed my information there to reflect that I wasn't at Cambridge anymore and that I'd recently cofounded my nonprofit lobbying group, Digital Asset Trade Association, whose purpose was to work with state legislatures to develop better policies around digital assets, including giving users more power over their own.

The note from Paul read, "Congratulations. Chat soon? It's good to see you building your empire."

The third, and truly the worst, wave of bad news for Cambridge arrived on the afternoon of that day, Monday, March 19.

England's Channel 4 had been conducting a four-month under-cover sting of Cambridge Analytica. The report, which chronicled meetings with Alexander Nix, Mark Turnbull, and Dr. Alex Tayler, was so damning that it was painful to watch.

Reporters posing as agents representing Sri Lankan billionaires looking to fund a dirty election campaign in their country had reached out to Cambridge. In the course of four separate meetings, all caught on videotape, CA had pitched the darkest of dark capabilities, activities, and operations on the razor's edge of law and ethics.

One reporter posed as a fixer and another as his assistant; each wore a wire. Meeting variously over time with Alexander Tayler, Mark Turnbull, and Alexander Nix in hotels, restaurants, and mirrored conference rooms in Knightsbridge and Belgravia, the reporters caught footage showing the CA people, and Mark and Alexander Nix in particular, eating lunch and drinking cocktails while boasting of Cambridge's secret capabilities.

In one segment, Mark asks about the "Sri Lankans'" interest in "intelligence gathering." He claims that CA has plenty of "relationships and partnerships with specialist organizations" that do that sort of thing. He meant MI5 or MI6, ex-spies, Israeli operatives—people, he said, who were good at digging up dirt and finding skeletons in the closets of opposition candidates.

Everything can be done without detection, the "Sri Lankans" were told. It was possible to set up contracts using different entities, with different names, and for them to pay in cash. "So, there's no record," Mark told the men, and then went on to describe a successful "underground operation" in an eastern European country where CA "ghosted in" and "ghosted out."

The company was used to operating through different vehicles and in the shadows, Alexander explained to them.

The CA people also boasted about their work in Kenya in 2013 and 2017, and told the "Sri Lankans" the story about Uhuru Kenyatta and the political party they invented for him.

It's important, Alexander and Mark told the clients in a face-to-face meeting, that any propaganda CA put out was unattributed, untraceable.

"It has to happen without anyone thinking, 'That's propaganda.'"

The company's psychographics, the "Sri Lankans" were told, were top notch. Nobody had what CA had. It operated on the premise that campaigns were not about facts; they were about emotions.

"Our job," Mark told the undercover reporters, "is to drop a bucket further down the well" of someone's soul in order to "understand what are those really deep-seated underlying fears, concerns."

CA could also bribe people to get what its clients wanted. It could "send some girls round to [a] candidate's house," get it all on tape, and inject that negative information into the bloodstream of the internet.

These are all "just examples of what can be and what has been done," Alexander muttered nervously on tape, as if there were no distinction between the two things. And when the reporter posing as the fixer asked about Trump and candidates in general—how much they themselves were involved in it all—Alexander answered blithely that the candidate wasn't involved at all. The candidate was merely "told what to do by the campaign team."

"That means that the candidate is just a puppet" of those who are funding him? the undercover reporter asked.

"Always," Alexander said with absolute conviction.

I sat back and looked at the screen. While everyone in the world watching this saw bad people doing and saying bad things, I saw former colleagues. I saw people with families, people who, up until fairly recently, I had believed were fundamentally good.

But there was no ignoring what this was, there were no shades of gray to this. Many of these actions, if they had indeed been carried out, constituted crimes. Never had I heard anything on this scale at any client meeting I'd ever been a part of. Yet, as deeply troubling as it was, it wasn't shocking. In many respects, everything at CA seemed to have been building toward this, toward some kind of dramatic moment that would lay bare the true risks Cambridge was willing to take in the name of victory. While one could state that this was a sting operation and a setup, the reality is that everything my former colleagues said on the tapes rang true for me, not because I'd heard it before—I most certainly hadn't—but because it was an extension of some of the case studies Alexander had described in the PRI pitch back in Mexico City. For a long time, he had danced around these issues in pitches and in private conversations. Now, on the tapes, he'd come out and said it.

When talking on the tape about what was done in Mexico, Alexander more than overstepped the truth. He claimed we did microtargeting when he never even gave me the budget to build a database. Microtargeting wasn't done; it wouldn't have been possible.

At one point on the tapes, Mark started to talk about playing on people's "hopes and fears." He even went so far as to say, "It's no good fighting an election campaign on the facts; it's fought on emotion." Hearing it worded like that made me cry. Was microtargeting just a way to play with people's emotions? Cambridge hadn't served persuadables the facts about candidates and their policies so they could make their own decisions. No, it had given them emotional garbage ads to stoke fear or give people false hope.

As the tapes continued, my CA colleagues admitted to using different entities under different names, with no way to trace them back to SCL or Cambridge. That I knew to be true. The first campaign I ever started was under the name "Nigeria Forward," which had a Web presence but was not traceable to an actual entity. It was a campaign "movement," I had been told, and could remain unattributed. That was preferable, Alexander said. At the time, I hadn't really considered what a big deal this was. I had known these tactics to be used to "protect the campaign team" or to get work visas for the SCL/CA employees without throwing up red flags, but hearing my colleagues describe them to the undercover reporters as a service we used to hide negative work, and hearing them say they used "different vehicles" to make sure their deeds remained "in the shadows," made my stomach turn. I imagined the negative cyberattacks on innocent citizens, and I thought about how easy it would be to funnel dark money into politics without a trace.

Was this a common practice at Cambridge? From my experience, using multiple commercial entities, and thereby claiming a contract was commercial when the work was in fact political, was commonplace. I was asked to do it on multiple occasions—first, in Nigeria and then again in Romania, Malaysia, and other countries—and I had always thought, Well, good, my colleagues will be safe working under unstable conditions in a place where political subversion is often punished with violence. But as I watched Alexander describe looking forward to a "long-term and secretive relationship" with the men in the video, I couldn't stop racking my brain, wondering about the implications of these revelations for upholding electoral spending laws. Were bodies such as the Federal Election Commission even equipped to handle the difficult-to-trace flows of dark money?

As if these thoughts were not enough to debilitate a stable person, the final blow nearly knocked me to my knees. In the tape, Alexander went straight to the subject of bribes and entrapment. Speaking of setting up scenarios with Ukrainian girls, he said, "I find this works very well."

I couldn't watch anymore. It was too overwhelming. How had I allowed a man like this to control my life for so many years? What else was I going to find out as the news continued to roll in?

Feeling shocked and alone, I went out and drank myself nearly blind again that night. When I woke on the morning of Tuesday, March 20, it was to the ear-splitting, relentless ringing of the phone. My head throbbed. I glanced at the screen and saw that the call was from Alexander. It was 7:30 a.m. He was calling on Telegram, an encrypted app he used only when he wanted to be certain no one would be able to hack in and hear what he had to say.

I didn't know if I should answer. What in hell was I going to say?

Finally, I picked up.

"Brittany. Hi. This is Alexander," I heard him say.

I stumbled. "I'm sorry," I said. "To see everything going on. In the press, I mean." I paused. "I hope you're okay."

"Well, yes, but what I'm calling about is that the *Guardian* has just sent a series of questions that are mostly about you," he said.

Me? Lord.

He said it had to do with Nigeria and that he didn't have the answers to what they were asking.

"They" was Carole Cadwalladr. In her article of March 17, she'd described materials Chris Wylie had shown her about the 2007 Nigerian election, in which CA had played a role. The materials had purportedly come from the campaign proposal. One slide, on so-called election-disruption techniques, detailed a "rumor campaign" CA had been behind. The rumors, sent out secretly, had purported that the Nigerian "election would be rigged."

It was the story Alexander had recounted to the Mexicans back in 2017, when he shared with them that Cambridge had the capability of inoculating voters with a small dose of bad news well in advance, so that they would become immune to it when it mattered most, on Election Day. It was the story he illustrated with the tale of the angry husband who walks in on his wife fucking another man and blows the lover's head off.

So, Alexander hadn't been exaggerating in that meeting. Such activities were in the Nigerian proposal. It was something that CA had done.

Now Cadwalladr wanted more information about Nigeria in 2015. Sometime before, she had already broken a story about the Israeli defense firm I had connected with the Nigerians, the firm that had infiltrated the Buhari campaign—she called them "hackers." Cadwalladr had falsely identified the firm, while also wrongly describing it as working for CA. Between that story and the suspect work Cambridge had done in Nigeria back in 2007, the waters were getting pretty muddy.

"Could I call you back about it?" Alexander asked. In just a little while, he said. He had to get his thoughts together first. "It was for the good of the company" that I comply, he added.

"Sure," I said.

I didn't have to look far to see that the world was closing in on him. In my email in-box was notice of another "All London Employees Town Hall" he must already have given. I couldn't image what it was like for him to face the CA team after the Channel 4 piece of the night before.

That morning, Cambridge had issued a statement that read, "We entirely refute any allegation that Cambridge Analytica or any of its affiliates use entrapment, bribes, or so-called honey traps for any purpose whatsoever."

It was a short while before Alexander called back. I answered his questions about Nigeria as best I could. They were about the meetings we'd had in late 2014 with the Nigerians and our work on Goodluck Jonathan's campaign in early 2015. I went through the chronology of CA's specific role in the campaign: my work with Prince Idris; my writing of the proposal; how I had flown with Alexander to Madrid to pitch the Nigerian representative; and how, after Christmas, I had flown to DC to pitch one of the Nigerian billionaires at the Four Seasons. After the signing of the contract, there was my disastrous experience with the hungry Nigerians at Davos.

I had helped hire Sam Patten to lead the Nigerian campaign along with Ceris; I had set up the first Twitter handle for Nigeria Forward; and I had been present at the initial planning meetings of the team that was to travel to Abuja. But because I had never gone with them to Nigeria, I didn't know all of what had happened on the ground.

I also recounted for Alexander how I'd met the Israelis, who told me they ran a defense company (both physical and cyberdefense), and I had introduced them to the Nigerians. I knew the clients had been angry at CA's performance and hadn't reupped their contract. Despite anyone's efforts, we had started too late in the game, and Buhari had won the election. Beyond that, I didn't have much more to add.

"Your name is going to be all over this," Alexander told me before we hung up.

It was the last thing I would ever hear him say to me.

As I was retelling Alexander the Nigerian story—from introducing defense contractors to the clients to setting up a Twitter account under an untraceable name—it sounded a lot worse to me than I had remembered it, and there were still so many things I'd not said out loud and that Cadwalladr wasn't even asking about yet. For example, I wasn't sure if there'd ever been a written contract; I certainly had never received a signature. The Nigerians had sent payment through a bank, but there might not have been real names or entities attached to the transaction. I remembered Ceris telling me how Alexander had scrimped on spending on the ground and then had taken an outsize profit.

And then there was the fact that Buhari had won. I had thought we'd been on the right side of that fight, not that Carole Cadwalladr cared—she was dead set on defaming me and probably knew nothing about the allegations of war crimes in Buhari's past. Even John Jones, one of the world's top human rights lawyers, had said that if we had to pick a candidate to back, Goodluck Jonathan was the lesser of two evils.

Restart Week was coming to a close, and I was scheduled to fly to San Francisco in an hour or two. I was headed there for some business meetings and a television appearance to discuss blockchain and artificial intelligence, but I knew that in returning to the mainland, I would be headed into the eye of the hurricane. The next few days would undoubtedly be a test of my mental strength. When Cadwalladr's Nigeria article came out, things would only get worse.

I didn't know what was going to happen. And I called my friend Matt to come over for moral support. He rushed over to give me a hug and help me get into the cab. I was about to do something big, I told him. I might not see him for a while.

On the way to the airport, I texted Paul Hilder. I had finally answered his "Congrats" note, quickly, a day or two before. Now I could see that he had been trying to reach me on two different platforms for two days.

"Hey, partner, you're ghosting me," he'd written.

"Just leaving Puerto Rico for SF. Let's catch up. Please brace yourself for what's coming out in the press tomorrow," I wrote.

I heard a bit more from Paul once I'd boarded the flight, before we took off.

"Bertie," he informed me, using Alexander's pet name, "is suspended by the board, pending independent investigation." He then reassured me that he was fully braced for any news that might come out about me. He told me to travel safely and said we ought to chat when I arrived.

"Sending strength," he wrote.

19

Of Truth and Consequences

MARCH 21–23, 2018

I arrived in San Francisco past midnight. It took forever, it seemed, to get to the West Coast from Puerto Rico. And when I checked my phone, I discovered that while I had been in the clouds, with a broad swath of a spinning globe below me, more than just the globe had been spinning.

It was early morning on March 21. Facebook's deputy counsel, Paul Grewal, had amended his original statement: he wanted to clarify that however egregious the data scraping had been, there hadn't technically been a "data breach."

Dr. Aleksandr Kogan accused Facebook and CA of scapegoating him.[1] He hadn't approached CA, he said. It had been the other way around. CA had helped him create both My Digital Life and the app's terms of service, which included assurances that Kogan and CA had been cleared for "broad usage" of the data. Oh, and Kogan hadn't made anything off the deal. CA, he said, had paid $3 to $4 for each survey taker, which amounted to $800,000. His profit, therefore, had been negligible.

Alexander hadn't had much of a chance to defend himself because

Channel 4 had aired a second segment of the sting. In it, Alexander, Dr. Tayler, and Mark Turnbull detailed to the undercover reporters Cambridge's role in the Trump campaign and the MAN1 super PAC. On camera, Alexander affirmed that CA had been responsible for every aspect of each effort—which was in complete contradiction to everything Brad Parscale and Donald Trump had averred since 2016. On tape, Mark Turnbull explained that the company could put out some of its messaging through "proxy organizations," and Dr. Tayler boasted that Cambridge had strategically decided that the focus of the campaign would be on mobilization, and the focus of the super PAC, on negative campaigning. The Channel 4 video went on to suggest that between the Turnbull and Tayler admissions were potentially very serious violations of election law and more.

In the middle of my catching up with this mess, Paul Hilder texted me from London. Cadwalladr's story about me and Nigeria hadn't come out yet, he said, but he thought the *Guardian* still had a treasure trove of Chris Wylie's materials to print out. "I don't think they're dropping anything new on you for the next three to four hours," he wrote.

"Oh, good," I replied, and told him I was going to try to get some "sleep before the bloodbath."

By the time I finally awoke, much later in the day on March 21, I saw that Mark Zuckerberg had emerged from whatever bunker he'd been huddled in to post to his Facebook page and give a couple of interviews: he was now admitting to Facebook's data breach, but he made sure to put it in the past tense.

"In 2015, we learned from journalists at *The Guardian* that Kogan had shared data from his app with Cambridge Analytica," he wrote. "It is against our policies for developers to share data without people's consent, so we immediately banned Kogan's app from our platform, and demanded that Kogan and Cambridge Analytica formally certify that they had deleted all improperly acquired data. They provided these certifications." The company had endeavored as early as 2014, Zuckerberg wrote, "to prevent abusive apps," and had changed its platform so that "apps like Kogan's," created in 2013, "could no longer harvest friends' data without their friends' permission." But even though Facebook had "made mistakes," Zuckerberg assured users that they could rely on him, his ingenuity, and his company's ability to protect its customers from all threats foreign and domestic. "There's more to do, and we need to step up and do it."

Both Zuckerberg and Sheryl Sandberg posted that when it came to inventing new ways to safeguard users' privacy, the company's ingenuity knew no bounds: it would seek out information about which app developers still had what the two called "identifiable information." It would ban them from the kingdom and let people know that they'd been at risk, but Facebook would also cut back on what users' data they were selling to third-party apps, and to make everyone more comfortable, they were going to give users an easier way to determine whom Facebook had sold access to.

Meanwhile, legislators in the United States wanted to cut the king's head off. They called for Zuckerberg to testify before Congress and Parliament. In the States, the Federal Trade Commission launched an inquiry into whether Facebook's failure to protect users' privacy had violated a settlement the company had reached with that body way back in 2011.

In England, everyone was trying to get ahead of the curve by proving that in comparison to the Americans, the country had always been at the forefront of protecting its citizens from bad actors. Op-ed writers extolled the virtues of a potentially powerful new data protection law that had been making its way through the legislative process. The DCMS noted that it had been examining fake news for a year. The ICO was determined to get in the door first, and had already been issued a warrant for CA's servers and its files to enable it to do so, succeeding in stopping a team of independent auditors, sent by Facebook, from storming into CA's offices.

Investors were taking revenge: Facebook stock fell by nearly twenty billion dollars in the first few minutes of trading on the NASDAQ, and a group of shareholders had rushed to file a suit against the company for "false and misleading statements."[2]

Meanwhile, users across the world were calling for an end to global dependence on social media, in particular, Zuckerberg's platform. On Twitter, the hashtag #DeleteFacebook was trending.[3] But nearly everyone also acknowledged, without coming right out and saying it, that Facebook had a monopoly on the market.

For me, there was a poignant moment here and there: a platform I had trusted with all my data (my hopes, my fears, my family photos, my life events) had become the arbiter of bad faith. Not only had it allowed all my data to be taken by any company around the world willing to pay for access, but it had also opened up its platform for interference in elections by powers foreign and domestic. Cyberwar crimes had been committed against the American people, and Mark Zuckerberg and Sheryl Sandberg were financially benefiting from them. Remorse was nowhere to be seen. Theirs was a modern-day dictatorship like the ones I used to lobby against in the European Parliament and the United Nations. How had it taken so long for me to see it?

Alexander had issued a statement: "I am aware how this looks," he said. But all he had been doing in the sting video—which had been seriously doctored, he assured everyone—was "playing along" with "ludicrous hypothetical scenarios."[4] Reuters posted a photograph of him trying to make his way through a scrum of reporters at the front doors of the SCL London office, a security guard gripping him tightly at the elbow to move him along. On Alexander's face was a look of almost childlike amazement. None of this could have been easy for him—it was so tawdry, so very un-Etonian and dark. It was Theater of the Absurd on steroids.

Technically, I stood apart from it. I no longer worked for Cambridge Analytica. I could watch it through the jaundiced eyes of a witness.

I texted back and forth with Paul.

"Were you fired?" he asked. "Or did you quit?"

Something of both, I wrote back. To borrow a Facebook expression, it was complicated. What was my place? And what, if anything, was my responsibility going forward? I honestly didn't know. I knew I was innocent of any crime. But I was in possession of proof that Dr. Alex Tayler, at least, had lied about the data erasure.

"I have a few things we should discuss," I wrote Paul. "Evidence about Facebook, emails in which CA promised to delete the data."

"Christ," Paul texted back. "If they're as bad as lying about Facebook, then there must be other stuff," he suggested, implying that written obstruction of the truth to a company as big as Facebook was so bold that they must be willing to hide much more than still meets the eye.

Strange as that might seem, it was the first time the thought had occurred to me.

It was shocking to discover that Alex Tayler hadn't been telling the truth. I had respected him. In my experience, he had been upright, responsible, and no-nonsense. I'd always seen him as separate and apart from the moneymaking aspects of Cambridge, the sales and the creative work. And I'd never seen him as an obfuscator or a bullshitter. He was the opposite of Alexander Nix. He never sold the "sizzle" instead of the sausage, and had seemed the opposite of morally reprehensible. Tayler *was* data: scientific and reliable.

Until he wasn't.

His lie seemed to change everything. Why had he lied? For the money? Because CA had forced him to? I couldn't know. But I felt something happen: Tayler's lie was like the single hanging thread you aim to tug off a garment but which unravels the whole thing into a tangled mess.

I, too, had lied, then. I had sold an idea to clients around the world that was in fact very much different from the reality. How much of Cambridge Analytica was built on lies?

"We should talk," I wrote Paul. There were things I wanted to tell him, things I needed to say out loud to someone.

"When are you going to tell your own story?" he texted back.

For three and a half years I had lived CA's story, not my own. I had participated in the company's spectacular rise. My own story was inextricably linked to Cambridge's. How was I even to begin to separate them out?

"Stop protecting old white men," a friend had said to me back in mid-March, when I told her about the impromptu termination letter. "They're good at protecting themselves; they don't need you"— another thought that hadn't occurred to me, and in so many years. I thought back to my days as a human rights activist, when I spent all my time holding people in power to account. What was stopping me now from calling these people out on their lies, on their bullshit, on their crimes? What did I gain from protecting people who had gladly thrown me under the bus? Who would win if I obstructed the light that I could instead shine on these dark places?

So, I asked Paul, "How would you suggest I go about it?"

He wasn't sure yet. He told me not think of that right now. He said that I ought to sit and write things down. "All the topics you think are really important." Everything—everything that had happened at CA, everything that I'd been a part of, "warts and all," he wrote. He wanted me to look inside myself, and he said that whatever I put down on paper should come from the heart.

So, I sat down and wrote everything I felt, everything I could think of that might be of use to the public. I made lists. I cried.

I had just finished writing when Paul got in touch again.

I had enough material to write an op-ed, I told him.

But he had a different idea.

Was I ready and willing to really put myself out there? If so, he knew a journalist named Paul Lewis. Lewis was the *Guardian*'s bureau chief in San Francisco. Paul Hilder trusted him; he sent me some links to a couple of Lewis's stories. One was recent, from just a day or so prior: a profile of Sandy Parakilas, a former operations manager at Facebook. In the wake of Chris Wylie's allegations, Parakilas had revealed that data harvesting of the sort that CA carried out had been routine at Facebook for years. In fact, tens of millions more users had had their private data scraped. The scandal was now of outsize proportions. Indeed, this stealing of data was so unethical that Parakilas had left Facebook because of it.

If I liked what I saw, and I was willing, Paul said he could introduce me to Lewis; he himself would get a flight out of London and be in San Francisco in thirty-six hours to help make sure the story was fair. Lewis was a serious journalist; he wasn't going to give me a pass. I might be innocent, but there was no telling what could happen, how it was all going to play out.

Did I understand that? Paul wanted to know. Was I ready?

I paused. I had signed an NDA on the first day I joined the company, which gave me pause, but I knew a little something about whistleblowers. As a high-schooler, I'd studied the case of Daniel Ellsberg and the Pentagon Papers. I'd written my undergraduate thesis using primary source materials leaked by Julian Assange. I knew what Assange had suffered. I'd visited him in his place of asylum. His seemed a terrible fate to me—held for years as a political prisoner. But I also knew what international law said about whistleblowers. In doing my graduate work at Middlesex, I had learned that whistleblowers were afforded protections under international and national laws. If a business broke the law, a former employee's coming out with evidence of this was considered as being in the public interest, and that act of self-sacrifice was protected in order to encourage and support those willing to hold bad actors to account.

I was also well aware that whistleblowers got plenty of blowback. They became lightning rods and scapegoats. If I came out about the company now, it'd be such convenient timing that I'd appear to be saving myself, one way or another—a rat leaving a sinking ship. And if I explained that I'd been unhappy for a long time, but that I'd already parted ways with the company before "Datagate" erupted, I'd be seen as the disgruntled employee with a convenient excuse for not being at the center of the scandal. I was in an impossible position.

Paul Hilder said that time was of the essence. If I was going to do it, it would be best if I met with Paul Lewis today.

Cadwalladr's Nigeria article in the **Guardian** had her byline, but it had been written with Anne Marlowe, a self-proclaimed journalist without any credentials, with whom Carole had tweeted viciously about me, even going so far as to tweet out my home address in London. The two "reporters" were out for blood, obsessed and unable to see straight. They piled on and made me out to be a warlord who had masterminded one of the dirtiest campaigns in the history of the African continent—that campaign of all of three weeks that they had barely bothered to investigate properly.

To them, I was a gadfly opportunist, a "prolific networker" who had choreographed a campaign marked by deceit and propaganda of a vicious sort.[5] Attached to the story was a Cambridge campaign video, an anti-Buhari ad I'd never seen before. It was filled with shocking, violent, bloody images of Buhari supporters wielding machetes on supporters of Goodluck Jonathan. One SCL employee had told Carole that the entire campaign had been horrifying and dangerous, and that the team *I* had sent to Abuja barely escaped with their lives before Election Day. I was confused, as none of this aligned with anything I had seen or was told about those few weeks Sam Patten's team spent on the ground partying with David Axelrod's staff. But I hadn't been there; the reality could have been anything.

When Paul Lewis drove up outside my hotel and I got in his car, he apologized about the *Guardian*'s Nigeria article. He hadn't had any control over the timing of it. It was a different bureau, lots of complicated relationships, he said. He wrote mostly about tech. He didn't have any pull.

Lewis was a thin, dark-haired man in his mid-thirties with a short, scruffy beard. Around my height, he looked directly at me when he spoke, with kind eyes. He appreciated that I was willing to be there, and he was taking me very seriously indeed.

He said he was too nervous to take me to the *Guardian*'s San Francisco headquarters. Someone there might recognize me or overhear us, and he didn't want that to happen. So, he drove us away from the city, past the tallest of buildings, from Google to Uber to Amazon, each packed with people at their desks finding new ways to collect data and monetize it. Soon, we had passed by rolling hills and through a looking glass, finding ourselves in the middle of Silicon Valley, the beating heart of the very technology platforms that had caused this mess in the first place.

Facebookland.

Paul Lewis had chosen a coworking space not too far from Facebook HQ, perhaps for irony or perhaps because he frequented this location with sources. It was a place packed with small companies and independent tech consultancies, somewhere we could be anonymous and go about our business undisturbed for as long as we wanted. Eerily enough, I had recently been invited to Facebook HQ by Morgan Beller, the woman who was building Facebook's blockchain now known as Libra. That I ended up in a WeWork nearby instead, about to change their narrative forever, is an irony in itself.

Once we got into a room of our own and shut the door, we both took a seat at a table. The room resembled the old Sweat Box at SCL in Mayfair. Lewis took out his laptop; I did the same. For more than a year, Alexander had forbidden me from speaking with reporters, and now there was more to say than ever.

I looked at Paul Lewis, he switched on his recording device, and I began to talk.

I started by showing Lewis the Trump postmortem, both the campaign and the super PAC materials. No one outside the company had ever seen this stuff, besides a few high-level clients. I showed him the PowerPoints from the campaign and the super PAC. The horrifying anti-Hillary ads, the targeting of African Americans, the data that divided Hispanics up into categories so specific that it was mind-boggling: Spanish-speaking, non-Spanish-speaking, Mexican, Puerto Rican, Cuban, and so on. I showed him the messaging with which the super PAC had targeted each group; the stats, the uplifts, the returns on investment. And I showed him the videos it had used for African Americans, which much of the public hadn't seen because they were dark, sent only to those categorized as persuadable.

I showed Lewis the charts and the graphs, the techniques the company had used, from the strategic segmentation of people of color to shocking negative campaigning materials and a clear strategy to send those ads to the "deterrence" group, those who could be persuaded not to bother voting. How had I never seen before that if these voters were deterred from voting for Hillary, perhaps they didn't vote at all? There was a very thin line between negative campaigning and voter suppression, and the mounting evidence before us suggested the latter.

I then walked him through the "impressive" numbers the company had achieved, the limited but effective psychographics used to target neurotics by the super PAC, the ugliness of the messaging.

I showed him the email chain between Alex Tayler and Allison Hendricks, the statement of so-called innocence, evidence of Cambridge's lies and Facebook's negligence.

I pulled up communications between CA and Arron Banks; a press invitation to the Leave.EU panel that indicated that CA was, in fact, part of the team; talking points that Harris had written out for me to give at the panel; the segmentation we'd done for them in the first phase of the project. There was an email from Julian Wheatland discussing the complicated and possibly illegal relationship between UKIP and Leave.EU, and a discussion about whether Leave .EU had lawfully used UKIP's data. I showed him the legal opinion on the matter that Matthew Richardson had coauthored, indicating that UKIP was in the clear—and exonerating his own party. I had an email from another organization that had written to me because Leave.EU had told them to coordinate with CA—it proved just how integral a part of the team Arron had considered us to be and how we had seen ourselves. I had an email from Julian about what "line" to take in the public panel presentation. Should we say where the data had come from that we had analyzed? He would rather I not mention it, to be honest, he had said. That was the best bit of honesty I had gathered from the slew of related emails.

At one point, Lewis pointed to a chain of emails I had shown him regarding the contracts between Leave.EU and UKIP, and he gasped. There it all was.

We talked about CA's specific focus on the vulnerable in both the United States and the United Kingdom; how so much of the campaign advertising had devolved into fear-mongering—because fear worked better than any other tool we had, even on those who weren't neurotic.

What else do you have? Lewis asked.

I had never even looked at my computer in this way. I had no idea what I had and what it meant when you examined it through a different lens, when you scoured it for evidence. There was so much.

That night, we stopped working only once, to go out to get a sandwich, but I couldn't eat a bite.

What did I know about Alexander's boasts in the Channel 4 sting videos? Paul asked: the bribery, the suggestion of honey traps. Had I ever actually seen him use women in that way?

I told Lewis I couldn't be sure. Alexander was prone to exaggeration. I'd never known if he was telling the truth or trying to impress clients. But it wasn't out of the question. There was so much I had written off as exaggeration that later had been borne out as something like fact. Still, I didn't know for sure.

I told him about Indonesia; about Trinidad and Tobago. I had a hunch something hadn't been right in Saint Kitts, but Alexander had always blamed the prime minister for anything that went wrong in those campaigns. There was also Nigeria, of course; Lithuania, Kenya, Romania: the creation of political parties; the invisible presences on Facebook and Twitter; the invention of Twitter handles and accounts—was all this merely crafty and strategic, or did it constitute crimes in those countries?

We talked and we talked, and I started to see things I had never allowed myself to see before.

Lewis then turned to Chris Wylie and the Facebook data set.

I didn't have access to the data itself, so we were mostly left with questions. So, he asked how much of what Chris Wylie had said in Carole's article was true—about the basics of the way the SCL Group had worked, the origins in defense work, and SCL Defense's psyops background. He wanted to know how I understood, or didn't understand, the relationship between SCL and AIQ. Had the Mercers really used two entities to launder data for targeting in both the Brexit and Trump elections?

If that weren't enough, there was the million-dollar question, of course: Russia. Did I, he wanted to know, have any evidence linking Cambridge Analytica to Russia? Did I have any evidence linking the Trump campaign to Russia? What about Arron Banks? What about Brexit? Bob Mercer? Bekah?

I had had a brief moment developing a relationship with Lukoil's Turkey office, and at the time I hadn't even known it was a Russian company. But SCL had spent a lot of time working that lead. Lukoil was the only Russia connection I knew of, but maybe it was relevant. I forgot about even mentioning Michael Flynn and the inscription in Alexander's copy of Flynn's book.

We scoured my laptop for more emails and documents, to find evidence linking any of these entities to one another—anything could be useful at this point, as there were so many accusations, so many possibilities for wrongdoing.

The more I told him, the more his jaw dropped, and the more his jaw dropped, the angrier *I* became at what I knew but hadn't allowed myself to register deeply enough to do something about it. It was just beginning to dawn on me how much I had conveniently chosen to ignore or rationalize.

I told Lewis about my training, about the very concepts behind psychographics: that what we did was find what made people thirsty and then turn up the heat.

It had never crossed my mind as something malevolent. I had seen it as savvy.

For so long, I had seen everything CA did the way Alexander saw it. His enthusiasm and the company's success were intoxicating. We were building a billion-dollar company. We were changing communications forever. I was a part of something unprecedented. I was special, smart as a whip. I was going to be CEO one day.

As my sister would later say: I drank the Kool-Aid. Or the Coca-Cola, so to speak, as Alexander had so often referred to it in his client presentations.

And not only did I buy into CA, I also went so far as to buy into what I had once abhorred. And I had done it all under the guise of "doing business."

With horror, I admitted to Paul Lewis that I had literally joined the NRA, and not just once but two years in a row! I had convinced myself that because I was going to be meeting with its executives, I ought to get the literature that came with the membership, to be able to understand the organization "from the inside out." I'd even gotten the hat, and had *worn* it! At the time, I had told myself that I was doing so ironically, but it had sat atop my head. There were pictures of me in it.

I had to admit that I had enjoyed moments like that over the past three and a half years. I had enjoyed what I thought was the joke of meeting Donald Trump and having him sign his own face on the cover of *Time* magazine. I had loved telling the story about meeting

Sheriff Joe Arpaio and about the pink boxers and the gaudy coins he gave out as souvenirs. With some glee, I had repeated the tale of Dick Cheney striding out onstage to the Darth Vader theme music in the Fantasia Ballroom at Disney World. I had relished the attention when I sat onstage at CPAC, live on C-SPAN, before a crowd of ten thousand, and I had worn my cowboy boots and vintage Texan suit, a symbol of my belonging to a cadre of Wild West renegades. I had once taken it as a point of pride that Alexander had thought me responsible enough to sit on a public panel, broadcasted on television, representing the company beside referendum expert Gerry Gunster. And I had prized and shown off my copy of *The Bad Boys of Brexit* with Nigel Farage's signature on the inside cover.

I'd be lying if I said I didn't indulge myself in it all at times, and without regret: I had loved the vintage champagne, the long lunches, the misty afternoons at polo parties on the Queen's grounds; the after-parties at Alexander's country house, the exclusivity of being among his "favorites"; the VIP passes; shaking hands with the likes of Ben Carson and Marco Rubio and, taken to the extreme, someone even once so abhorrent to me as NRA chief Wayne LaPierre. I had stood next to Ted Cruz and had my picture taken with him. I had rubbed elbows with the richest people in America, cocktail in hand, celebrating a shared victory. I had, for a brief moment, been elevated up and out of my circumstances, and I had thought of myself as important and as powerful and as in-the-know. I had fooled myself. I had betrayed myself. And I had represented myself as someone else to others.

Perhaps I was the one who had thrown myself under the bus, even more than Alexander had in Parliament.

I had, in Alexander's words "sold myself." And I had sold myself out.

Somehow, without thinking I had chosen to do so, I had tuned out the rest of the world's noise, and like people who watch only *Fox*

News or read only Breitbart, I had tuned in to one channel only: the Cambridge Analytica channel, all its programming hosted by a man named Alexander Nix.

I had believed we were *leveling the playing field*. And instead of seeing the warped rules of the game as unethical or even criminal, I saw them as the cost of doing business with savvy in the modern world.

I chose to judge and then ignore the fact that Alexander had profited so excessively off a deal, in Nigeria and in Mexico. I had reasoned his lack of ethics away: There really hadn't been enough time for the team on the ground in Abuja or the State of Mexico to carry out all those plans I'd put in the proposal; it was the fault of the client for having come to us so late in the game, so close to Election Day, and wanting us to do so much in so little time. I had been up front with them, hadn't I? I had warned them we might not be able to deliver everything we promised.

I had been horrified at the materials I saw in the two-day Trump postmortem, but horror had been only enough to make me flee the country, not the company.

"Well, I guess that's not the way they sell soda, huh?" chief revenue officer Duke Perrucci had said to me after the debrief. He and I and our colleague Robert Murtfeld had been shocked by the two-day series of extravagant revelations. But I had excuses for everything, including the fact that I'd been unaware of the tribalistic and ugly content of our materials or the tone of the election itself and how it had led to violence.

I hadn't seen the content because of the firewall, I could tell myself and others. And I could also say that in the run-up to the general election, I didn't even have time to watch TV.

I could say that I was focused on the commercial side of Cambridge Analytica. I could say that I was traveling all the time. Just look at my daily calendar from 2016 and 2017, and you'll see that I was almost always in the air! *You* try to keep up with the news with that kind of crazy schedule. I didn't have time to watch the *news*!

And I explained to Lewis how I had given up my vote and contributed in no small part to the general lack of support for Hillary in the primaries and even the animosity toward her in the general election—all of which had led ineluctably to her defeat.

I had flown to Chicago expressly to vote for Bernie Sanders in the primaries. Then, in November, I told myself I was too busy to fly back there again for the general. I had just been there to see my father. I hadn't had time to get an absentee ballot. Besides, Illinois wasn't a swing state. It hadn't occurred to me to register to vote in Virginia, which was not only a swing state but also where our Cambridge Analytica "DC" apartments had been.

Over and again, I had told myself that any ugliness I encountered in my time at Cambridge Analytica had left me untouched. I had principles. I was a good person. I had been nothing more than a "dirty Democrat spy" embedded in a conservative empire.

I had helped to empower voters to engage in a fairer and more equal "democratic" process by giving them the critical tools they needed to fight the other side. But I had not aided and abetted them in any sinister ventures. I did not ascribe to their beliefs. I had remained agnostic in the face of virulent racism, sexism, and assaults on civility.

My failure to stand in opposition to what I encountered wasn't a failure at all, I'd told myself. It was a triumph of impartiality. I had been trained in international human rights law, and impartiality was its hallmark. The best barristers, domestic or international, didn't judge their clients. At a war crimes tribunal, the purpose wasn't to impugn the character of those on trial, but to uphold the sacred principles of the law itself. I had made John Jones, my dear departed friend, a paragon of those principles, and the patron saint of my twisted logic: I would not judge those whose behavior was indefensible. I could stand next to criminals and think, I am still good and righteous.

I had made choices in all this. But not unlike the very people who were the targets of Cambridge Analytica's devious and brilliant messaging, I, too, had been a perhaps unwitting victim of an influence campaign. As with so many others, something had made an impression on me, I clicked on it, and that had sent me through a wormhole of disinformation, and I made choices I never would have thought I was capable of making.

It had happened as equally to me as to the country I was born in and the country I'd adopted as my own. I was a proxy for each of those nations, willingly hoodwinked, living in an echo chamber, and never even knowing it.

On March 21, the earth spun again, and Paul Lewis and I worked past midnight into March 22, and then got up and did it again.

That day, in the news, the "brilliant" Steve Bannon, who had been cast down from the heavens, nonetheless defended himself and his gods: he never knew anything about Facebook mining, he claimed, and neither he nor CA had had anything to do with "dirty tricks" or swaying elections.[6]

And then he brought moral relativity into the mix: Besides, he said, "Facebook data is for sale all over the world."

And then propaganda: Cambridge hadn't swayed the election, he said. "Here's what won it for Trump: economic nationalism" and speaking in plain language to the American people. Populism, Bannon said, not microtargeting, had won the day.

Paul Hilder arrived in San Francisco late on the twenty-second. By then, Paul Lewis and I had gone through everything we could. I was exhausted, and at this point, the two Pauls could together begin to try to make sense of the story. It was going to have to be more than one article, they said. They didn't know how many yet. The unraveled sweater was so tangled.

We left the coworking space, grabbed food, and went to Paul Hilder's hotel room, where we holed up to work.

I had been in and out of touch with my sister. I called her to let her know that I was okay. I hadn't told her much yet, but now, breathlessly, I explained to her what I was doing. She wanted to know what I was planning to do afterward.

She meant after the news came out.

What was my exposure? Being innocent of a crime didn't matter. There were two powerful governments that could choose to do anything they wanted with me. I had to be prepared for the worst-case scenario. Was I? she wanted to know.

I couldn't breathe.

I had to protect my family first. "Don't tell Mom anything except that I'm fine," I said. No one needed to know where I was, where I was going to be. That could be a liability to my parents. Any number of powerful people and their henchmen could decide to try to find me after the news hit.

The two Pauls were still hard at work at the desk in Paul Hilder's hotel room. I sat on the bed, then slumped down, and from time to time, I fell asleep and then woke again, each time catching snippets of their conversation.

They were trying to take it all in. In my sleep, I thought I heard them cry out in wonder and sigh with exhaustion. Sometimes they roused me in order to ask a specific question or check a fact. I'd sleep again, and then I'd wake to find one of them pacing the room, the other typing frantically.

At around five or six in the morning, I was dead to the world, in a deep but disturbed sleep. When I finally woke up again, the sun had been up for a while.

It was March 23.

"Good morning," the Pauls said.

I rubbed my eyes. They were looking at me with concern.

Paul Lewis had bad news. It wasn't going to be possible, he said, to hold the article. It was in his editor's hands now, and he had no control over it. It was going to come out that day.

That had not been my plan. I had wanted to be somewhere far away when the news broke, but I didn't feel betrayed. I understood. And strangely, thinking back on it now, I thought to myself, Better sooner than later. News like this is so ephemeral. People will be over it in a day.

Little did I know.

It was time to figure out what to do, though, going forward. It was possible that CA could sue me for breach of contract, libel, or slander. And if there was a Russia connection between any of the entities, then I possibly had a great deal more to worry about.

I had to find a safe place to go. It had to be outside the United States and Britain. It had to be someplace where it wouldn't be easy to find me.

I hadn't been paid in two months. I had nothing in the bank. Somewhere, I had a small stash of Bitcoin, but I wasn't sure how that would get me where I needed to go. At least my location couldn't be traced while using it, and no government could freeze my account, but it wasn't enough to get me very far away.

I got in touch with Chester, the person with whom everything had begun on a winter's day in 2014. I'm in trouble, I told him. A lot of things were about to come out, and I needed to leave the country.

He didn't even pause. "Where to?" he asked.

I said Thailand. There was a certain island I could go to.

We got off the phone, and within an hour he'd booked and paid for a flight; he sent me the confirmation number. In the meantime, I'd hide out.

I called my sister and asked her to liquidate the Bitcoin I had, explaining to her how to do it, where to go to a Bitcoin ATM near her, and how to send it to me via Western Union, so I wouldn't create as much trackable data by swiping my bank card. My Bitcoin savings amounted to about a thousand dollars. It would get me through for a little while.

When the first of many articles based on my evidence and interviews came out in the *Guardian* that day, I forwarded it to her. I was crying.

"Look what I did," I wrote.

I hoped she would read it, understand, and support me.

I also sent it to Facebook's Morgan Beller, now cofounder of their blockchain concept Libra, who had invited me to come to Facebook HQ while I was in Silicon Valley to discuss their early thoughts on blockchain development. While I desperately wanted Facebook to implement technology to track data better and to compensate their users for how much they had taken, I decided instead to whistleblow against them.

She read the article and responded, "Wow." Maybe now she understood why I couldn't make the proposed meeting, and why data companies such as Facebook needed blockchain so badly.

I hoped everyone would read it and understand what was at stake.

I headed to the airport to board another plane, this time having no idea when or if I could come back, or what was in store for me or the powers that be. I had taken the matter into my own hands, taken the first step. Whatever came next would be up to the people who read the article. Would they care? Would they take action?

Would you?

20

The Road to Redemption

MARCH 23, 2018–PRESENT

Finally, I was free.

Those who have ever bottled something up until they just couldn't take it anymore will know what I mean. I had spent years looking forward to the future, and every time something incredibly exciting came along—a promotion opportunity or a promising client I wanted to work with—the rug would be pulled out from under me. Another man hell-bent on holding on to power would be put above me, telling me what to do, in control of my life yet again. I would keep on taking "a beating," so to say, to my pride, to my spirit, and to my own decency.

The dark discoveries I made while riding the roller-coaster of Cambridge Analytica more than nauseated me. I had spent my whole life dedicated to finding solutions to the world's problems, working for free or next to nothing to achieve my lofty goals, partnering with unfunded organizations, nonprofits, and charities. And when external forces pushed me to make the metaphorical "golden handcuffs" decision, I had compromised myself and thrown away my moral compass—and I had not even been paid well to do it. How had I been so blind?

Looking down at the country I was leaving behind, my home, I couldn't help but wonder how we had gotten here. I was leaving behind a country where divisive rhetoric had become commonplace, and where the political correctness that used to protect the public from extremism, sexism, and racism had begun to fall apart. How had I ended up playing a role in the degradation of our civil society, and of civil discourse? I remembered what I had to deal with on the Obama campaign: the constant influx of racial hatred on our social media pages, and we had chosen censorship over allowing those ideas to run rampant—and somehow, through many years of allowing myself to be targeted, I had ended up at a company running campaigns that gave a platform to the hate that I used to help stamp out. And America wasn't the only place suffering in the wake of this return to radical populist rhetoric—the Brexit campaign in the UK led to the rise of extreme nationalist and fascist leaders coming out of the woodwork across Europe and Latin America, calling for suppression of the progressive ideals that have defined the human rights and the fundamental freedoms we should be protecting. I found myself deep in a nightmare—and had finally just woken up. It was time to take action and begin cleaning up the messes that had been made—that I had a hand in.

As I flew through the clouds, hurtling away from the country that had been turned upside down by the Trump campaign, I began to consider the scope of what had just happened: darkness had crept into our lives through our phone screens, laptops, and TVs. People had been targeted, and now we were more divided than ever. In the United States, hate crimes had risen dramatically, and from the start of the Brexit campaign, the United Kingdom had descended into similar fits of racial-fueled conflicts and crimes against immigrants or those perceived to be "the other." The tribalism in two of the most developed Western societies had become so very extreme, and this was only the "tip of the iceberg," as Alexander used to say. He also said that he had run campaigns in more than fifty countries. How much more was there for the world to know, across all the nations in the world in which SCL had worked, besides the devastating consequences in the two countries that I knew, loved, and understood best?

The problem was bigger than Cambridge; the problem was Big Data. It was that Facebook, in particular, had enabled companies like Cambridge to harvest the data of billions of people, and how, in turn, those companies had sold that data, promiscuously, to anyone who could pay for it; and how *those* parties had abused it without anyone ever knowing how or for what purpose. All this has been going on since the beginning of our digital lives, without our knowledge, and without government oversight. Even the few laws governing the use of data were completely unenforceable, with no technology in place to allow for the transparency and traceability that would be required to confirm that individuals or companies were obeying the law.

The problem also lay in how easy it was for Facebook, Twitter, and the like to become the globe's new town hall, and what happened there: the devolution of civility; the rise of tribalism; and how an online war of words and images escaped the bounds of the internet and altered the moral landscape of the real world.

The problem was that bad agents could poison minds, and that that poison had led to bloodshed. Fake news infiltrated our phone screens and laptops and made us deaf, dumb, and blind to reality—and willing to kill each other for causes that were not even real. Hatred poured out of those who were usually peaceful. The dream of a connected world instead tore us all apart. And where was it going to stop?

I had kept all these negative thoughts and feelings in my head, allowed them to stew, to consume me from the inside out, until there was so much poison deep within me, and a hollowness, that my only choice was to crumble or explode.

And explode I did, all over the international press. The reaction was raw, it was damning, and it was everywhere.

Picking up the pieces of my former self, I landed in Thailand unsure of my next move. Some whistleblowers, I knew, were revered for their heroism, and went on after their revelations to live happy, safe lives with their families—Daniel Ellsberg, for example. After reading the Pentagon Papers he'd leaked, the world rejected the war in Vietnam and replaced Richard Nixon with a leader who deserved to be called president of the United States. Others, such as Julian Assange and Chelsea Manning, ended up losing large parts of their lives to vilification and incarceration. They were celebrated for their attempts to let the world see the truth. But unlike in the case of Ellsberg, those in power at the time of their leaks were not replaced, and the whistleblowers paid a price, rewarded only with the knowledge that when government crimes were committed, they had stopped at nothing to expose the perpetrators.

I knew the stakes, but somehow I felt confident, and willing to accept either path, come what may. I had made my bed and could be forced to lie in it; only time would tell.

In the meantime, I was heading to a remote island where no one could find me, from which I would wait to see how the international community took the news, but especially people in the two countries I called home. And it was there, on the royal docks of Phuket Harbour, that the film crew rolled up.

In the hours before my plane took off from San Francisco, my story had exploded across the media world, both mainstream and social, and the messages began to pour in. Some people were mad and took an "I told ya so" view of what I had exposed.

You're a liar and so were they! I knew it!

Some told me to be careful, that powerful people would come after me. I couldn't tell if these were veiled threats or just the scared well wishes of acquaintances who would never have allowed themselves to be in my shoes.

Then there were the golden few who told me they were shedding tears on my behalf and were so very proud of me. Matt, whom I had told in Puerto Rico that I was about to do something big, posted one of the articles from my *Guardian* interview, and commented, "Brittany Kaiser is my heroine." I blushed when I saw this, heartened that some of the people who mattered realized that what I had done was right.

And then the phone rang. It was Paul Hilder.

"Brittany, there are some serious filmmakers that have been working on a documentary about the data crisis, and they want to talk to you. Can I put them in touch? I have vetted them; they're the real deal."

Within a few hours, both he and one of the directors were on a flight, Thailand bound, to join the mission.

There on Phuket Harbor, I had my first face-to-face with the film crew: Karim Amer, one of the directors and producers, had been researching how to explain the data crisis to the world. In the wake of the 2014 Sony hack that saw millions of people's personal data exposed, he and his partner, decorated filmmaker Jehane Noujaim, had been interviewing people around the world, from Sony execs to Steve Bannon to Chris Wylie, but they hadn't found a voice through whom they could tell the story. Then they read the Pauls' *Guardian* articles, Karim told me, and they knew that I could be the one.

And now here we were, about to take a speedboat to the private island where I had arranged to hide out for a while, and from where I would view the fallout, judging how safe it was to go back, or not, to the places I called home.

Fresh off the speedboat on that blazing hot day, we nestled into the pool, with Karim's videographer and sound guy leaning over the water, and began our first interview.

Where were we, Karim asked.

"I'd rather not have geolocation on for this, if you don't mind," I said. "Just me, sitting here, the person trying to overthrow two administrations with one . . . disjointed but soon-to-be-seamless narrative."

He laughed, but went further: "Why are you concerned about the two administrations?"

The Trump and Brexit campaigns had likely been conducted illegally, and I had evidence of it. It went without saying that I was likely unsafe, and I had no idea how things would play out.

Then, we dived deep and tried to touch every topic we knew to be revelatory: Cambridge's database, the data sources, the cut corners, the shady dealings with morally vacant clients, and the aftermath. What had we done, what did I know, and what did that mean now? What we'd planned to last thirty minutes turned into three hours, and Karim and I, our faces sunburned, emerged from the pool mentally exhausted. There was too much to cover today, but he and his crew were not leaving me anytime soon. We knew one thing for sure: this was the beginning of something great.

I had planned to be in Thailand for a while. My life had been . . . well, less than pleasant for many years, and I needed a break, somewhere to clear my head, where I had zero influences. I yearned to free my mind from the shackles of my recent past and sink into the reality of what I had just decided to do.

Unfortunately, that ideal scenario didn't last too long. While the film crew and I were exploring the islands of Thailand, I received an invitation: the British Parliament had requested that I testify as a witness in the DCMS's public inquiry on fake news. What had I seen? What did I know? Could I call out these injustices publicly? Did I know what to do with everything I knew? Luckily, I was surrounded by the film crew and Paul, and we began to explore not only my own memories, but my computer and my evidence. We tried to make sense of so many things that had been inexplicable. It was like having an external hard drive to my own brain, with multiple minds to contemplate what I had experienced and to map out both what had actually occurred and where that left us to contemplate action.

Without hesitation, my answer to the invitation was yes. I replied almost immediately, confirming my interest and asking how soon I needed to be in England, my adopted home, which had recently been torn to shreds by the lies of a few. I had to go back and help it heal. It was my duty. To me, it wasn't a choice; it was a privilege and an honor.

While flying back there, I heard it announced in the press that Alexander Nix would be testifying the day after me.

"It's all real now," said Paul, at my side as we flew back to what was left of my life in Great Britain.

I had already written to the best British lawyer I knew, Geoffrey Robertson QC, founder of the Doughty Street Chambers, the place where I had once dreamed of being a barrister myself someday. Geoffrey had spent some time doing pro bono work under my late friend John Jones and the illustrious Amal Clooney, working to free political prisoners who were dying behind bars for their efforts to make the world a better place.

Within an hour or so of my email, I received a reply, with Geoffrey's cell phone number and a request to please call him. I did so, of course, and he invited me to Doughty Street, a place that elicited so many strong emotions in me. It had once been where I hoped to contribute to protecting clients. But now the world was flipped upside down: I was the one being brought in and shown to the client chair (for the first time in my life), and as I sank into the leather seat cushion, the heaviness of my situation began to finally weigh on me. I had not returned to Doughty Street as a barrister as I had always meant to, but as a client. Thank god I had done my pro bono time and now had the opportunity to be represented by them pro bono in turn, as a show of respect.

To help with the case, Geoffrey brought in the infamous Mark Stevens, one of the top data lawyers, who was also known for representing dissidents and human rights activists from all walks of life. Mark was ready to fight against the Brexiteers who had held his country hostage. I was in the best of hands.

"You know you have the best lawyers in Europe, right?" a friend of mine from the BBC chimed in. "The Leave.EU guys and Alexander should brace themselves for what's coming!"

Meanwhile, with newly born confidence, I began working with Paul Hilder on my "coming out" strategy: We knew we needed to mobilize the masses, and with my upcoming appearance on TV in British Parliament, not to mention the inevitable rush of global media attention that would follow, it was the right time to grab ahold of a catchphrase and push it out into the universe. We brainstormed: How could we sum up the need for transparency, ownership, and accountability? We began writing down some ideal policies, the changes we wanted to see in the world, and racked our minds for the right slogan.

Suddenly, it came to me: Own Your Data. It was simple, short, and direct. "'Own Your Data,' Paul! It's 'Own Your Data'!"

Paul grinned widely, with the all-knowing expression of an experienced campaigner who can recognize a winning slogan from a mile away. "It's perfect!" he said excitedly, and we began to put together the messaging, the content, and then the initial team. We had our rallying cry, and with the final touches on a Change.org campaign and some creative materials pressuring Mark Zuckerberg, it was nearly time for launch.

My parliamentary testimony ended up scratching the surface of the biggest scandal of my lifetime. Once the authorities saw how open I was about everything—and I mean *everything*—the requests started pouring in: Could I assist the Senate Intelligence Committee? The Judiciary? House Intel? The DOJ—aka Special Counsel Robert Mueller's investigation into Russian interference in the U.S. election? The Information Commissioner in the United Kingdom? In Trinidad and Tobago? The list went on. I opted into it all, openly consenting to share my information, time, conscience, and memory.

It was time to go home and do for my native country what I had just done for the British government, authorities, and public. Americans deserved the truth about how everything had happened. Indeed, citizens of the United States are more vulnerable to their data being weaponized against them than in Britain: in the United States there were so many more data points available on each person, and hardly any legal or regulatory constructs to manage data or trace how it was used (or abused) by private and government entities alike. The ability to have full transparency or traceability was next to impossible. That needed to change.

When I got back to the States, and before I had my first round of meetings in DC, I went to New York. Some of my blockchain friends were building technology solutions to the problems I had been outlining, and they wanted to hold a press conference. Their organization had booked a room at the Roosevelt Hotel in Manhattan, where they'd gathered many of the top journalists in tech, especially the ones working on the abuses by Cambridge Analytica born from the ruthlessness of the recent elections. With some advisory board members assembled in front of a giant backdrop reading, "RIP: STOLEN DATA 1998–2018 #OWNYOURDATA," we broadcast on fifteen different media networks our intention to build technology-driven solutions to protect the data that government had left wide open for pillaging.

It was that same week that, after the onslaught of press resulting from the Roosevelt Hotel press conference, Karim and his film team wanted me to hire a PR strategist. And where better to meet such a person than at Daniel Ellsberg's keynote speech on whistleblowing at a human rights law conference?

Though not an official delegate to the conference, I made my way to the Hilton Midtown—funnily enough, a place I hadn't been to since Alexander gave a talk there on behavioral microtargeting—not knowing what to expect, but dying to meet one of my heroes. Inside, I made my way to the back of the conference room, from where I listened intently to Ellsberg's words.

"What would you do if you were a young professional working at your dream job," Ellsberg said, "and you discover that your employer was lying to the public, promoting a disastrous foreign war, and steadily expanding a weapons program that threatened to destroy human life on earth?"

I was taken aback. It felt too close to home.

When Ellsberg got offstage, he was surrounded: everyone from lawyers in slick New York suits to grandmotherly looking women in knit dresses moved in to shake his hand and thank him for taking such a great risk in the face of adversity. Ellsberg was calm, considerate, and open to every question, and I simply couldn't wait for my opportunity. It soon came when he made his way over to me.

I am not someone who is often starstruck, but I quickly went into full fan-girl mode: my palms were sweaty, I muddled my words, and stared at him, waiting for the wisdom to pour out.

And that it did. Upon being introduced to me by the film crew, Daniel—as he asked me to call him—sat next to me, so close I could feel his warmth, and asked me calmly, "So, how old are you?"

"I'm thirty years old," I muttered quietly.

"Wow," he exclaimed, "I was thirty when I decided to become a whistleblower, too—when I released the Pentagon Papers. I suppose bravery runs strong at that age."

I was still glowing from meeting Ellsberg when I arrived in DC—for the first time in a while. My last trip there had been back in February, for a breakfast meeting with officials from the Securities and Exchange Commission, the Commodity Futures Trading Commission, and the Federal Reserve, to discuss blockchain policy, the catalyst for the launch of Digital Asset Trade Association (DATA), the first blockchain lobbying organization. DATA had already helped pass eight new laws over the past few months in the State of Wyoming by putting boots on the ground in the State Congress, following the lead of the fierce expert Caitlin Long and the hardworking people of the Wyoming Blockchain Coalition. DATA was also working with legislators across the country to implement other laws and regulations for the greater good—what I like to call "blockchain-positive laws" to differentiate them from legislation that hampers innovation, such as New York State's BitLicense.

Now, back in DC for a new reason, I was seeking to level the playing field for my native country: What in hell had happened in the 2016 election and why; and if it was nefarious, how would we prevent it from happening again? Paul Hilder and the film crew came along with me, helping me—again, as with my appearance before the British Parliament—to prepare my thoughts by interviewing me, investigating my evidence, and providing moral support.

This time they had set up a meeting for me with another epic hero of mine, Megan Smith, former chief technology officer at the White House under Obama and the top technology policy figure in the country for many years. She met us in a room that Paul had decked out with core political and ethical reading materials. He had been traveling with a suitcase of these books to many of the cities we were visiting, offering me one here and there for guidance, or pulling one out and reading me inspirational quotes at times of emotional strife. The books provided the perfect welcome for Megan, who keenly admired the titles displayed before her.

Seated on the couch with her, I found her a consummate professional, but it was obvious that she was an activist, in a perfectly pressed suit but comfortable walking shoes—a woman who most likely put in long days running around DC getting more done than the average government official. I explained how I had gone from being an Obama girl to Cambridge Analytica whistleblower. It hurt me deeply to discuss this with an Obama administration official—how far south the country had gone since then. But Megan didn't flinch or appear to judge me. Instead, she took out her laptop and pulled up an image showing the way Congress had voted from the 1920s until now. The two sides used to vote together, as one could see from the nearly indistinguishable blue and red dots sharing space all over the infographic. Then, as the decades grew closer to the present, the blue dots and red dots began to separate, like water from oil, moving, as if almost physically repelled, onto opposite sides of the graph.

"It is the use of data," Megan proclaimed. The algorithms drive us apart because we get pushed far into our own rabbit hole of beliefs, directly in confrontation with the people we are supposed to be working with.

I knew she was right. After all, I had seen it with my own eyes.

After I shared my story, she took my hand in hers and said she forgave me. It wasn't my fault, she reminded me; sometimes good people get wrapped up in dark things. Also, it's easy for a young woman to get taken advantage of—that I had been, but there was now an opportunity for me to use my experience to change what we had in store for us for the future.

I was blown away by Megan. Taking the hand she was holding, she pulled me to my feet and gave me a hug. She then reached in a pocket and pulled out an enameled coin: "This is the White House CTO coin. I'm gifting one to each of you, as it will remind you of your strength, your intelligence, and that we can solve any problem we put our minds to if we work together. You as individuals and we as collective societies have been taken advantage of. There is a lot we can do to combat it, and we need to work hard every day to do so."

At this point, Paul and I had tears streaming down our cheeks, and we each accepted from her a bronze coin enameled in red, white, and blue, with ones and zeros all over it—a data coin, a symbol both of the problem we needed to fix and of the campaign we had ahead of us.

After meeting with Megan and members of a variety of government agencies and congressional committees, we headed back to New York. There was someone there who wanted to discuss Facebook with us, someone who had almost as much insider knowledge as

Mark Zuckerberg himself. He had been one of Facebook's earliest investors, and a mentor to both Zuckerberg and Sheryl Sandberg. A few years back, he had also exploded onto the press scene, as an outspoken critic of Facebook. Now I wanted to know why.

While waiting inside his fancy residence in New York with the film crew, I watched a video of the now-infamous Roger McNamee. Like me, McNamee had played a significant role in the growth of a tech company that had taken the path less traveled, and that had made all the difference. No one knew better than he the dangers that lurked behind the rapid growth of a firm with zero competition, with nothing else like it in the marketplace. Both CA and Facebook had been led by privileged white men who thought nothing of exploiting people in the name of advanced communications, never stopping to wonder if their algorithms were intrinsically flawed or if what they were bringing to the world did more harm than good. In the video, Roger was on CNN, explaining how he couldn't keep silent any longer.

When McNamee walked in the room, I put down my phone and shook his hand, all on camera, but as genuine as anything off camera would have been. He was neatly put together, but leaning over hard onto the table, tired from a very long day, with the bloodshot eyes of someone who has been tossing and turning in bed for a long time. After some initial pleasantries, we sat and talked about being a part of building something that became a monster, and how despite our concerns, expressed privately over and over and over, the CEO in charge of that monster had balked at our constructive criticism.

"I wanted to bring it to Mark first," Roger said, "as I thought he would be happy to see the cracks in the system I had pointed out. I saw the darkness in the algorithms, I saw people's data being used against them, and suggested so many ways to fix it. Unfortunately, he wanted nothing to do with it, and passed me off to lower-level employees to 'hear me out.'"

Zuckerberg had ignored Roger's warnings, as had Sheryl Sandberg, and by pawning him off to other departments underneath them, they had shown him the truth: as long as Facebook experienced sustained growth in value, they didn't care.

"What's happened to Facebook is the saddest case of a company getting blinded by its success that I've ever seen," Roger said. "And I'd like to think it's still fixable. I've spent years trying to convince them. First, privately and quietly. And now, not so quietly. It's frustrating because they've achieved more than their wildest dreams, and now they're having a fight over pride. They're basically asking us to challenge them because they're too proud to admit that they made mistakes. That's too bad. It's our job to see if we can fix the problem."

It had all gotten a bit out of control, and at this point, McNamee had a duty to speak out, as the private approach had borne no fruit and everything at Facebook was getting worse. "I helped build this thing," he told me. "My fingerprints are all over it! I just want to be able to sleep at night, ya know?"

Armed with confidence and the knowledge that I had some of the best and brightest behind me, and that what I was doing was right, I persevered with my #OwnYourData campaign, racking up hundreds of thousands of supporters worldwide, and millions of views of my videos and articles. So many people tried to access the online video of my parliamentary testimony that the video crashed the British Parliament's website upon publication. The race was on to speak truth to power, and the campaign consumed me 24/7.

One of my first big appearances was at the European Parliament, the day before the General Data Protection Regulation was enacted, the first important change to data privacy policy in twenty years. I also spoke on the opening panel of the biggest blockchain conference they had ever had, which was moderated by the former prime minister of Estonia and where I was flanked by a minister of finance and the head of FinTech for the European Central Bank. I appeared at data privacy events and tech meetups, high-level press conferences and news shows. I participated in closed-door meetings with legislators and policy makers worldwide, and became a confidante of reporters around the globe who needed insider information off the record.

The speaking engagements were not only informational in nature; by default, I often ended up serving as an expert witness in cases of data crimes. In at least twelve individual investigations and multiple trials, I provided expert witness testimony, much to the thrill of my supporters and the legislators. The best example was *McCarthy v. Equifax*, in which my colleagues at the law firm Madgett and Partners sued the company that is now infamous for one of the biggest data breaches in history. At the time that it was hacked, Equifax had let more than three hundred security certificates expire, which the prosecuting attorney in the case, David Madgett, called akin to "leaving the door open with the lights on and the alarm off." Madgett prosecuted Equifax for damage to property as a result of its exposing the personal data of 157 million Americans to a lifetime risk of fraudulent activity and identity theft. With his victory in the case in the state supreme court, your data is now your property in the State of Minnesota, and we are all better off for it. With the Equifax trials—and with new bills being presented to the British Parliament, the U.S. Congress, and the legislative bodies of other governments around the world—data protection case law is progressing.

What did all these investigations and trials find? At the time of this writing, it is not yet solidified. Only the Mueller Report has been released, with many redactions, and without a straightforward conclusion—although, I believe Robert Mueller was quite clear for those who like to read between lines:

If the president weren't a criminal, he would tell us so =
The president is a criminal.
If the president didn't have a sealed indictment waiting for
him, he would tell us so = As soon as we get Donald Trump
out of the White House, he's going to jail.

Why the American public, and the world at large, needed a degree in cryptography to squeeze that out is beyond me, but it got through to me, and I hope it got through to everyone else.

Many similar investigations are still in progress, from the FTC negotiation of a $5 billion fine for Facebook's negligence and inability to protect consumers, to the criminal investigations of the Brexiteers. And of course, the House Judiciary and Intelligence Committees' hearings on the Mueller investigation into Russian election interference and possible obstruction of justice by President Trump are ongoing at the time of this writing.

One morning in March 2019, I woke up to a flood of texts and emails: Congressman Jerry Nadler had tweeted a list of eighty-one people who were to be called as witnesses in his investigation into whether President Trump was fit to serve. I was number nine.

I shouldn't have been surprised. I had been one of the enablers. I had helped build up the machine, and borne witness to Trump, Facebook, and Brexit breaking democracy in front of my very eyes, hacking our digital lives and using our data against us. Now it was time to stop it from happening again.

As for Trump, nothing has changed, but the Mueller Report has come out. Mueller testified in Congress and solidified his ask: Get him out and I will arrest him.

As for Facebook, it has had to change some of its policies: We now have disclaimers for fake news and edited video content, and notifications label political advertising and where it has come from. It has been convicted of breaking data-protection laws in so many countries, and has just received a fine of $5 billion from the Federal Trade Commission—an all-time high—which will hopefully become a government budget for technology that can protect consumers.

As for Brexit, there is still no deal, a people's vote is possible. The Brexiteers have been found guilty of breaking both data-protection laws and violating election-spending regulations.

It is not a set of final results, but despite what the critics say, it is never too late to do the right thing. Our choices every day make us a part of the problem or a part of the solution. I have decided to be a part of the solution. What about you?

Now where do we look next? How do we make sense of all of this? Is it possible to have a free and fair election ever again, or even to have self-determination in our daily lives? Let's look at the key players and where we can expect to see still more of the same, for the sake of group vigilance:

Cambridge Analytica and The SCL Group have been dissolved, but what does that mean? Many of my former colleagues are still out there, consulting on elections and working in data analytics. This includes Alexander Nix, who, according to press reports, met with former prime minister Theresa May upon her exit and the newly minted prime minister Boris Johnson. Given the unfinished business of the ICO and parliamentary inquiries, I am concerned about where the Brexit and campaign support conversation has gone. And, besides Alexander, while many former Cambridge Analytica staff were bright, well-meaning professionals, some were definitely the opposite—and they are up to their old tricks and have not yet been brought to account for their actions.

The Mercers, while having fallen out of favor with Trump, are still influential in the political scene and will likely be funding plenty of causes, some of which may be using divisive and inflammatory materials, given the history of the rhetoric. I would watch where the money goes through nonprofit 501(c)3s and 4s, and both PACs and super PACs. Their influence is not lost on us yet.

Facebook, while having made a dirty laundry list of cosmetic fixes, has not made any progress on policing fake news, algorithms that prioritize inflammatory and false information, or the ability to really block bad actors from targeting users on the platform. While they allow you to see your data and to see the labeling of political ads and edited creative content (such as Nancy Pelosi's doctored video), they are wholly unprepared for the next election, let alone daily user activity. I recently shared a stage with Ya'el Eisenstat, who after a career in the CIA and counterterrorism and counterpropaganda work, was recruited by Facebook to be head of elections integrity. She quit after six months, refusing to take any salary or shares for her time, as Mark and Sheryl would not implement any of her recommendations to protect citizens ahead of the next election cycle. I needn't say more.

On the legislative side, we are getting the groundswell of support needed to make real changes this year, but the laws are only as good as the technology behind them. Luckily, blockchain solutions, which I always hoped could help fix the problems of Facebook, will now have the opportunity to turn the entire data industry on its head, returning the value produced by individuals every day back to them, and empowering the world to enter a new global economy previously accessed only by the world's most powerful organizations.

Big Data, Trump, and Facebook have broken our democracy. It lies in pieces at our feet, with individuals left struggling to piece it back together.

We now have a window of opportunity: we can begin to put those pieces back together into the mold of an ethical, just, and stable global community that will dedicate time and decision making toward positive change, and reimagining a more ethical world—or we can leave our societies in pieces at our feet, bracing for impact every day, expecting those pieces to become so damaged that we can no longer put them back together.

The choice is ours: we have a man in the White House likely with a sealed indictment awaiting him—trust me, the dictator that scrambles to stay in place is more dangerous than ever. He may go to jail if he loses this next election: consider that for a moment. He refused to interview with Mueller and instead just slanders him on social media. You may be guaranteed that he will wield any tools possible to retain power.

Secondly, we have a man in Menlo Park who is also in power-grab mode: his latest announcement of Libra, a blockchain payments ecosystems I wish I could support, but cannot. Libra, a consortium of big corporations, such as Facebook, Uber, and Visa, that want to launch their own financial system, would allow for data abuse so rife that governments around the world have risen up to stop our generation's most negligent manager of our digital assets from becoming the world's new digital central bank. Imagine a dystopia where you could be sold products at a different price because the seller knows how much you have in your bank account. It's already happening, and Libra will hurtle us into a connected world we never hoped for or dreamed of—a nightmare is more like it.

And lastly, there is the endless flow of data, still unregulated, and mostly untraceable. Once it's out there we cannot get it back. We have to demand change, and rights to our data, before this ecosystem breaks beyond repair. As Paul Hilder once said, "I'm an optimist, I believe that you can fix things that are broken." I want to see this attitude in the next wave of politicians that bid for our attention. Give us something to hope for again, and give us the tools to empower ourselves. We need legislative and regulatory change, and real investments in the technology solutions that will allow us to implement these new standards.

Now is the time. We must come together to pick up the pieces of our digital lives and build toward protecting our future.

Epilogue

ENDING THE DATA WARS

We will have to want peace, want it enough to pay for it, in our
own behavior and in material ways. We will have to want it
enough to overcome our lethargy and go out and find all those
in other countries who want it as much as we do.

—ELEANOR ROOSEVELT

Ultimately, the question of data rights is the pivotal issue of this generation. Data, our intangible digital assets, is the only asset class to
which the producers have no rights to its value or consent to its collection, storage, trade, or ultimately any profits from its production.
Throughout history, we have looked back with disdain at the crusad-
ers' exploitation of land, water, and oil from indigenous owners, not
as powerful as those who forcibly take their valuable goods, and we
have considered it a stain on our past.

How, then, have we blindly allowed Silicon Valley to evade us so
silently? While we proudly post and share our digital lives on their
platforms, we have been complicit in our own targeting. On our
watch we have seen the rise of racism and intolerance, the dissolu-
tion of civil society, the viral growth of fake news, and the repercus-
sions in the physical world when they result in violence and murder.
How now, with twenty-twenty hindsight, do we see the "never again"

sentiments we so strongly proclaimed after learning of atrocities in our history lessons?

The truth is that now we have a golden opportunity that comes once in a lifetime. It's our choice to seize it or forever be seen in history as the armchair activists who let a bright future slip through their fingers. We have so many ways to take charge of our digital lives, to own our data, to demand transparency, and to end the murky kleptocracy that the tech industry has become.

I am an eternal optimist, or I wouldn't be issuing this warning: We must move quickly while the momentum is in our favor. If we choose to sit idly by, then the dystopian realities of *1984* and *Black Mirror* will become even more real than what we experience today. Tribalism will grow, the line between truth and manipulation will blur, and our rights to our digital identity, the world's most valuable asset, may never be recoverable. The time to act is now.

We have a big job to do, and making these issues tangible has become my raison d'être, my calling. After reading this book, you can now see how even an open-minded intellectual can be easily tricked by nothing more than a sleight-of-hand and the misinformation that is spoon-fed to us daily.

So, how do we protect ourselves? How do we protect our democracy? We stand up, speak out, and act. It is the duty of a every good citizen not to be silent.

You can start today with the following:

1. *Become digitally literate.* It's time we educated ourselves and others so that we understand what we are up against: how our data is collected, where it goes, where it's held, and how it can be used against us (or to make the world a better place). I started in the data game with the highest of hopes to use data for good, and I saw what happens when unethical practices permeate the

upper echelons of power. Some of the best tools for fighting back can be found at the DQ Institute's website. There you can learn why digital intelligence is essential in the digital age and how to get up to scratch to protect yourself and those around you. Visit http://www.dqinstitute.org.

Additionally, I recently cofounded the Own Your Data Foundation to raise awareness of the need for data rights. This nonprofit is promoting digital literacy through STEM education, so that one day all people will understand how to own and protect their digital lives. For resources and opportunities, visit: http://ownyourdata.foundation.

2. *Engage with legislators.* While I recognize that writing and passing more laws is not an immediate solution, it is a tangible way to work toward a better future, to protect our society for generations to come. There are many great people in government and in civil society organizations working on laws to protect us. Inform yourself about upcoming legislative initiatives and get involved! Call and write to your legislators (you can find their details at https://www.usa.gov/elected-officials) and tell them that you support new, common-sense data-protection legislation, including the following pending bills and initiatives currently being debated, both in Congress and in the court of public opinion:

   a. *Senator Ed Markey's CONSENT Bill* would flip the script, requiring companies to obtain opt-in consent from users (rather than their being automatically opted in), develop reasonable data security practices, and notify users about all data collection and any data breaches.

   b. *Senator Elizabeth Warren's Corporate Executive Accountability Act* would make corporate executives criminally liable for data breaches that occur as a result of negligence, as in the Equifax and Facebook data breaches.

c. *Jim Steyer's "You Are the Product" Legislative Initiative* would enshrine legal recourse for abuse of your data and ownership rights. The related bill(s) have not yet dropped but are something to look out for, given that Jim and the Californians for Consumer Privacy were instrumental in translating GDPR into the California Consumer Privacy Act (CCPR), the most comprehensive data legislation in the United States.

d. *California governor Gavin Newsom's Data Dividend Law*, which has been introduced and is being debated, recognizes that people from whom personal data has been collected should be compensated for its use.

e. *Senator Mark Warner's DETOUR Act* and associated bills that aim to regulate big tech by providing transparency into the value of consumers' data, and to block manipulative "dark patterns" in the use of algorithms.

f. *The state of Wyoming's Digital Asset Legislation*, which includes thirteen new laws already passed, and has many more in consideration during the upcoming legislative cycle. The benefits include definitions of your digital assets as intangible personal property, thereby ascribing rights to, and legal recourse for, their use. Learn more about the new tech capital of the United States here: http://www.wyoleg.gov.

g. *The Government Accountability Project's Scientific Integrity Act* supports science whistleblowers by protecting those who hold power to account for abuse, waste, and negligence. We want more strong individuals to come forward for the greater good and to feel comfortable in doing so. Get involved here: http://www.whistleblower.org/supporting sciencewhistleblowers.

3. *Help companies make the ethical choice.* Plenty of companies are looking to offer easy-to-implement, affordable solutions

to the problems in our digital lives. We must make it easier for new and smaller companies to conform to new laws and encourage them to bring about essential changes to their business models. Companies as big as Facebook and Google don't need such hand-holding, as they often have more expertise than regulators in how to fix these problems. While the regulators deal with the bad actors appropriately, show you care by implementing some of the ethical technology solutions listed at: http://designgood.tech. For an example of corporate thought leadership, check out Phunware (NASDAQ:PHUN), a Big Data company that is returning the data they hold to consumers and rewarding them for its use: http://www.phunware.com.

Additionally, I eagerly await the first beta coming out of Voice, a new social media platform that lets you own your data, get rewarded for the content you produce, and blocks bots and fake accounts with legitimate KYC/AML identity verification. Thank you to BlockOne for building the prime example of what Facebook and Twitter should strive to become: http://www.voice.com.

4. **Ask regulators to hold abuses of power to account.** The main issue with long, protracted investigations is that the individuals, campaigns, and companies at fault are often embarrassed but not punished. Many of them will not make ethical decisions unless forced to; hence my stress here on legislation and regulation. As such changes don't happen internally, external pressure is needed. The Brexit and Trump campaigns did not follow existing laws and regulations, and imposing mere fines on entities with deep pockets does not discourage them from breaking the law again. If we want to fix our broken democracy, we have to stand up and make our voices heard. Contact the Federal Election Commission, the Federal Trade Commission,

and the British Electoral Commission to let them know you demand real solutions and a satisfactory completion of current investigations before the next elections.

5. ***Make ethical choices in your own digital life.*** Choose to question negative news articles. Refrain from sharing messages that incite anger or fear. Choose not to engage in the negativity, the harassment, or the targeting. If you run a company, give your customers transparency and opt-in consent. Explain to them the benefits of the data they are sharing; you will reap greater rewards with open communication. Do not engage in trickery, and do not sell data to third parties without letting your customers know and giving them the choice to opt out. Do not use underhanded tactics to get people's attention; dark ads and divisive rhetoric have driven our societies apart too easily, and with just the click of a button. Dedicate yourself to not falling into the trap of convenience. This is not a time to remain idle— we need action from every person.

As Albert Einstein said, "I am not only a pacifist but a militant pacifist. I am willing to fight for peace. Nothing will end war unless the people refuse to go to war." We must fight to fix our democracy before it breaks beyond repair.

We can only do this together.

Remember: you have agency! It is not only up to big tech and our governments to protect us. We have to stand up for ourselves as well. You do not need that viral Facebook app, or to answer that quiz, or to give away the value of your facial-recognition data to see what you look like when you are older. San Francisco was the first city in the United States to ban facial recognition altogether, and that city knows its dangers better than any other.

Every day you can make the personal choice to use that new app for convenience, or if you can live with traditional website and phone options. See for yourself: does that app take your data, and if so, who does it share your data with? For what purposes? These choices have consequences. One easy example are your daily messages. I'll just come out and say it: use Signal, not Whatsapp! Mark Zuckerberg weakened the encryption to pull data from it for targeting. And you can prevent being targeted by making a simple choice.

I should know, it happened to me. I was targeted and I lost my way. It likely has happened to you in one way or another, my reader. And I do not want you to leave this page feeling helpless, but rather empowered. You can own your data and harness your own value, but we all need to opt in and build a world based on transparency and trust. If we do, I guarantee we are right on time, with all the momentum around the world, to re-envision what our ethical future will look like, together.

Acknowledgments

I am humbled every day by the opportunities I have been given by those around me and the unconditional support that has come my way from both loved ones and those I haven't yet met. Therefore, making this list comprehensive is nearly impossible, but I will try my best to recognize the most important people and organizations in my life. Thank you to everyone that has helped, and will help, along the way. You inspire me, and the differences you are making are so important. Together we can lead our world into a more ethical digital future.

With special thanks to:

My family; firstly to my sister and cofounder, Natalie, who jumped into data-rights activism and hit the ground running. Your love, intention, and of course diligent organization are responsible for so much of the impact we are making together. To my parents, for always believing in me and for encouraging me to strive for excellence. You raised me to do the right thing and to work hard for what I believe in, and I cannot ever thank you enough. To my grandparents, aunts, uncles, cousins, and extended and adopted family members: I love you so much. I am so happy you are a part of my journey.

The Digital Asset Trade Association (DATA), especially David Pope, Alanna Gombert, Jill Richmond, and Brent Cohen, for working diligently pro bono since January 2018 to move the needle in new legislative initiatives to define and protect digital assets worldwide. Your energy and support for me know no bounds.

Paul Hilder, I struggle to put into words how important your friendship and belief in me have been—not only to me but to the world. I thank you for caring so deeply about important causes that you dedicate your life to. Thank you for solving problems on behalf of the greater good and never stopping until you win. You are an expert at turning ideas into action, and you are the reason why the #OwnYourData campaign exists. You never gave up on me and always believed in me. I will continue to make you proud of the time you donated to this cause.

The Great Hack and Netflix teams, especially Geralyn Dreyfous for your unrivaled support, and to the brilliant Karim Amer, Jehane Noujaim, and Pedro Kos for telling part of my story to the world in a way that has been so incredibly impactful. To Elizabeth Woodward, Bits Sola, Basil Childers, Matt Cowal, and the rest of the beautiful (and patient) film and Netflix teams that created and pushed out the incredibly viral social impact campaign led by *The Great Hack* and our partners.

Harper Collins and Eileen Cope, for giving me the special opportunity to tell my story around the globe through a personal memoir, and for the ability to finally get out the truth of what happened and why, and to give the tools to the public to make tangible change.

Julie Checkoway, for supporting the creation of *Targeted* in a way I could never have imagined. Your fierce intellect, thoughtful reflection, and emotional support have changed my life forever. I could never thank you enough.

Julia Pacetti, for not only becoming my protector, my second adopted mom, and one of my best friends but for your professional dynamism and unmatched ability to turn important conversations into global phenomena. Your ability to reach legal, political, and commercial leaders so that they get behind important initiatives stuns me every time. You are a force of nature!

My lawyers Geoffrey Robertson QC, Mark Stephens, Jim Walden, and Amanda Senske, who each gave me so much of their time pro bono, and gave me the guidance and support I needed to be effective in bearing witness in countless testimonies around the world. Your expertise in holding truth to power has advanced so many causes, and I am honored to be represented by you all.

The great state of Wyoming and the people who have made it the forward-thinking capital of digital asset protection. With special recognition to Caitlin Long, Representative Tyler Lindholm, Senator Ogden-Driskill, Rob Jennings, Steven Lupien, and the rest of the Wyoming Blockchain Task Force, the Wyoming Blockchain Coalition, and the forward-thinking legislators that have voted to pass all thirteen of these new laws that protect your citizens and residents. I am proud to call this beautiful place my new home!

The U.S. Congress and its top thought leaders, for pushing forward with the regulation of big tech and the protection of the digital assets of the citizens and residents of the United States. With special thanks to Senator Mark Warner, Senator Ed Markey, and Senator Elizabeth Warren. You are a guiding light for others to see how important this is to the future of our country.

Matt McKibbin, for being an incredible friend, partner, and thought leader. Your love and support have kept me sane and helped me become more open-minded, effective, and thoughtful. You've taught me to question everything I have ever been told and reinvent a better world built on more ethical principles. We are changing the world together, and I cannot wait to see what the future holds.

Lauren Bissell, for being my globetrotting partner and badass entrepreneurial and adventurous best friend that I not only love, but need! I cannot wait for all the exciting things we are doing together now and in the future.

Chester Freeman, for your brilliant mind, for your friendship, and for opening up my world to this crazy journey. I love you and want you to know how important you have been to me for more than a decade.

To the rest of my friends, colleagues, activists, whistleblowers, and supporters around the world: Thank you for everything you have done to advance these causes and to support me and this campaign. We have a very bright future ahead of us because of your efforts. #OwnYourData lives on and grows more effective because of you!

And to my readers: Thank you for caring and for reading my story. I hope you are inspired to make a change in your own lives, and to join the movement to create positive change in our digital lives.

Notes

1: A LATE LUNCH

1. Ari Berman, "Jim Messina, Obama's Enforcer," *The Nation*, March 30, 2011, http://www.thenation.com/article/159577/jim-messina-obamas-enforcer.
2. David Corn, "Inside Groundswell: Read the Memos of the New Right-Wing Strategy Group Planning a '30 Front War,'" *Mother Jones*, July 25, 2013, https://www.motherjones.com/politics/2013/07/groundswell -rightwing-group-ginni-thomas/.

3: POWER IN NIGERIA

1. Julien Maton, "Criminal Complaint Against Nigerian General Buhari to Be Filed with the International Criminal Court on Short Notice," Ilawyerblog, December 15, 2014, http://ilawyerblog.com/criminal-complaint-nigerian -general-buhari-filed-international-criminal-court-short-notice/.
2. John Jones, "Human Rights Key as Nigeria Picks President," *The Hill*, February 20, 2015, https://thehill.com/blogs/congress-blog/civil-rights /233168-human-rights-key-as-nigeria-picks-president.

4: DAVOS

1. "Our Mission," World Economic Forum, https://www.weforum.org /about/world-economic-forum.
2. Jack Ewing, "Keeping a Lid on What Happens in Davos," *New York Times*, January 20, 2015, https://dealbook.nytimes.com/2015/01/20/keeping-a -lid-on-what-happens-in-davos/.
3. Ibid.
4. Strategic Communications Laboratories. *NID Campaign January-February 2015 Final Completion Portfolio*. London: Strategic Communications Laboratories, 2015.
5. Agencies in Abuja, "West Criticises Nigerian Election Delay," *Guardian*, February 8, 2015, https://www.theguardian.com/world/2015/feb/08 /nigeria-election-delay-west-us-uk.
6. Ibid.
7. Ibid.
8. Nicholas Carlson, "Davos Party Shut Down After Bartenders Blow Through Enough Booze for Two Nights," *Business Insider*, January 23, 2015, https://www.businessinsider.com/davos-party-shut-down-by-swiss -cops-2015–1.

6: MEETINGS AND REUNIONS

1. Joseph Bernstein, "Sophie Schmidt Will Launch a New Tech Publication with an International Focus," *BuzzFeed*, May 1, 2019, https://www.buzzfeednews.com/article/josephbernstein/a-google-scion-is-starting-a-new-publication-with-focus-on.
2. https://www.bluestatedigital.com/who-we-are/.
3. https://www.bluelabs.com/about/.
4. https://www.civisanalytics.com/mission/.
5. Rosie Gray, "What Does the Billionaire Family Backing Donald Trump Really Want?" *The Atlantic*, January 27, 2017, https://www.theatlantic.com/politics/archive/2017/01/no-one-knows-what-the-powerful-mercers-really-want/514529/.
6. Mary Spicuzza and Daniel Bice, "Wisconsin GOP Operative Mark Block Details Cambridge Analytica Meeting on Yacht," *Journal Sentinel*, March 29, 2018, https://www.jsonline.com/story/news/politics/2018/03/29/wisconsin-operative-mark-block-details-meetings-between-cambridge-analytica-and-its-billionaire-back/466691002/.
7. Erin Conway-Smith, "As Nigeria Postpones Its Elections, Has It Chosen Security over Democracy?" *World Weekly*, February 12, 2015, https://www.theworldweekly.com/reader/view/939/-as-nigeria-postpones-its-elections-has-it-chosen-security-over-democracy.
8. Vicky Ward, "The Blow-It-All-Up Billionaires," *Huffington Post*, March 17, 2017, https://highline.huffingtonpost.com/articles/en/mercers/.
9. Ibid.
10. Ibid.
11. Ibid.
12. "We Need 'Smith,'" video, Promise to America, http://weneedsmith.com/who-is-smith.
13. Rebekah Mercer, "Forget the Media Caricature. Here's What I Believe," *Wall Street Journal*, February 14, 2018, https://www.wsj.com/articles/forget-the-media-caricature-heres-what-i-believe-1518652722.
14. Ibid.
15. Quinnipiac University Poll, "Walker, Bush in Tight Race among U.S. Republicans, Quinnipiac University National Poll Finds; Clinton Sweeps Dem Field, with Biden in the Wings, *Quinnipiac University Poll*, March 5, 2015, https://poll.qu.edu/national/release-detail?ReleaseID=2172.
16. Timothy Egan, "Not Like Us," *New York Times*, July 10, 2015, https://www.nytimes.com/2015/07/10/opinion/not-like-us.html?_r=0.
17. Dolia Estevez, "Mexican Tycoon Carlos Slim's Camp Calls Ann Coulter's Wild Allegations Against Him True Nonsense," *Forbes*, June 9, 2015, https://www.forbes.com/sites/doliaestevez/2015/06/09/mexican-tycoon-carlos-slims-camp-calls-ann-coulters-wild-allegations-against-him-true-nonsense/#694892fc654f.

7: THE FACE OF BREXIT

1. Naina Bajekal, "Inside Calais's Deadly Migrant Crisis," *Time*, August 1, 2015, http://time.com/3980758/calais-migrant-eurotunnel-deaths/.
2. "The Dispossessed," chart, *The Economist*, June 18, 2015, https://www.economist.com/graphic-detail/2015/06/18/the-dispossessed.
3. "Forced Displacement: Refugees, Asylum-Seekers, and Internally Displaced People (IDPs), Factsheet, European Commission, n.d., https://ec.europa.eu/echo/refugee-crisis.
4. Louisa Loveluck and John Phillips, "Hundreds of Migrants Feared Dead in Mediterranean Sinking," *Telegraph*, April 19, 2015, https://www.telegraph.co.uk/news/worldnews/africaandindianocean/libya/11548071/Hundreds-feared-dead-in-Mediterranean-sinking.html.
5. "What's Behind the Surge in Refugees Crossing the Mediterranean Sea?" *New York Times*, May 21, 2015, https://www.nytimes.com/interactive/2015/04/20/world/europe/surge-in-refugees-crossing-the-mediterranean-sea-maps.html.
6. European Union, "European Union Receives Nobel Peace Prize 2012," European Union, n.d., https://europa.eu/european-union/about-eu/history/2010-today/2012/eu-nobel_en.
7. Stephen Castle, "Nigel Farage, Brexit's Loudest Voice, Seizes Comeback Chance," *New York Times*, May 14, 2019, https://www.nytimes.com/2019/05/14/world/europe/nigel-farage-brexit-party.html.
8. Thomas Greven, "The Rise of Right-wing Populism in Europe and the United States: A Comparative Perspective," Friedrich-Ebert-Stiftung, May 2016, https://www.fesdc.org/fileadmin/user_upload/publications/RightwingPopulism.pdf.
9. Charlie Cooper, "Trump's UK Allies Put Remain MPs in Their Sights," Politico.eu, November 20, 2016, https://www.politico.eu/article/trump-farage-uk-brexit-news-remain-mps/.
10. Ed Caesar, "The Chaotic Triumph of Arron Banks, the 'Bad Boy of Brexit,'" *The New Yorker*, March 25, 2019, https://www.newyorker.com/magazine/2019/03/25/the-chaotic-triumph-of-arron-banks-the-bad-boy-of-brexit.
11. Simon Shuster, "Person of the Year: Populism," *Time*, http://time.com/time-person-of-the-year-populism/.

8: FACEBOOK

1. Harry Davies, "Ted Cruz Using Data Firm that Harvested Data on Millions of Unwitting Facebook Users," *Guardian*, December 11, 2015, https://www.theguardian.com/us-news/2015/dec/11/senator-ted-cruz-president-campaign-facebook-user-data.
2. "The Facebook Dilemma," *Frontline*, PBS, October 29, 2018.
3. Ibid.
4. Mark Sullivan, "Obama Campaign's 'Targeted Share' App Also Used Facebook Data from Millions of Unknowing Users," *Fast Company*, March 20, 2018, https://www.fastcompany.com/40546816/obama

-campaigns-targeted-share-app-also-used-facebook-data-from-millions
-of-unknowing-users.

5. "The Facebook Dilemma," *Frontline*, PBS, October 29, 2018.
6. Ibid.
7. Ibid.
8. Ibid.

9: PERSUASION
1. James Swift, "Contagious Interviews Alexander Nix," Contagious.com,
   September 28, 2016, https://www.contagious.com/news-and-views
   /interview-alexander-nix.

10: UNDER THE INFLUENCE
1. Jane Mayer, "The Reclusive Hedge-Fund Tycoon Behind the Trump
   Presidency," *The New Yorker*, March 27, 2017, https://www.newyorker
   .com/magazine/2017/03/27/the-reclusive-hedge-fund-tycoon-behind
   -the-trump-presidency.
2. Jim Zarroli, "Robert Mercer Is a Force to Be Reckoned with in Finance
   and Conservative Politics," NPR.org, May 26, 2017, https://www.npr.org
   /2017/05/26/530181660/robert-mercer-is-a-force-to-be-reckoned-with-in
   -finance-and-conservative-politic?t=1562072425069.
3. Gray, "What Does the Billionaire Family Backing Donald Trump Really Want?"
4. Matt Oczkowski, Molly Schweickert, "DJT Debrief Document. Trump Make
   America Great Again; Understanding the Voting Electorate," PowerPoint
   presentation, Cambridge Analytica office, New York, December 7, 2016.
5. Lauren Etter, Vernon Silver, and Sarah Frier, "How Facebook's Political
   Unit Enables the Dark Art of Digital Propaganda," Bloomberg.com,
   December 21, 2017, https://www.bloomberg.com/news/features
   /2017–12–21/inside-the-facebook-team-helping-regimes-that-reach
   -out-and-crack-down.
6. Nancy Scola, "How Facebook, Google, and Twitter 'Embeds' Helped
   Trump in 2016," *Politico*, October 26, 2017, https://www.politico.com
   /story/2017/10/26/facebook-google-twitter-trump-244191.

11: BREXIT BRITTANY
1. Jeremy Herron and Anna-Louise Jackson, "World Markets Roiled by
   Brexit as Stocks, Pound Drop; Gold Soars," Bloomberg.com, June 23, 2016,
   https://www.bloomberg.com/news/articles/2016–06–23/pound-surge
   -builds-as-polls-show-u-k-to-remain-in-eu-yen-slips.
2. Aaron Wherry, "Canadian Company Linked to Data Scandal Pushes Back
   at Whistleblower's Claims: AggregateIQ Denies Links to Scandal-Plagued
   Cambridge Analytica," CBC, April 24, 2018, https://www.cbc.ca/news
   /politics/aggregate-iq-mps-cambridge-wylie-brexit-1.4633388.

13: POSTMORTEM

1. Nancy Scola, "How Facebook, Google, and Twitter 'Embeds' Helped Trump in 2016," *Politico*, October 26, 2017, https://www.politico.com /story/2017/10/26/facebook-google-twitter-trump-244191.
2. Sentiment analysis has its roots, interestingly enough, in the innovations Robert Mercer pioneered years before at IBM. For the campaign, it measured not only if people liked tweets or retweeted them but something more nuanced: whether tweeters were feeling positive or negative when composing their tweets.
3. Glenn Kessler, "Did Michelle Obama Throw Shade at Hillary Clinton?" *Washington Post*, November 1, 2016, https://www.washingtonpost.com /news/fact-checker/wp/2016/11/01/did-michelle-obama-throw-shade-at -hillary-clinton/?noredirect=on&utm_term=.686bdca907ef.

14: BOMBS

1. Hannes Grassegger and Mikael Krogerus, "The Data That Turned the World Upside Down," *Vice*, January 28, 2017, https://www.vice.com /en_us/article/mg9vvn/how-our-likes-helped-trump-win. For the original German, see https://www.dasmagazin.ch/2016/12/03/ich-habe-nur -gezeigt-dass-es-die-bombe-gibt/.
2. Information Commissioner's Office, "Investigation into the Use of Data Analytics in Political Campaigns," November 6, 2018, ICO.org.uk, https:// ico.org.uk/media/action-weve-taken/2260271/investigation-into-the-use -of-data-analytics-in-political-campaigns-final-20181105.pdf.
3. Ann Marlowe, "Will Donald Trump's Data-Analytics Company Allow Russia to Access Research on U.S. Citizens," *Tablet*, August 22, 2016, https://www.tabletmag.com/jewish-news-and-politics/211152/trump -data-analytics-russian-access.

15: QUAKE

1. Luke Fortney, "Blockchain Explained," Investopedia, n.d., https://www .investopedia.com/terms/b/blockchain.asp.
2. Ellen Barry, "Long Before Cambridge Analytica, a Belief in the 'Power of the Subliminal,'" *New York Times*, April 20, 2018, https://www.nytimes .com/2018/04/20/world/europe/oakes-scl-cambridge-analytica-trump.html.

16: BREAKUP

1. Paulina Villegas, "Mexico's Finance Minister Says He'll Run for President," *New York Times*, November 27, 2017, https://www.nytimes .com/2017/11/27/world/americas/jose-antonio-meade-mexico.html.
2. "Ex-Daughter-in-Law of Vincente Fox Kidnapped," *Borderland Beat* (blog), May 1, 2015, http://www.borderlandbeat.com/2015/05/ex-daughter-in -law-of-vincente-fox.html.
3. María Idalia Gómez, "Liberan a ex nuera de Fox: Mónica Jurado Maycotte

Permaneció 8 Meses Secuestrada," EJCentral, December 16, 2015, http://www.ejecentral.com.mx/liberan-a-ex-nuera-de-fox/.

4. Eugene Kiely, "Timeline of Russia Investigation," FactCheck.org, April 22, 2019, https://www.factcheck.org/2017/06/timeline-russia-investigation/.

17: INQUIRY

1. Alexander Nix, "How Big Data Got the Better of Donald Trump," *Campaign*, February 10, 2016, https://www.campaignlive.co.uk/article /big-data-better-donald-trump/1383025#bpBH5hbxRmLJyxh0.99.

18: RESTART

1. Paul Grewal, "Suspending Cambridge Analytica and SCL Group from Facebook," Newsroom, Facebook, March 16, 2018, https://newsroom.fb .com/news/2018/03/suspending-cambridge-analytica/.

2. Alfred Ng, "Facebook's 'Proof' Cambridge Analytica Deleted That Data? A Signature," CNet.com, https://www.cnet.com/news/facebook-proof -cambridge-analytica-deleted-that-data-was-a-signature/.

3. Matthew Rosenberg, Nicholas Confessore, and Carole Cadwalladr, "How Trump Consultants Exploited the Facebook Data of Millions," *New York Times*, March 17, 2018, https://www.nytimes.com/2018/03/17/us /politics/cambridge-analytica-trump-campaign.html.

4. Carole Cadwalladr, "'I Made Steve Bannon's Psychological Warfare Tool': Meet the Data War Whistleblower," *Guardian*, March 18, 2018, https:// www.theguardian.com/news/2018/mar/17/data-war-whistleblower -christopher-wylie-faceook-nix-bannon-trump.

19: OF TRUTH AND CONSEQUENCES

1. Matthew Weaver, "Facebook Scandal: I Am Being Used as a Scapegoat— Academic Who Mined Data," *Guardian*, March 21, 2018, https://www .theguardian.com/uk-news/2018/mar/21/facebook-row-i-am-being-used -as-scapegoat-says-academic-aleksandr-kogan-cambridge-analytica.

2. Selena Larson, "Investors Sue Facebook Following Data Harvesting Scandal," CNN, March 21, 2018, https://money.cnn.com/2018/03/20/technology /business/investors-sue-facebook-cambridge-analytica/index.html.

3. Andy Kroll, "Cloak and Data: The Real Story Behind Cambridge Analytica's Rise and Fall," *Mother Jones*, May/June 2018, https://www .motherjones.com/politics/2018/03/cloak-and-data-cambridge -analytica-robert-mercer/.

4. Ibid.

5. Ibid.

6. Joanna Walters, "Steve Bannon on Cambridge Analytica: 'Facebook Data Is for Sale All over the World,'" *Guardian*, March 22, 1018, https://www .theguardian.com/us-news/2018/mar/22/steve-bannon-on-cambridge -analytica-facebook-data-is-for-sale-all-over-the-world.